The
Ayatollahs'
Democracy

BY THE SAME AUTHOR

The Ayatollah Begs to Differ

The Ayatollahs' Democracy

An Iranian Challenge

HOOMAN MAJD

W. W. NORTON & COMPANY
New York   London

For information about permission to reproduce
selections from this book, write to Permissions,
W. W. Norton & Company, Inc.,
500 Fifth Avenue, New York, NY 10110

For information about special discounts for bulk
purchases, please contact W. W. Norton Special Sales
at specialsales@wwnorton.com or 800-233-4830

Manufacturing by Courier Westford
Book design by Helene Berinsky
Production manager: Devon Zahn

Library of Congress Cataloging-in-Publication Data

Majd, Hooman.
The Ayatollahs' democracy : an Iranian
challenge / Hooman Majd. — 1st ed.
p. cm.
Includes bibliographical references and index.
ISBN 978-0-393-07259-4 (hardcover)
1. Iran—Politics and government. 2. Democracy—Iran.
3. Islam and politics—Iran. I. Title.
DS318.9.M355 2010
955.05'4—dc22

                                                2010018481

W. W. Norton & Company, Inc.
500 Fifth Avenue, New York, N.Y. 10110
www.wwnorton.com

W. W. Norton & Company Ltd.
Castle House, 75/76 Wells Street, London W1T 3QT

1 2 3 4 5 6 7 8 9 0

CONTENTS

EVERYTHING IS TRUE;
NOTHING IS PERMITTED

There are several peculiar features about writing any detailed account of the recent political events in Persia which make necessary some slight explanation. The first point is that Persian political affairs, fraught as they are with misfortune and misery for millions of innocent people, are conducted very much as a well-staged drama—I have heard some critics say, as an opéra bouffe.

—WILLIAM MORGAN SHUSTER, *The Strangling of Persia*, 1912

DRAMATIS PERSONAE

Mahmoud Ahmadinejad, 53: The President

HIS CHALLENGERS:

Mir Hossein Mousavi, 68: Prime Minister of the Islamic Republic of Iran, 1981–1989. An architect by profession, an artist, and onetime president of the Academy of Arts.

Mehdi Karroubi, 72: Mid-level liberal cleric, two-term Speaker of Parliament, and two-time presidential candidate from the National Trust Party (*Hezb'e Etemaad'e Melli*).

Mohsen Rezai, 55: Conservative politician and teacher, Secretary of the Expediency Discernment Council. Commander of the Revolutionary Guards, 1981–1997. Also on the official Interpol wanted list, for allegations of involvement in the 1994 bombing of the Jewish Cultural Center in Buenos Aires.

THE PRINCIPAL PLAYERS:

Supreme Leader Ayatollah Seyed Ali Khamenei, 70: The *valih-e-faqih* since 1989, the highest authority in the Islamic Republic.

Ayatollah Ali Akbar Hashemi Rafsanjani, 75: Speaker of Parliament, 1980–1989. President of Iran, 1989–1997. Chairman of both the Expediency Discernment Council and the Assembly of Experts, and one of the principal architects of the Islamic Revolution and Republic.

Hojjatoleslam Seyed Mohammad Khatami, 66: Two-term President of Iran, 1997–2005. Father of the reform movement and founder of the Foundation for Dialogue among Civilisations.

Ali Larijani, 51: Speaker of Parliament, Supreme Leader's representative to the Supreme National Security Council. Son and son-in-law of two Ayatollahs, and brother of Judiciary Chief Ayatollah Sadeq Larijani. Holds a PhD in Western Philosophy, Tehran University.

ACT ONE:

Everything Is True

5:00 p.m., June 12, 2009: Mousavi Campaign Headquarters, Tehran. Mir Hossein Mousavi, President Mahmoud Ahmadinejad's chief rival in the presidential election, has just hung up the phone. Ali Larijani, the powerful speaker of Parliament and close ally of Supreme Leader Ayatollah Khamenei, was on the line, calling to congratulate him on his victory. The polls haven't closed yet, but the mood is jubilant, and Larijani's call is a confirmation of what Mousavi's aides already believe: the next president of the Islamic Republic of Iran will be their man. This despite the fact that all day they have been calling Speaker Larijani, Interior Ministry employees, and various other officials to report irregularities in the election process—everything from a shortage of ballots to their campaign workers being denied access to polling places, from a shutdown of the nation's SMS text-messaging network (which the campaign was going to use to report in from the field, since there is no widespread mobile data service in Iran) to pro-government websites announcing a win for Ahmadinejad before any official results have been announced. There are still long lines at many polling stations and voting hours have been extended, but everyone knows there has been an unprecedented voter turnout. Mousavi cannot lose.

But how does Larijani *know* at this early hour? Results are trickling in to the Ministry of Information—maybe better than trickling, given that there are tens of thousands of polling stations across the country and each is responsible for only a few thousand votes, which can be counted quite easily and entered into computers on the spot, to be transmitted to Tehran electronically, or called in by phone. Larijani knows because he has access to "firsthand and classified information and news." *Really?* According to a hard-line website, he most definitely had such access. And according to that same website, in its clumsy attempt to implicate Larijani in the unrest that followed, the phone call from him began the process by which Mousavi and the other losing candidates questioned the results of the election. The website, Rajanews.com, is run by one of Ahmadinejad's strongest supporters, Fatemeh Rajabi, the wife of former archconservative government spokesperson Gholam Hossein Elham and a journalist who has personally attacked any official who has even hinted at a disagreement with the conservative administration in power. Her previously printed attacks have been full of speculation and downright falsehoods, so maybe Larijani never made the call. But curiously, Ms. Rajabi, known sometimes as *Fati-ar'reh* (*Fati*, the "Saw") for her merciless cutting down of public figures, must not have been aware that her accusation was actually an accusation against her beloved president, for if, as she claims, Dr. Larijani made the call and had access to "firsthand and classified information," presumably from the Ministry of Information (which would have of course provided polling figures to him had he asked), then she was *confirming* that Mousavi was indeed on his way to a win, a win so big that by 5:00 p.m. there was no longer any doubt about the results, even as polls remained opened. How then did President Ahmadinejad emerge the winner? The Saw, normally one who cuts to the chase, never quite answered that question.

12:00 noon, June 12, 2009: A Polling Station, Midtown Tehran. A long line of voters snakes around the corner. Some of those already in the room are casting their ballots, but the last of the blank ballots have just been handed out. "We need more ballots!" screams the young woman into the phone. "We never had enough, and now we're already out," she continues, speaking to an official at the Interior Ministry. Fifty-eight million ballots were printed for an election where some fifty-two million Iranians were eligible to vote, and yet at this station, and others across the country, ballots are inexplicably running out. "They said they're on their way," the woman tells her colleagues and those waiting to cast their vote. "We'll have to be patient." Some leave the room, others leave the line outside, but others replace them, waiting patiently for their chance to exercise their right to vote. "If the majority doesn't vote, the minority rules" read one poster all over Tehran in the weeks leading up to the elections, and the message must have sunk in.

4:00 p.m., June 12, 2009: The blank ballots finally arrive. "How many do we have?" asks a poll worker, as she begins handing them out. "Fifteen hundred," replies a colleague. "That's *it*? You better call now and get some more, we're definitely going to need them."

6:00 p.m., June 12, 2009: The last of the ballots is handed out. "I said we need more ballots!" the young woman again screams into the phone. "You only sent us fifteen hundred, and we still have a long line of people waiting to vote." She hangs up and turns to another worker. "They said they didn't have any more ballots. Can you believe that?" The polling station remains open, as voting hours have just been officially extended, but no more ballots will be cast at this location. A *glorious* election, with a turnout of over 80 percent, as the state media claims? Yes, but not all of those 80 percent were able to vote, for this polling station is one of many reporting similar problems with ballots. How do I know? My cousin's daughter was in charge here.

4:00 p.m., June 12, 2009: The Hyatt Hotel at Grand Central Terminal, New York City. The Islamic Republic has set up polling stations across the world for Iranian expatriates, usually at Iranian embassies or consulates, but in the United States, where Iran has no diplomatic representation other than at the United Nations, a few polling places have been organized in major cities with the help of the Iranian Mission to the UN and the Iranian Interests Section at the Pakistani Embassy in Washington, D.C. The ballots are identical to those used inside Iran, and the results are to be sent to Iran by the end of the evening, by e-mail, I understand. I join a dozen or so Iranians and cast my vote, writing "Mir Hossein Mousavi" as legibly as I can in Farsi. The mood is lively, and reports from Iran, eight and a half hours ahead of our time, so far indicate only that the turnout is massive. We all have a knowing look on our faces, a sort of half-smile that indicates we know—we *know* that our vote, and the votes of our compatriots, will end the presidency of Mahmoud Ahmadinejad. I have been back from Tehran for only about ten days, still wearing the green silicone wristband I picked up at a Mousavi rally, and still wondering if the results, which I expect to hear the next morning, will mean a second-round runoff or an outright win for Mousavi. Given reports of the massive turnout, it appears that perhaps former president Seyed Mohammad Khatami was right when he told me, as I was leaving Tehran, not to bother if I was expecting to return for a second-round vote. "I'll come back for the inauguration, then," I replied. There are other Iranians mingling outside the small conference room on the mezzanine of the giant hotel, which sits atop a railroad station in midtown Manhattan, and still others coming up the escalators. A couple of camera crews, one from the Islamic Republic of Iran Broadcasting (IRIB) network, are filming the scene, a stark contrast to the one four years ago when a much smaller room was booked at the Marriott a few blocks away, and where hardly a soul showed up to vote. It's working, I think, this Islamic "democracy." At least those of us voting think so.

1:00 p.m., June 10, 2009: Revolutionary Guard Headquarters, Tehran. Brigadier General Yadollah Javani, head of the Guards' Political Bureau, has issued a statement, posted on the Revolutionary Guard website. "The presence of supporters of Mir Hossein Mousavi on the streets are part of the velvet revolution," it reads, two days before voters go to the polls. You're kidding, right? Javani *can't* think that Mousavi is seeking to overthrow the system, can he? "Using a specific color for the first time by a candidate in this election shows the start of a velvet revolution project," it goes on. Ah, that's it. He's just a little worried about the whole green thing, all those kids I saw on the streets of Tehran a week ago, partying and rallying every night, all wearing green. "Any attempt at a velvet revolution will be nipped in the bud," Javani insists. Well, since there *is* no velvet revolution, and he will see that on election day, this is no big deal. Javani takes his orders from his commanders, who take their orders directly from the Supreme Leader. No, no velvet revolution here, nothing to see, move along now.

11:00 p.m., June 12, 2009: Mousavi Campaign Headquarters, Tehran. Mousavi has written two letters to the Supreme Leader, which were delivered by hand. In them he asks his former boss to intervene, to do something about the massive fraud he and his campaign officials believe is being perpetuated. In the 1980s when Mousavi was prime minister, then-President Khamenei had tried to have him removed but Ayatollah Ruhollah Khomeini, the Supreme Leader at the time, threw his support behind his protégé Mousavi and not his own successor, Khamenei, and Mousavi remained in his post for a full eight years. (The position of prime minister was eliminated after the founder of the Islamic Republic, the first valih-e-faqih, died.) The relationship between Khamenei and Mousavi had been tenuous at best, but that was twenty years ago. Islamic democracy had many layers then, more than today. Did Khamenei still hold a grudge? Whether he did or not, Mousavi's letters don't have an effect. Iran's conservative press will announce Ahmadinejad's re-election by an overwhelming margin in the morning papers, and Mousavi is expected to fade into oblivion, once again. But he is unwilling to do so. Meetings go on through the night, with the candidate insisting that he will challenge the election results if they hold, as they are expected to do. The phone rings constantly, supporters and the press wanting to know what has happened and what will happen. No one knows, and among the tears and forlorn faces, and anguish even, only Mousavi appears resolute.

8:30 p.m., June 3, 2009: IRTV 3 Television Studios, Tehran. It's the one everyone has been waiting for—the first live televised debate between the two front-running candidates for president in the Islamic Republic's brief history. Mohsen Rezai has already debated Mehdi Karroubi, and all four candidates will debate each other over the next few days, but this is the one, the debate that will give us the opportunity to see the two men most likely to be Iran's next president duke it out. It's an American-style campaign debate; no holds barred, and to the winner, if there is a clear one, will probably go the spoils. There are at least four IRIB cameras: one facing each candidate; one stationary for a wide shot of the two men and the moderator, seated between them at a round table; and one overhead, which zooms in every now and then for dramatic effect. Clearly visible by Ahmadinejad's left hand is a stack of manila file folders; Mousavi glanced at them as he walked in to take his seat. One of them has his wife's name, Zahra Rahnavard, on it.

Ahmadinejad begins his allocated ten-minute introduction presenting himself as a victim. He is not running against Mousavi, he claims, but against three men—Rafsanjani, Mousavi, and Khatami, two former two-term presidents and a prime minister—and three administrations. Ayatollah Ali Akbar Hashemi Rafsanjani is their leader, he claims, and had long ago formed a cabal to keep power in the hands of the few and away from pious, hardworking, incorruptible people like himself. It is business as usual for the president, to always portray Rafsanjani, his family, and his allies as corrupt politicians out to get him, Mahmoud, the savior of the ordinary Iranian. If one of the basic precepts of democracy, and Iranians understand democracy, is equal access to power, then Ahmadinejad is accusing Mousavi and his cohorts of being *anti*-democratic, for they want to deny power to anyone but themselves, he claims. They have ganged up on him from the very start of his presidency, he cries, and they are now mounting vicious attacks on him. It's a message that resonates with his audience and with his supporters, perhaps even with some Iranians more ambivalent about his presidency. Ahmadinejad, like the Glenn Becks and Sarah Palins of America, appeals to every Iranian who is either envious or contemptuous (or both) of the highly educated elite— Iranians who believe themselves entitled to govern over the masses of less educated and less sophisticated people. "A worthless, torn piece of paper," Ahmadinejad had once said of a college degree, when one of his ministers was accused of forging his. Economic theory was just that to Ahmadinejad—theory—and a regular guy could do as good a job with the economy of the country as could a professor, because, after all, *regular* guys understood *regular* problems.

Mousavi speaks in his slow, deliberate, even boring way, but he methodically counters every Ahmadinejad accusation. One wonders if it is having any effect, this professorial tone of his. He accuses Ahmadinejad of mismanaging the economy, hinting that regular guys might not, in fact, have all the answers. Gee, but does Mousavi have to be *boring*? Well, this debate isn't going to be, not by a long shot, and not if Ahmadinejad, hardly someone to be accused of being boring, has his way.

We don't have to wait too long for the excitement to begin, the moment when Ahmadinejad starts waving Zahra Rahnavard's file in the air, *Stasi*-style. Wait, what is *this*? Debates are unusual in Iranian politics, but *this* is going way beyond what anyone could have imagined. From the expression on his face, Mousavi is clearly pissed, and the television audience is riveted. Is it a sign of desperation on Ahmadinejad's part? Zahra hides no secrets—a rumor had been making the rounds of Tehran salons that she donned miniskirts when she was a college student, before the revolution; perhaps the file contains the photographs to prove it? A week before at her office she had readily admitted as much to me though, so who would really care? After all, she *chose*, she said, to adopt the hijab, also before the revolution. It's a choice, she emphasized, and her personal belief is that the government should not be in the business of mandating clothing laws, although she also emphasized that it is not within a president's mandate to change those laws. She said all this quite freely, so what does Ahmadinejad's file contain, *other* than photos of a young Zahra *mal*-veiled? It is a weak moment for Ahmadinejad, even among his staunch supporters. No one likes files kept on them—*no* one, not even in the Islamic Republic.

But no, it's not Zahra's skimpy dress or the allure of her bare head he wants to embarrass Mousavi with. It is her college degree, or, as Ahmadinejad claims, her *lack* of one, despite her being a college professor. Waving the file, Ahmadinejad coyly says, "Shall I tell? Shall I tell?" like a high school student teasing a classmate. He *did* tell, of course. Whatever happened to his equating a diploma with a "torn piece of paper"? Since the impeachment of his interior minister for lying about his, we all thought Ahmadinejad viewed college degrees as an unnecessary distraction, but I guess he's trying to point out the corrupt ways of the elite, not necessarily their lack of qualifications.

Mousavi's anger shows; but he brushes aside the accusation (which no one really believes) and berates the president for his foreign policy—his adventurism, as he calls it—and his failure to deliver much of anything to the Iranian people. The oil wealth never did quite make it to the dinner table of ordinary Iranians, as Ahmadinejad had promised four years ago, but he did provide some services to the poor and working classes during his first term, which has ensured at least some measure of support from them. Ahmadinejad counters, mostly by leveling more accusations against Mousavi's supporters, particularly the Rafsanjani family, who he claims is bankrolling his opponent's campaign. Corruption is a favorite topic among working-class Iranians, who have seen little improvement in their lives as the Tehran elite grow richer and richer. Perhaps Ahmadinejad's vicious attacks are working. It's hard to say, but the audience seems divided by the end of the broadcast. There has been no real knockout blow, both men (and their supporters) claim to have come out on top, and little will be remembered of the debate except for the president's meticulous file-keeping on all enemies, real or perceived, and their spouses.

6:00 p.m., June 9, 2009: Ministry of the Interior, Tehran. By now a leak from the ministry in charge of the elections has made the rounds of Tehran, creating a buzz and some concern in the campaign headquarters of Mir Hossein Mousavi and Mehdi Karroubi. Ayatollah Mohammad Taghi Mesbah-Yazdi, the most radically hard-line of the hard-line clerics in the holy city of Qom, and Ahmadinejad's mentor and spiritual adviser, is said to have issued, in an open letter addressed to ministry officials in charge of the vote and leaked by one or more of them, a *fatwa* allowing the manipulation of the election results in favor of the candidate truest to the principles of Islam. Although Mesbah-Yazdi is not mentioned by name, information provided by ministry officials implicates only him, and although he is not a *Marja-e-taghlid*, or Grand Ayatollah, and therefore technically not able to issue a fatwa (which can have the force of law), his words have a chilling effect on all who read them. "For you," his letter states in reference to ensuring that a true Muslim wins, "as administrators of the election, *everything is permitted.*"

8:20 p.m., June 8, 2009: IRTV 3 Television Studios, Tehran. The final debate of the presidential campaign is about to begin. Mohsen Rezai, a former commander of the Revolutionary Guards and Ahmadinejad's only conservative rival, walks past the president's stack of files. The top one has the name of Rezai's son on it, the son who a few years earlier had made his way to the United States and decided to stay, requesting political asylum. He changed his mind quickly though, and returned to Iran after a few months. The affair was silenced, and Rezai's son suffered no consequences of his betrayal and disloyalty. The political elite take good care of each other in the Islamic Republic, particularly the Revolutionary Guard elite. But Ahmadinejad, who had already shown a willingness to sling mud in his debate with Mousavi, seems like he's going to do the same with Rezai, a *Sepah* veteran. The *Sepah-e-Pasdaran*, the Revolutionary Guards, are his main backers, after all, and he would be nowhere without their support. Rezai glares at Ahmadinejad. "You bring up my son, one mention, and I'll bring up your entire family," he says, according to a witness present in the studio. He uses the Farsi *toh* rather than the more respectful *shoma*, similar to the difference between *tu* and *vous* in French. "You think *you're* the only one with files?" Rezai continues, before taking his seat. Rezai, of course, has plenty of files. You don't get to be commander of the Guards, for eight years no less, unless you know a lot about your enemies *and* your friends. Ahmadinejad, needless to say, does not raise the issue of Rezai's son and why he did not pay a price for his defection. Perhaps this exchange didn't happen, perhaps the witness is exaggerating, or making it all up. But it is more than likely to have.

6:00 p.m., June 13, 2009: North Tehran. Ayatollah Rafsanjani is huddled in a room with his family and some of his aides. Rafsanjani, known as the second most powerful man in Iran, is calm. The Supreme Leader has already congratulated President Ahmadinejad on his re-election, essentially validating the results of the election before the Guardian Council, the body that certifies elections, does. More than a week ago, Rafsanjani had written to Ayatollah Khamenei, the *Rahbar*, asking him to ensure that the election would be a fair one. Some viewed that letter as a threat—that Rafsanjani was suggesting that if there were to be fraud, he would hold Khamenei responsible. And Rafsanjani arguably had the power to do something about it, but Khamenei must not have cared. No one in the opposition, not even some supporters of Khamenei, believes the results of the election exactly as announced. So now, while many on both the left and the right are confused and unsure of what their next steps should be, it is up to Rafsanjani, easily the most powerful politician opposed to Ahmadinejad, to make his move. He knows it, but he also knows how dangerous it can be in the waters he's about to venture into. Not one to make mistakes, Rafsanjani is cool and collected as he considers the best way of thwarting the Ahmadinejad putsch, for that's what he believes it to be. Mousavi's headquarters have been raided, his communications network shut down, and Iran is in a state of shock. Ayatollah Khamenei, the man Rafsanjani shoe-horned into the job of Supreme Leader twenty years ago, was once his friend and ally, but he has now made it clear that he is backing Ahmadinejad all the way. It is still unclear which way the political pendulum will swing, and Rafsanjani, sometimes known as the *Kuseh*, or the "Shark," won't take any chances. It's finally decided. He will quietly make a trip to two cities, Qom and Mashhad, visiting clerics and members of the Assembly of Experts, of which he is the chairman, to see which way the wind is blowing. Nothing is to be disclosed publicly, not his itinerary, not who he is meeting with, not even that he's left Tehran. And that's the way it will be, except for the Tehran rumor mill, which continues to grind away with reports of Rafsanjani's every move, all unconfirmed, but all believed. Everything *is* true.

8:00 p.m., June 15, 2009: North Tehran, Iran, and Brooklyn, New York. I am on the phone with Ali Khatami, former president Khatami's brother and longtime chief of staff. "My sense," I say, "is that people are really just protesting the vote, not looking to start another revolution."

"Exactly!" he says. "That's exactly what is happening, and nothing more. It just doesn't make sense to most people, and they are frustrated and angry. We have to support them, as they have supported us."

"You know, some are calling it a revolution here and in the West in general," I say.

"No!" says Khatami. "All we're asking for is what is legal in Iran, for the law to prevail. Karroubi, you know, can be hot-headed, he's a Lor after all, but we're all just asking for the law to be applied to the elections."

"What's going to happen?" I ask, on a day when Iran has seen the largest demonstration in its history as an Islamic Republic.

"I don't know," Khatami replies, "but we can only hope that everyone comes to their senses."

1:45 p.m., June 19, 2009: Tehran University Campus, Friday Prayers, Tehran. The Supreme Leader of the Islamic Revolution, Ayatollah Seyed Ali Khamenei, delivers his sermon. The entire world has been waiting for this moment, waiting to hear Iran's most powerful man weigh in on the biggest internal crisis to face the nation in thirty years. Khamenei tells the audience how humbled he is by the turnout in the election a week ago—almost 85 percent and forty million souls—and how the people are still committed to the Islamic Revolution. "This election put religious democracy on display for the whole world to witness," he says, and "all ill-wishers of the Islamic establishment saw for themselves the meaning of religious democracy." It is not what voters opposed to the government of Mahmoud Ahmadinejad want to hear, not by a long shot. *Religious democracy?* "This is an alternative path in the face of dictatorships and arrogant regimes on the one side and democracies devoid of spirituality and religion on the other," the

Ayatollah continues. "This is religious democracy. This is what brings the hearts of people together and draws them to the scene."

What has been "drawing" people "to the scene" in the last week—the scene being the streets of the capital and other cities—has been allegations of fraud, but he is right that the notion of democracy brought people to the ballot box. It is becoming clear, though, that the Supreme Leader means to draw a line in the sand. While he praises all the candidates who ran for president, and dismisses notions that any of them are "outside" the system or anti-revolutionary, he also admits that President Ahmadinejad's ideas "are closer to mine" than anyone else's. Never before has a Supreme Leader so openly played favorites among the many powerful politicians vying for power under his leadership. It is the end of the game as far as many Iranians are concerned: as long as Ali Khamenei is alive or occupies the post of Supreme Leader, Ahmadinejad and perhaps even his chosen successor will enjoy the protection of the valih-e-faqih. That, it seems, is this Ayatollah's version of an Islamic democracy.

As for the opposition, Khamenei warns them in no uncertain terms. "Post-election rivalry on the streets is not the right way to go," he says. "It only challenges the election. I want all sides to put an end to this. If they do not stop such actions, then they will be responsible for the repercussions of such incidents." "Repercussions," all Iranians know, is the code word for state-sanctioned violence. "It is also wrong to assume that street riots can be used as leverage to pressure the establishment and to force officials to listen to them for what they believe is in the interest of the country," the Ayatollah continues, trying to put an end to any ideas Iranians might have that their protests will have an effect. "Giving in to illegal demands under pressure is in itself the beginning of dictatorship. This is a miscalculation and the consequences will be directed at those who orchestrated them." The Ayatollah has spoken, and his word is law.

1:50 p.m., July 17, 2009: Tehran University Campus, Friday Prayers. Ayatollah Rafsanjani is the prayer leader today, a little over a month after the election, a month during which he has been remarkably quiet, at least publicly. Everyone in Tehran knows that he believes the election results to be fraudulent, that he probably spent the last four weeks trying either to unseat the Supreme Leader or to gather enough support among fellow critics to persuade him to change his mind about Ahmadinejad and the election of 2009. The crowd is overflowing; it looks to be one of the biggest crowds to attend Tehran Friday prayers in years, and many attendees will have to listen and pray on the grounds or on adjoining thoroughfares like Enghelab Street. The last time Rafsanjani delivered the Friday sermon in that huge ceilinged but otherwise open-air hall was on May 22, three weeks before the election. Rafsanjani, leaning on a Kalashnikov rifle, had exhorted the much smaller crowd, and whoever was listening on the radio then, not only to chant "Death to America" and "Death to Israel" but also to participate in the upcoming vote. I was present for that sermon, but none of my many cousins attended. This time, they are all there. For many of the tens of thousands of people in the hall and outside, it is their first time attending a Friday prayer, certainly for many of the women (who are segregated) and the secular Tehranis who on a normal Friday holiday would be engaging in less religiously themed enjoyments. But they are here to hear what Rafsanjani says, for this, they recognize, is a momentous occasion in the history of their republic, and for the notion of democracy in Iran. Friday prayer sermons are supposed to reflect the Supreme Leader's views. Will Rafsanjani cave and express his support for Khamenei, or will he challenge him in a way no one has ever done in the Islamic Republic's thirty-year history? Millions of Iranians are waiting to see, perhaps oblivious to the irony that their hopes for a more democratic Iran are resting with one of the pillars of the regime many have grown to hate—a two-time president, an Ayatollah, and a person in whose interest it has always been to preserve the regime at all costs.

Rafsanjani doesn't disappoint. Ignoring any directives from the Supreme Leader, he challenges his own regime to make the changes needed to avert what he calls a "crisis." "The legitimacy of the country comes from its people's consent," he says, quoting the founder of the republic, Ayatollah Khomeini. "When we were writing the new constitution," says Rafsanjani, referring to the founding of the Islamic Republic, "we asked the Imam [Khomeini] for advice. He put a lot of emphasis on the role of the people. He also knew that people's vote was the most important thing inside our country—everything depended upon the people's vote. People should directly elect the president, the Parliament, the local council—it was all about the vote of the people. This is a theocracy—a theocratic republic." The audience is again chanting, drowning out his words. "Be patient," Rafsanjani exhorts. "Be calm," he pleads. "If the government is not Islamic, then we are heading nowhere. If it is not a republic, then it doesn't amount to anything." There is more chanting and the atmosphere is getting more tense by the moment. The supporters of the regime, hoping that Rafsanjani might use the nation's most influential pulpit to throw his full support behind the Supreme Leader, are unhappy. "We need to have an open society in which people can say what they want to say," Rafsanjani continues, ignoring them. "We should not imprison people—let them rejoin their families." The pro-government crowd inside the hall tries to shout him down, with chants of "Death to America!" and "Death to Israel!" but supporters and pro-reform Iranians counter with their own idea of to whom death should pay a visit. "Death to Russia!" they shout, a reference to the fact that President Dmitry Medvedev was the first foreign leader to congratulate Ahmadinejad on his re-election, and that Ahmadinejad's first foreign jaunt was to Russia, only days after the disputed election. There are clashes outside, between Basij, police, and

a pro-Ahmadinejad crowd on one side, and anti-government demonstrators on the other. A number of people are arrested, including the
sons of that other pillar of the establishment, Speaker of Parliament Ali
Larijani. It is an electrifying day for Iranians, who have not seen this
kind of debate, disagreement, and public questioning of the direction
their country is headed in years or, in fact, ever. Everything is *not* true.

ENTR'ACTE

While the battle over the presidency and the future of Iran continues, we consider the political landscape.

The Supreme Leader. The Guardian Council. The Assembly of Experts. The Expediency Discernment Council. Corps of the Guardians of the Islamic Revolution (The Revolutionary Guards, Sepah-e-Pasdaran), Islamic Consultative Assembly (Majles, *or Parliament*). The president, *any* president, important as he is, would not be president if the Guardian Council hadn't approved his candidacy *ahead* of time; he would not be able to take office if the council and the Supreme Leader had not certified his election; and he would not be able to form a cabinet without the confirmation process of the Parliament. And then, if he is able to get legislation passed by the Parliament, he has to await the Guardians' approval, and if it is not forthcoming, await the Expediency Council's arbitration of any dispute. And then there's the Supreme Leader's opinion.

"Everything is true; nothing is permitted." That statement can often be not just the Supreme Leader's opinion but his edict as well. It is the obverse of a cryptic phrase attributed to Hassan'e Sabah, the eleventh-century Persian leader of the Nizari Ismaili Shia sect (better known as the "Assassins"), which he uttered on his deathbed at his fortress at Alamut and which the American beat generation, most notably William S. Burroughs, widely propagated in its original form: *nothing is true; everything is permitted*. Which can *also* be the Supreme Leader's edict, when it suits his purposes.

One can be forgiven for thinking the government, and even the military of Iran, sound rather Orwellian. And it's not only as in George Orwell's *1984*; how about the commandment in his *Animal Farm* that "all animals are equal, but some animals are more equal than others"? Muslims are more equal than non-Muslims in the Islamic Republic, aren't they? Shia Muslims are even more equal than Sunnis, clerics more equal than laymen, and Ayatollahs the most equal of all. Or are they? Neither the Orwellian nomenclature (or nature) of the governmental bodies, nor the *Animal Farm*–like hierarchy of its citizens tells the whole story of Iranian politics, as tempting as it is for some to reduce Iran to a caricature of a Stalinist dictatorship. While the names given to the governmental bodies sound Orwellian, their functions, at least as originally intended, were meant to ensure a form of *mardomsalari*, or democracy. "Supreme" is a word added on in English; in Farsi the title of the Leader is just that, *Rahbar*. He is the jurisprudent at the head of the *velayat-e-faqih*, the "guardianship of the jurisprudent," or as some prefer in the practical case of Iran, "*rule* of the jurisprudent." But if the Supreme Leader were a Stalin-like figure who tolerates no dissention or debate, no breaks from his orders or philosophies, then the various Orwellian bodies of government would be stacked only with his most loyal lieutenants. The Guardian Council is arguably the one body (other than the Guards, who are loyalists by definition and are by law to remain neutral in political matters) that is effectively appointed directly by the Supreme Leader, and it has always reflected his conservative bias. A twelve-member body—six Islamic jurists appointed by the Supreme Leader and six jurists elected by Parliament from a list of names provided by the chief of the Judiciary, who is in turn selected by the Supreme Leader—its primary function is to interpret the constitution and to approve or veto bills passed by Parliament, judging both the Islamic and constitutional suitability of any law. Its other function, what it is best known for in the West, is approving or disqualifying candidates for public office, from the presidential level on down, and certifying all election results. *Everything is true.*

Undemocratic? You bet. Mohsen Rezai, the losing conservative

challenger to President Ahmadinejad in the 2009 election, has suggested that future elections be handled by an independent "National
Election Commission" to ensure fairness, from the vote count itself
(now handled by the Interior Ministry, whose head is appointed by the
president and therefore is likely to be biased) to the certification of the
results. Whether that will come to pass or not, the likelihood of some
change in the electoral process is high, given the dissatisfaction with
the way the 2009 election was handled, on the part of both reformers *and* conservatives. Some reformists in Iran have suggested that
the Guardian Council be eliminated altogether, and that this unlikely
scenario is even on the table, discussed openly in a place where *nothing
is permitted*, is perhaps of some solace to those who want democratic
change in the Islamic system.

The Assembly of Experts, perhaps the most Orwellian sounding
of the various governmental bodies, is actually, in a typically Persian
way, simultaneously the most and least important branch of the government. The assembly, composed of eighty-six Islamic scholars elected to
eight-year terms, meets quietly twice a year and is charged with monitoring the Supreme Leader's performance. The clerics in the assembly,
all elected by direct vote of the people, pick the Supreme Leader and
can remove or impeach him, but since the Islamic Revolution of 1979
they have had to consider a new Leader only once, after Khomeini's
death, and perhaps consider action once, in the aftermath of the 2009
election. Otherwise, they are essentially irrelevant to the day-to-day
functioning of the republic, and no one pays any attention to their
twice-yearly meetings. The chairman of the assembly, Ayatollah
Rafsanjani, has many allies in that body, including Hassan Rowhani,
the former nuclear negotiator under President Khatami and someone
close to the reformers as well as the pragmatic conservatives, but of
course there are hard-line clerics in the body, too, who are resistant to
any change in the system of leadership (some of whom, like Ayatollah

Mesbah-Yazdi, would very much like to become the Supreme in that leadership one day).

After Khomeini's death, a proposal to replace the Supreme Leader with a council of three (or more) jurists was floated and rejected, but Ayatollah Rafsanjani has revived this as a possibility. In the aftermath of the 2009 election, many analysts and anti-regime Iranians pointed to the shadowy Mojtaba Khamenei, the Supreme Leader's son, as the man responsible for ensuring an Ahmadinejad win, partly because of his own ambitions to succeed his father in the post of Rahbar. If true, at least the ambition part, he is probably in for a major disappointment. For Khamenei Jr. has neither the religious credentials (his father didn't either, but at least he had the respect of his fellow clergy) nor the political acumen to maneuver around the likes of Rafsanjani, or, more important, conservative and hard-line clerics who want the job for themselves.

In order to ensure some form of democratic control over the office of the Supreme Leader, reformist politicians have indicated that they wish to amend the Iranian constitution to allow non-clerics into the assembly, and to remove the Guardian Council's veto on who can run for election to the body. Again, it is unlikely that their efforts will be successful, certainly not while they are the minority in Parliament and excluded from the executive branch, but in what they call the necessary "evolution" of the Islamic Republic, they view the acceptance of their concepts of Islamic democracy as inevitable for the long-term survival of the Islamic system. If they can get some of their top politicians out of Evin prison before the next round of parliamentary elections, and if the Guardian Council allows more reformists to run (if only to avoid incurring the wrath of the people yet again), perhaps they will be in a position to convince their conservative colleagues of the same. If past civil rights movements in other countries are any indication, Iran's own movement may have far-reaching implications for a new kind of democracy established without the wholesale removal of a political system (which some insist is the only real reform possible in Iran).

The Expediency Council, not very Orwellian but beautifully named (who *wouldn't* want a council charged with expediency in government?), is an important body that was set up under the revised constitution of 1988. However, it is little understood, even in Iran. Officially it is charged with resolving differences and conflicts between the Guardian Council and the Parliament, although as an advisory body to the Supreme Leader, who appoints its members, it has far greater power, and in fact, the Supreme Leader gave the Expediency Council supervisory authority over the executive branch after the election of President Ahmadinejad in 2005. (Ahmadinejad has chosen to ignore the council with apparent impunity.) The longtime chairman of the council is Ayatollah Rafsanjani, and among its members have been Hassan Rowhani, Ali Larijani, and Mir Hossein Mousavi (who is *still* a member, believe it or not), all opposed to the hard-liner Ahmadinejad. Ahmadinejad and his allies had hit hard at Rafsanjani after the disputed election because of his initial unambiguous stand on the results and the government crackdown that followed, but the Supreme Leader made very clear the importance of the council and Rafsanjani to the continued stability of the Islamic Republic. In November 2009, after more attacks on Rafsanjani, Khamenei stated that "reports that tarnish the reputation of prominent figures of the establishment are unacceptable, whether these reports are about the president, or the speaker of Parliament, or the head of the Expediency Council." He even said that accusations against Rafsanjani were part of a foreign plot, a "soft war" on Iran, he called it: "Such actions are in line with the wishes of the enemy because the country's officials, including the president, the Majles speaker, the Judiciary chief, and the Expediency Council chairman are at the helm of the country, and people should trust them."

So THERE are *four*, not three, branches of government in *this* Ayatollah's democracy—five, if you include the Leader himself—and they are often at odds with each other. All throughout the summer Ahmadinejad and his friends had been accusing the reformists of being a "part of the enemy's soft war"; now *they* were being included in the list of Iranians who were doing the enemy's bidding. One could be forgiven for wondering if there was no one left in Tehran in late 2009 who *wasn't* a part of the enemy's plot to overthrow the Islamic regime. Ali Larijani weighed in a few days later, criticizing those who criticized Rafsanjani, and at the Tehran Friday prayers the same week, an archconservative ally of Ahmadinejad's, Ayatollah Ahmad Khatami (no relation to former president Khatami), who ironically was leading the important Eid-ol-Adha (Muslim holiday) prayers for the first time—traditionally the role of Ayatollah Rafsanjani—repeated the Supreme Leader's admonition by advising his flock to respect the heads of the three branches of government *and* the chairman of the Expediency Council, Ayatollah Rafsanjani, "per guidelines of the Supreme Leader of Islamic Revolution Ayatollah Seyed Ali Khamenei." It must have pained him to say so, but say it he did, even as he emphasized the *three*, and not four branches of government Khamenei had apparently outlined.

A FEW DAYS earlier, Hassan Taeb, a former commander of the Basij but at that time the deputy for intelligence in the Revolutionary Guards, had accused Rafsanjani's oldest son, Mehdi, of running a prostitution ring in the 1990s, for the purpose of espionage, and Taeb claimed that only his father's influence guaranteed his immunity from prosecution. Mehdi Hashemi, as he is known, has been the longtime head of the Tehran Metro (my cousin Mohammad Majd, also former President

Khatami's cousin, is his longtime deputy). In this role, Hashemi runs a multi-billion-dollar project that has built and is expanding Iran's first subway system, and the Ahmadinejad administration has been trying, unsuccessfully, to have him removed from the post from almost the day the president was first inaugurated.

Taeb and his supporters in the Basij, the Guards, and the Ahmadinejad government were no doubt shocked to hear that they too, by disparaging Rafsanjani, might have been a part of the enemy's soft war on Iran, a war that they had responded to, up until then, in an aggressively vicious fashion. Everything is true; *everything is forbidden*. With prostitutes in tow or not, corrupt or not, Rafsanjani, the chairman of the Expediency Council, and his family would remain untouchable, at least for now, and the Supreme Leader, by his own decree, would have to countenance his dissent, which Rafsanjani, undaunted by Taeb or anyone else, repeated only a few days later. By emphasizing in a speech at a university that the regime needs to respond to the protests, needs to "open the sphere of criticism over shortcomings and weaknesses of the regime," and needs to recognize the importance of "the irrefutable role of the public in providing legitimacy to the regime," Rafsanjani showed not only his independence from *all* branches of the government, however many there are, but also his confidence in the power he wields in *his* version of the Ayatollahs' democracy.

THE CLERICS and people in Iran have their differing ideas of what "Islamic democracy" means, or what it should look like, but they almost all agree that the foundations of that democracy were laid down by the revolution of 1979. Perverted perhaps by individuals with unchecked power or sometimes by the very bodies that were intended to ensure a form of democracy, it is not a form of government to write off just yet. Mehdi Karroubi, who like Rafsanjani was jailed on numerous occasions during Shah Mohammad Reza Pahlavi's time, has often said that he did not expect the Islamic republic he helped found to become the autocratic and intolerant government he believes it now to be. Islamic democracy, as he and other clerics have avowed, is possible because there are republican aspects of Islam and Islamic aspects of republicanism, such as respect for and protection of the rights of the people, and the ability of the people to choose their leaders. That's far too vague to be a description of a political system, and one that melds theology with governance, but perhaps it's that vagueness—and the anomalous nature of the Ayatollahs' democracy—that has allowed its survival this long.

ACT TWO:

Nothing Is Permitted

10:00 p.m., September 25, 2009: The Intercontinental Hotel, New York City. President Ahmadinejad and his entourage, in town to attend the UN General Assembly, are in residence. Ahmadinejad, as he does every year he comes to the United States, holds a dinner for Iranians living in this country, and this year is no exception, despite an election widely seen as fraudulent and the massive unrest that ensued, resulting in deaths, detention, forced confessions, and allegations of torture and rape. However, this year the dinner is a more intimate gathering, held in two small adjoining conference rooms on the ground floor of the hotel, which is located on Lexington Avenue, a few blocks away from the UN. There are protesters outside, and those of us attending had to pass through heavy security to get in. Nonetheless, before dinner starts, an elderly gentleman neatly dressed in a gray suit stands up and yells at the top of his voice, *"Marg bar Jomhouri-e-Eslami, Marg Bar Khamenei!"*—"Death to the Islamic Republic, death to Khamenei!" It seems we can't get away from death, not even here, not even among Iranians who had perhaps hoped and voted for a less pugnacious administration in Tehran. The room is awkwardly silent as the man is gently escorted away by American security officials under the glare of their Iranian counterparts.

The Iranian foreign minister, Manouchehr Mottaki, a holdover from the first Ahmadinejad administration, stands up to speak. President Ahmadinejad himself is a no-show, owing to an emergency dinner he is having with UN Secretary-General Ban Ki-moon, to discuss the latest element in the nuclear crisis: the revelation of a previously undisclosed enrichment site, which was made public this morning. Lucky A-jad! He won't have to face any tough questions from his carefully screened guests, for he has to leave for Tehran this evening—right after his tête-à-tête with the secretary-general—and the FAA has given his jet a short window of opportunity in which to take off.

During his talk Mottaki makes no mention of the lone protester, who will not, it seems, get his fifteen minutes of fame right here in Andy Warhol's town, and certainly not in Tehran where his defiance will go unreported. The foreign minister is smiling just as uncomfortably as the rest of us, and even sweating, it appears. "The elections," he says, "were an affirmation of our democratic process." I turn to look at Eshagh Al'e Habib, the ambassador and deputy permanent representative to the UN, and an intelligent, mild-mannered diplomat, who is sitting next to me. He also smiles, almost apologetically I think. "Over 13 million people voted for the loser!" exclaims Mottaki, not able to bring himself to mention that loser's name, Mir Hossein Mousavi. It is almost as if he is afraid to, here in front of Ahmadinejad's top aides, including the mastermind behind his first legitimate electoral win, and possibly his second questionable one, Mojtaba Hashemi-Samareh. "And some presidents in the Islamic Republic's history have actually *won* with less than that," continues the foreign minister, "with only 11 million votes!" The official tally in 2009 had been 24 million votes for Ahmadinejad and 13 million for Mousavi, while Ahmadinejad in his previous victory had received only 17 million votes. I wonder if Mottaki realizes that in trying to convince what he knows is a tougher crowd than what he would face back home, if only because they live in New York, he is begging the question, *so where the fuck did A-jad's extra few million votes come from?*

3:00 p.m., July 29, 2009: Iranian Mission to the United Nations, New York City, Office of Ambassador and Deputy Permanent Representative Eshagh Al'e Habib. Permanent Representative Mohammad Khazaee has been back and forth to Tehran for weeks, and is largely absent from the offices in New York and from the UN building. Al'e Habib and I are sitting in his spacious office suite, sipping tea.

"I've asked Counsellor Alavikia to join us, if you don't mind," he says. Majid Alavikia, a relative newcomer to this diplomatic outpost of the Islamic Republic, walks into the room, almost on cue, and sits down on the couch next to me.

"I have my opinions," I say, "but I'm still trying to understand what's going on in Iran. You know of my relationship with Mr. Khatami . . ." I am interrupted by Al'e Habib.

"Of course!" he exclaims. "I have the utmost respect for Mr. Khatami and Mir Hossein Mousavi," he continues, "but you know, when you leave Tehran, you see how much support President Ahmadinejad has."

"I was in Iran for over a month, right before the elections, and I traveled around the country," I say, "but I have to differ with you on the level of support the president had in the provinces." Al'e Habib and Alavikia smile uncomfortably. Neither has been back to Tehran, or anywhere else in Iran, for over a year. These foreign ministry employees must be facing the most difficult period of their careers, I think, especially since they are posted in the United States. Not only is it the one country in the world where antagonism with their government is the highest, but also the U.S. government restricts their movements to a twenty-five-mile radius of Columbus Circle, making them and their families virtual prisoners of New York. "But leaving aside whether there was any fraud in the elections or not," I continue, "what is happening in Iran with respect to the arrests, the killings, and so on, makes it impossible to not believe that something has gone horribly wrong."

"The media is being unfair," says Alavikia. "All they want to report on is what the opposition is saying, and what the protesters are saying." He pauses for a moment. "Of course, we respect the opposition, the people," he adds.

"With all due respect," I say, "you're not allowing the press to cover anything at all, so they cover what they can."

"The media has shown its bias," says Al'e Habib, "all this talk of revolution, of toppling the system . . ."

"I know, and I disagree with the idea that there's a revolution brewing in Iran," I reply, "but throwing journalists in jail doesn't help your cause. Maziar Bahari, for example." (Bahari was the *Newsweek* reporter who spent 118 days in Evin prison.) Al'e Habib nods his head.

"This will all pass," he says. "Things will settle down once the authorities in Tehran are satisfied. You know, Roger Cohen was here a few days ago, asking for a visa to return to Tehran. He promised he would be fair in his coverage from now on, but really, I cannot imagine that he'll be welcome for a while." Cohen, who writes for the *New York Times*, had provided eyewitness accounts of the post-election unrest in Iran and had defied the authorities' prohibition on reporting from the streets until his visa ran out and he was forced to leave the country.

"Yes, Mohammadi [Mohammad Mohammadi, the spokesman for the Iranian Mission at the time] told me," I said. "He also told me he challenged Cohen, demanding to know why he thought the election was stolen, and Cohen asked him if he had been in Iran during the vote. No, Mohammadi had said, but he was Iranian, had lived in Iran for over forty years, and expected he knew a little more about Iran than Cohen, who had spent all of four weeks in Iran in his entire life." Al'e Habib and Alavikia laughed. "I know it's a problem, this idea that foreigners don't understand Iran," I said, "but Iran doesn't make it easy, either."

3:00 p.m., September 30, 2009: Iranian Mission to the United Nations, New York City. I am in a reception room, handsomely and appropriately furnished in faux Louis Quinze. The floor is covered with a huge Persian carpet, one of many extra-large rugs scattered about the half-floor of a high-rise on Third Avenue that has long served as Iran's diplomatic offices. "It's better," says spokesman Mohammad Mohammadi, "if you avoid *mocking* President Ahmadinejad in your writings." I pick up the obligatory glass of tea from the coffee table, not sure how to respond. I, like many other Iranian writers, have been invited to appear on count-less television and radio programs, and have written a number of essays on Iran in the months following the presidential election. My tone, I'm sure, has offended on more than one occasion.

"I don't think I've ever intended to mock," I say with a wince after a gulp of the scalding hot tea, "but you know my opinions on what has transpired."

"Of course," says Mohammadi gently. He has mellowed somewhat since June 13, the day after the election when all hell broke loose in Iran. Always an Ahmadinejad supporter, he was convinced that not only did Ahmadinejad win by a large margin, but also the West, along with its media, had conspired to create the unrest the world had witnessed. We have had many long phone conversations in the past three months, some as long as two hours, where I swear I could *hear* the frothing at his mouth and the tears of anger in his eyes. "After five years, I thought I understood the workings of the U.S. media," he once told me in a fit of rage, "but I realize now I was taken in just like everyone else. All of them are working against Iran, and in coordina-tion with the U.S. government." Mohammadi had staunchly defended the Basij, telling me on numerous occasions that their crackdown was justified, that the media ignored the fact that rioters and protesters killed many Basij, and he became, in telling me that he was duped by the media he believed he had been helping all these years, the *victim*, like his Basij brethren. Shiite victimhood never goes away, not even after spending five years in New York without leave to go home.

"I know we disagree on the election itself," I say to him, "and I appreciate your openness . . ."

"There's never a problem with disagreeing among ourselves," he interrupts me. "Nobody ever said there was!"

"Yes," I say, "but this ongoing violence in Iran, these prisoners . . . one of my friends is in jail right now, a musician, and I can tell you for a fact that he is *not* guilty of anything, much less of trying to overthrow the system."

"Really, your friend?" Mohammadi leans forward, genuine concern showing in his face.

"Kamran Jahanbani," I reply. "You can check him out; he was seated in the second row during the televised trials."

"I'm sorry," says Mohammadi. "I'm sure he'll be released soon; it's just a process that has to be completed."

"I hope so," I say. "But what is going on in Tehran? When can we expect this violent reaction to protests to end?"

Mohammadi begins a long monologue, explaining why the government has to work diligently to foil foreign plots, that Mousavi and Karroubi and Khatami—and he emphasizes Khatami because he is well aware of my relationship with him—need to understand that they are being used as pawns of the West and of subversive elements. But as he begins to talk about the Basij and the Revolutionary Guards, I sense his discomfort. A Basij himself once, one who served on the front lines of the Iran-Iraq War and lived to tell about it, he is fiercely loyal to the militia and to their military bosses in the Guards. "You don't know, Mr. Majd, what it's like to hold the head of your best friend in your arms as he takes his last breath." He's fighting back tears as he tries to explain to me what it means to be a Basij, what many of them have gone through in defense of their country, and how unfairly they are portrayed. "All he wanted was water, and I couldn't give him any," he says of his wounded friend. I let him continue, and as he speaks I am more and more convinced that he is having a terrible time reconciling his beloved Basij with the images of their brutality against their own countrymen and women beamed to television sets around the world. I can sense his doubt, his discomfit. "He died in my hands, Mr. Majd. And there was nothing I could do about it." *This,* he must know, what he is seeing on his television every night and far away from home, is not what his friend gave his life for. Perhaps that explains his tears, plainly visible in the corners of his eyes, for he has told me the story of his friend before, a few times. Dry-eyed, that is.

August 20, 2009: Tehran Television Studios. President Ahmadinejad is presenting his cabinet choices for a new administration directly to the Iranian people. He is proposing three women to replace three men, and if Parliament confirms any of them, it would be a first in the history of the Islamic Republic, since no women have ever served in any cabinet position. Some say it is a cynical attempt to woo Iranian women (who generally have been more liberal than men) to his side, others say it is an attempt to reach out to liberals in general, but whatever Ahmadinejad's motivations, there are fierce arguments within the regime about whether the women will, or should, be confirmed.

One of the women he proposes, Marzieh Vahid Dastjerdi, is for the post of minister of health, but he defends his previous minister, Kamran Lankarani, while still insisting a change is needed at the ministry. He begins in a serious tone, describing Lankarani's service in glowing terms, adding that he has a "special, personal affection for him." And then his voice changes. "I said somewhere," Ahmadinejad says, his voice cracking and a few decibels lower, almost child-like, "that he is like peach—you just want to *eat* this man." He is using a Farsi expression reserved exclusively to show admiration and love for babies, or for a female lover. Except, presumably, it is used for gay Iranian men too. No one remembers Ahmadinejad having ever said such a thing about Lankarani, or indeed any other man. Inquiring Persian minds want to know: Could it be that Ahmadinejad, if not a self-hating Jew, is a closet *queen*? Could it be that the "somewhere" he said he would like to eat Dr. Lankarani was at a tryst? *Nah* . . . but Ahmadinejad proves that he is still capable of providing Iranians with the next laugh, the next moment of levity, in the Persian theater of the absurd.

9:00 p.m., July 5, 2009: North Tehran. Former president Khatami and his family and aides are under close observation by the government; their movements, their phone calls, and all other communications are monitored carefully. So far, despite new rumors every day, he hasn't been arrested or called in for questioning. "Every single day I expect I'll be taken away," he repeats to his aides, also almost every day and only half-jokingly. I am on the phone from New York with his chief of staff and brother, Ali Khatami.

"It's tense," he says, "but we're okay so far. We'll see in the future." His voice, albeit calm and reassuring as it always is, betrays his concern.

"But no one's done anything wrong!" I protest.

"The old story is that a hare was running through the forest," Khatami tells me, "and another hare rushes up alongside him, asking him what he's running away from and what the great hurry is. 'They're castrating every hare with three testicles,' the first hare responds, continuing on his way. 'But you don't have three testicles, do you?' asks the second hare breathlessly. 'They castrate first, and count later,' says the first hare as he disappears into the trees. *That*," says Khatami, laughing, "is what's happening in the Islamic Republic right now." *Un opéra bouffe*, indeed, but we still don't know how many acts there are. *Nothing is permitted*.

10:00 a.m., October 29, 2009: Tehran, Iran. Yesterday, IRIB televised an annual students' and intellectuals' audience with the Supreme Leader. The broadcast was cut short when one student, Sharif University sophomore Mahmoud Vahidnia, launched into a twenty-minute criticism of the Ayatollah, questioning the Supreme Leader directly and to his face for what Iranians believe to be the first time ever. *Nothing is permitted.* The entire session was captured by cell phone video, and the news has rocketed around a captivated Tehran. Even the Supreme Leader's own website has news of the exchange, which *Kayhan*, the nation's leading conservative and pro-government newspaper, describes this morning as "The Revolutionary Leader's Fatherly Response to Critical Youth." *Critical?* How's this:

> Why can't anyone in this country criticize you? Isn't that ignorant? Do you think that you make no mistakes? Why have they made an idol out of you that is so unreachable and that nobody can challenge? I have never read an article about your performance in any newspaper because you have shut down all the media that is against you in the country. Why does national TV show all the events untruthfully? For example, all the events after the election: why do you support them [national TV shows], when everyone knows they are lying? Since the president of national television is directly selected by you, you are thus responsible for all this.

It is, for some Iranians, a moment of truth. It is as riveting to Iranians as Joseph Welsh's outburst directed at Joe McCarthy was to Americans in 1954, which put an end to government purges and anti-communist paranoia not wholly dissimilar to the government purges and anti-Western paranoia evident in Iran in the last four months. "Have you no sense of decency, sir?" Vahidnia might have asked if he had been a history student rather than a scientist. It is a question many Iranians, even some who supported Ahmadinejad (but not the brutality of the government crackdown), *wanted* to ask. *"At long last, have you left no sense of decency?"* Reports that Vahidnia was

arrested after his monologue have proved untrue, which has led some
to believe that the whole exchange was staged, to show Iranians that
even the Supreme Leader allows criticism and dissent and that free
speech is allowed in Iran's Islamic democracy. It *can't* be staged, most
argue; nothing like this would ever cross the minds of government
propagandists. Besides, few would have dared to suggest a script that
called for crossing previously red lines in a public setting. Khamenei's
obviously uncomfortable responses and his early exit from the audience with the students also indicate that Vahidnia acted on his own.
But Vahidnia remains free, and uncastrated. *Nothing is permitted?*
Except when it is.

8:00 p.m., July 24, 2009: Fars News Agency, Tehran. The Supreme
Leader's letter has just arrived, been scanned, and is going up on the
news agency's website. In his brief missive addressed to the president, the Rahbar describes Ahmadinejad's appointment on July 17
of Esfandiar Rahim Mashaie as his first vice president—that is, the
person who would assume the presidency should Ahmadinejad become
incapacitated—to be "null and void." The letter is dated July *18*. For a
week Tehran has been abuzz with rumors that the Supreme Leader had
instructed Ahmadinejad to reverse his decision to appoint Mashaie, the
former vice president for tourism who also happens to be his friend and
in-law. Mashaie once described Iran as "friends of the Israeli people,"
which theoretically disqualifies him from this sensitive post, at least
in the eyes of most Ayatollahs. That the Supreme Leader would have
to resort to making his instructions public in order to force the president to obey his commands is astonishing, more astonishing even than
Ahmadinejad's blatant disregard of his allies' sensitivities in appoint-
ing Mashaie, the bête noir of conservatives, in the first place. He still
appears to be on shaky political ground, only a little over a month after
his allegedly rigged re-election. Ahmadinejad, a believer that the best

defense is a strong offense, has seemingly forgotten that one has to possess the ball to play offense, and neither the opposition nor his onetime allies were allowing him much possession time. Reminiscent of his brazen first term, and when only intervention by the Supreme Leader finally persuaded his vice president (but not Ahmadinejad) to apologize for his pro-Semitic faux pas, the president's behavior, his baiting of not just the Supreme Leader but every other conservative cleric and politician he relies on for his dwindling support, is fueling rumors that he will not survive a full term. Ahmadinejad has annoyed conservative clerics in the past, in his "more Catholic than the Pope" moments, such as when he declared, without checking with the guardians of the faith, that women should be allowed into soccer stadiums, or when he claimed he had a special relationship with the Mahdi (rumor has it that he leaves a place setting at his dinner table for him, you know, just in case he arrives suddenly and is hungry, after an eleven-century fast), leading some mullahs to warn him of veering dangerously close to heresy. At times Ahmadinejad has seemed to be almost taunting the mullahs and Ayatollahs, behaving more like a fundamentalist Sunni who believes he is as qualified to interpret his faith as any imam, and less like a pious Shia who should accept an Ayatollah's directives just as a believing Catholic must accept his Pope's. But Ahmadinejad's disdain for the clergy, or at least for mullahs he disagrees with, has always been shared by many Iranians, pious and secular alike.

12:15 p.m., April 21, 2010: Office of former President Khatami, Jamaran, Tehran. I am sitting across from Khatami in his office, drinking tea. Khatami is calm and collected, even cheerful. We are making small talk, asking each other about family and discussing non-political issues. At one point, I ask him a more specific question. Khatami pauses and then waves one hand toward the ceiling and the walls, and says, "You know how it is." Yes, I do. His offices are thoroughly bugged, his every conversation monitored, his every movement tracked. The security services and hard-line papers have repeated, virtually word for word, things said in this very office by accused seditionists, those labeled Green, probably sitting in my chair. But finally, Khatami lowers his voice to a whisper. "Things have never been this bad in the Islamic Republic," he hisses. He knows the microphones can pick up the sound anyway, but he is unconcerned. I'm reminded that only hours before I went to JFK for my April 15 flight to Iran, Khatami—who was due to attend a nuclear summit in Hiroshima the same day I attended one in Tehran—was barred from leaving the country. *Nothing is permitted.* Khatami is actually less pessimistic about the future of the republic than his short outburst would indicate, and agrees that on the surface, Tehran seems normal and the republic is in no danger of imminent collapse. He tells me of plans to travel abroad in coming months, *insha'allah*, and has taken in stride the indignity of being forbidden to travel, an unprecedented act on the part of the government, as he has all the other indignities he's suffered in the ten months since the June elections. This morning the government, perhaps embarrassed by the international coverage his travel ban has received, simply denied its existence. "There is no official ban on Mr. Khatami traveling abroad." *Everything is true.*

8:00 p.m., January 14, 2010: IRIB Channel 3 Television Studios, Tehran. The government-controlled media has begun broadcasting live debates between conservative and reform politicians and thinkers, an opening of Iran's airwaves demanded by the opposition, the "Green Movement," and also supported by conservatives who think that seven months of unrest is harming the republic. Millions are tuning in to the show *Rou be Farda*, "Facing Tomorrow," witnessing again, as they did in the live debates between the candidates before the election and rarely since, the paradoxical nature of Iranian politics that can sometimes simultaneously allow open and deep criticism just as it stifles any dissent. *Everything is permitted; nothing is true.* Tonight, a professor of political science at Shahid Beheshti University, pro-reform Javad Etaat, is debating conservative MP Ali Reza Zakani, and he is merciless in his critique of both the government and the state television it controls. The screen doesn't go black at the first mention of "green," no harsh words are bleeped, and the discussion proceeds as if everything the government has forbidden in the last seven months is now permitted. "I was once invited to give a speech about the attempt to topple Iran's political system through a 'velvet revolution,'" says Etaat in the debate, "but we all know that 'velvet revolutions' always occur in dictatorships. So when you say that some forces are planning to create a velvet revolution, you have indirectly admitted that your system is not democratic."

For months now the government has leveled the accusation that the Green Movement is pursuing a "velvet revolution," but until this moment no one has argued the point Professor Etaat is making. "When elections, discussions, and competition take place in a free atmosphere," he continues, "why should people want to make a revolution? People make revolutions perhaps only every hundred years or so, and only when they are totally fed up with a situation. It doesn't matter whether the revolution is violent, velvet, colored, white, black, red, or yellow. So when the Islamic Republic talks about a 'velvet revolution,' there is an unintended admission that Iran is not a free country, and that people cannot achieve their goals through the institutions the system offers." How can anyone refute *that*? The hardest of hard-liners never cared to describe Iran as a democracy, but most government officials always have, and Etaat is challenging them to either admit they were wrong and then face a real revolution, or allow the constitution—its democratic principles, which he describes article by article—to prevail. The government, already cognizant of this logic, has in the last few days stopped referring to a "velvet revolution," instead calling the unrest *fetneh*, a word that can mean sedition or something softer, such as "troubles." This followed Supreme Leader Khamenei's admonition to the security forces, in the wake of violence and the killings of demonstrators at the end of 2009, to not "take the law into their own hands." *Everything is true.*

Tamam (Na)shud—(Not) The End

PROLOGUE

The sitcom that was the regime of President Mahmoud Ahmadinejad in Iran, entertaining as it was for four years—with halos surrounding his head when he first addressed the United Nations, repeated Holocaust denials and international conferences in Tehran dedicated to the topic, anti-Semitic cartoon festivals sponsored by his government, the removal of countries' names from world maps, ministers not without portfolio but without the university degrees they claimed, the uniqueness of a pure Persian society with a complete absence of homosexuals, and, of course, a president who claimed the Mahdi would appear before the end of his first term—was finally voted off the air, according to many Iranians, in June 2009. It could be said that it jumped the shark *after* its cancellation, taking the Supreme Leader with it, but Ayatollah Ali Akbar Hashemi Rafsanjani (who is actually known in Farsi as the "Shark" for many obvious reasons, including his genetic inability to grow a beard) did everything in his power to prevent the republic *itself* from doing the same.

At one point in the summer of 2009, when what was transpiring in Iran appeared to some to be a new revolution and to others an affirmation of the iron grip of the Revolutionary Guards on an irredeemable system, it was Jon Stewart, the American comedian, who put what was happening best when he asked, "Does *anyone* know what's going on in Iran?" Hardly anyone—no, let's say no one—had predicted the outcome of the election (and certainly no one had predicted the possibility of widespread fraud or an outright manufacturing of results). Fewer still had predicted there would be such large demonstrations every day, bringing new news that made yesterday's analysis seem hopelessly wrong. And the machinations of Ayatollahs like Rafsanjani and Supreme Leader Seyed Ali Khamenei, never transparent in the past, were more opaque than ever.

Years ago, President Seyed Mohammad Khatami had told me that elections in Iran were generally fair—fair, that is, if the winner of any election won by more than three or four hundred thousand votes, since fraud or ballot stuffing on that level was not only possible, but even likely. In the aftermath of the election that no one predicted, the Supreme Leader upped that figure—to one million in a defense of Ahmadinejad's eleven million margin of victory—a new revelation about this particular Ayatollah's democracy. The Guardian Council, however, discovered in its investigation of fraud days later that as many as *three* million votes were suspicious—not, however, including the ballots it showed on television, which were neatly rolled up as opposed to folded (as I had to do to mine to slip it into the ballot slot) and with suspiciously similar handwriting spelling out Ahmadinejad's name—revealing a new level of brazenness thought impossible until now. The focus of the Western media, indeed even Iran's media, was on Mir Hossein Mousavi's loss to Ahmadinejad, but while it would have been impossible to prove that Mousavi was more popular than the president, it was also a virtual impossibility that Mehdi Karroubi, a former speaker of Parliament and liberal cleric, could have received only one-twentieth the votes he did four years ago, and less votes than there were card-carrying members of his own political party. Did Iran's

propagandists engineer a "big lie," which I thought was the only explanation of the vote tally, or was there a silent majority in Iran disinclined
to the kind of giddiness for change that I had witnessed on the streets
of Tehran and other towns during the campaign season? Giddiness,
we later discovered, is not an option in the Islamic Republic.

BEGINNINGS CAN be long. The Islamic Republic's beginnings turned
thirty years old in 2009. It was a new beginning after an end, a long
end, to twenty-five hundred years of monarchy. The end of the monarchy lasted almost a hundred years and, without foreign interference,
might have been much shorter. Without the existential election crisis
of 2009, the beginning of the revolution might have dragged on, with
Iran still searching for its soul, its definition of democracy, and its place
in the world. But the crisis brought the first chapter of the republic's
history to a very Persian ending. It doesn't matter who is president of
Iran in 2013 (or even earlier), whether the *velayat-e-faqih* is embodied in one person or in a committee, or whether the Revolutionary
Guards are really in complete control of Iran or not. Democracy, or
at least *Islamic* democracy, became more clearly defined in 2009, not
just by Mir Hossein Mousavi, Ayatollah Rafsanjani, or former president
Mohammad Khatami, but by the *people*, conservative, liberal, and
everyone in between. A democracy, they cry, that does not remove
religion from the public sphere, but that still must allow the people
to choose their government. And the Green Movement, as the challenge and opposition to the government of Mahmoud Ahmadinejad
became known, led by the reformists but also a spontaneous creation
of its own—a sort of immaculate conception of the political kind—was
Iran's first real civil rights movement, one not so unlike the civil rights
movement in the United States a short half-century ago. While there
have been democracy movements in Iran in the past one hundred

years, nothing has had this kind of momentum or showed such resilience, despite government pressure on protesters perhaps equally as
intense as that exhibited in the American South in the 1960s or at the
anti-war protest at Kent State in 1970. And just as Martin Luther King
and Malcolm X, two very different civil rights leaders in the United
States, had extensive FBI files and were under suspicion of having
communist sympathies and were thought to be a threat to American
national security (as were leaders of the American anti-war movement),
so too did the Iranian regime treat its Green Movement leaders as if
they were a threat to the national security of the nation.

By the end of 2009, however, those leaders had not faced the kind
of charges some of their unfortunate lieutenants and supporters had,
and the government continued to walk a thin line between accusations
of sedition and pleas for the leaders, children of the revolution, to come
home, safe into the bosom of the velayat-e-faqih they had once helped
to create. But at the end of Iran's theocratic beginning, the Greens
no longer sought such safety, and probably never would again. At a
minimum the Green Movement, they knew, had ensured that there
would never be a repeat of the debacle of the 2009 election in Iran,
and with its continued existence, Green also ensured that the country
would not readily become another Burma. But it is also unlikely that
there will be a revolution along the lines of Iran's own in 1979, or of the
more subtle Eastern European type in the post-communist years. Iran
will, however, continue to defy the odds and the experts, as it always
has, and the future of the Ayatollahs' democracy, their Shia *Islamic*
democracy, will be inextricably tied to Iran's power, influence, and its
challenge to Western hegemony, not one of which will dissipate or
disappear with the changes the Green Movement demands.

Iran is complicated, like every culture, and it defies any attempts to
describe it, its people, or its politics, in red, white, or Green. Journalists
and writers rely on their experiences, as I do, to relate a story, and

Iran has a thousand and one of them. Although as an Iranian I am emotionally invested in the politics of the country, that investment was not the motivating factor in writing this book. Nor have I wanted to allow my biases to color, excuse the pun, the truth about Iran, a truth that is as elusive to most people as it might be to American talk-show hosts. The Green Movement may have started as a symbol of opposition to a government, but in reality it is more symbolic of a desire for something better than what Iran now has, a desire to move forward and not backward, and the hope of reform politicians and clergy is that *all* Iranians, not just angry protesters, might one day be able to call themselves Green. My name is Green, yes, but only as long as it can be for all Iranians. It is that embrace of Iran and Iranians, of the good and the bad, of the Green and of those who fear it, that inspired me to tell my stories, from well before Green was a name.

There are, of course, many books on Iran and on the Islamic regime, and there will be many more, some quite valuable for the insight they provide into a frustratingly mysterious place. No book, article, or essay, however, can ever completely unravel the mystery of Iran for a reader, or fully explain either the country or its people to his or her satisfaction, especially not after the often confusing events of 2009. At times it has seemed that for every event that signals the demise of the Islamic Republic, there has been another that reinforces its longevity. For every protest that has brought demonstrators to the streets demanding an end to oppression by the state, there have been long stretches of days when Iranians woke up, went to work or school and came home, watched television, laughed and cried, and lived their lives pretty much as people do everywhere else. For every story on Iran printed in our newspapers there have been thousands ignored, and forgotten. Iran, despite what we're told is its prominent role in our lives and in our security, continues to be woefully misunderstood, and in some cases woefully misrepresented, and while not every question on Iran can be answered or every facet of the Iranian character can be explained, my hope is that this book might illuminate some of the darker corners of Iran's political and social topography, and perhaps even reveal just a few truths, truths about Iran, Green and every other hue, and the Ayatollahs' democracy.

MY NAME IS GREEN

I have bad memories of this place, but this is my land and my
*country; Iran is the **only** reason for my existence.*

—Yas, twenty-eight-year-old Tehran rapper,
in his song "Be Omid'e Iran"

It is autumn and I am as the rain,
It is autumn and I am as the rain
Imprisoned by my rage.
What a beautiful tomorrow we dreamed of,
It was all in vain.
What great times and what dreams we saw
Searching for a reawakening
Me and you!
We were the wingless generation
Me and you!
We were the generation that could not fly!

—From a speech by Hilla Sedighi,
a female student in Iran, Autumn 2009

For two weeks in 2009, from June 12 until June 25, a frenzy of Western media attention centered on the Islamic Republic of Iran, where President Mahmoud Ahmadinejad's staggering landslide re-election resulted in general disbelief that quickly turned to anger, and then to street protests on a scale as yet unseen in the history of the republic. The focus of international news organizations, diverted only by pop-singer Michael Jackson's untimely death, was more intense for this new development than it had been for any of the venom that had spewed from Ahmadinejad's Holocaust-denying, Great Satan–baiting lips, or even for the worrisome nuclear ambitions of the mullahs who rule Iran.

We in the West were fascinated by this nascent revolution, just as the image we had of Iran and Iranians—dark, brooding, and reflexively anti-everything—was shattered by the reality of a people, looking very much like us, pleading on our television screens that all they really wanted was what *we* did: a right to determine their own destiny. Thirty years before, we had been fascinated by a people demanding to be led not by a suave, Westernized, and modernizing king, but by austere men in turbans and robes who promised the kingdom of God on earth, a God some imagined never felt comfortable outside the Middle Ages. And here we are, three decades later, believing we might be witnessing the beginning of the end of rule in God's name—*b'esm'allah*—that few could reconcile with *rahman'o rahim*, merciful and beneficent.

But as the government (or really, the Ahmadinejad regime), initially caught off guard, put its strategy into place—one that included zero tolerance for the kind of "people power" that it owed its *own* existence to—the massive protests became less frequent, foreign reporters either left as their non-renewable visas expired, or were arrested and jailed, and it appeared for a moment that Tehran might slowly be returning to normal just as Iran slipped from the front pages of newspapers and from nightly newscasts. The rumors of the Islamic Republic's death, it seemed, had been greatly exaggerated. But *normal*? Normal, perhaps, as far as we were concerned, with the abnormal President Ahmadinejad large and still very much in charge, and Iran once again the belligerent wannabe nuclear player we all imagined it to be. *That* was Iran, we thought: the despotic theocracy that was incompatible with democracy, and the proof was in the pudding of blood and guts spilled on the streets of Tehran. But for the cries of *Allah-hu-akbar!* shouted from rooftops every night as faithfully reported in blogs, on Twitter, in Facebook, and to any mainstream media that might still pay attention, Iran's latest revolution, it seemed, had retreated in the face of a massive crackdown on any dissent, repression redolent of military dictatorships—states and nations that Iran had been at pains to distinguish herself from since her rebirth as a republic after twenty-five hundred years of absolute monarchy.

The chants of "God is Great!" were reminders that He, Allah, was not dead—not to the regime, we already knew, but not to the opposition either. They were also reminiscent of the slogan Iranians shouted at the time of the Islamic Revolution in 1978 and 1979; just as young Iranian soldiers, Muslim themselves and mostly conscripts, struggled emotionally with punishing those proclaiming the greatness of Allah thirty years prior, today's protesters assumed that government forces would again find it hard to arrest or beat citizens uttering the most Islamic of phrases. In the intervening years, rooftop cries of Allah-hu-akbar could be heard only during the "Ten Day Dawn," the yearly anniversary marking the days between the arrival of Ayatollah Khomeini on Iranian soil and the fall of the Shah, and most loudly on the eve of the twenty-second of *Bahman*, the national holiday celebrating the culmination of the revolution. It was always a remembrance of how a people brought down a tyrant, not unlike an American Fourth of July fireworks display, but it was largely ignored by upper-class Iranians, some of them oblivious to the sound reverberating in their neighborhoods. And it was a remembrance in 2009 too, one that neither the government nor the formerly apathetic elite could ignore. Like the color green chosen by the opposition for its direct link to Islam, Allah-hu-akbar was a defiant cry of protesters signaling their devotion to the faith of the oppressed. I had wondered out loud in the past why Iranian protesters in the intervening years, between 1979 and 2009, had not resorted to the same tactic, but organized protests against the regime in the past had been limited to demonstrators from specific groups, such as students or women's rights activists or trade unions, with little support from the general masses (and none from the media), whereas the Green Movement spanned the entire political and social spectrum. More important, it included many of the architects of the Islamic regime itself. *Allah is Great,* alive, and well in the Islamic Republic. Yes indeed, He *has* to be, for however great the discontent of the Iranian people, they are still resoundingly religious and, of course, *Shia.*

Early in the summer of 2009, death of the King of Pop might have temporarily pushed Iran's internal crisis and the images of a young girl, Neda Agha-Soltan, who was brutally murdered on the streets of Tehran, off the network news and the front pages of our newspapers, but the Iranian government and the opposition to it were still hard at work trying to figure out their next moves. Both sides recognized, perhaps too late, that this was an existential crisis. While the Western media, if only for a few days, was fixating on the tragi-comedic life and death of the man who was once the world's biggest pop star, the Iranian political system itself had fractured, with various politicians, Ayatollahs, and clerics taking sides, but it wasn't broken, not yet. Jackson, as popular a star in Iran as anywhere else, would have ordinarily received much attention by the youth and those older who remembered his groundbreaking work, but in 2009 Iranians were pre-occupied with their own drama, more tragic than comedic.

The government, having realized that the initial burst of citizen fury was not limited to the privileged and secular classes or students, groups they have never relied on for support and who bore little resemblance to the rest of its citizens, began a campaign to persuade *those* Iranians that the unrest was being guided by Iran's enemies—namely, the West, which was one reason why Western reporters were subsequently barred from Iran. Meanwhile, the opposition, mindful that the accusation could very well stick, formulated a strategy of opposing any govern-ment moves through legal challenges and emphasizing the rule of law, and of Islam itself. But containing its citizens' anger, no longer limited to dismay at the results of the presidential election, was not going to be easy for the government, and no less difficult for the opposition whose initially peaceful protests soon threatened to turn violent. Fresh bouts of street protests took place in July commemorating the tenth anniversary of the student rebellion on the eighteenth of *Tir* (Persian month) in 1999, despite the main opposition figures remaining silent in the face of government threats, intimidation, and the closure of many of their channels of communication. The subsequent televised mass trials of detained protesters, journalists, and reform politicians, many of whom "confessed" to the crime of working with foreign forces to overthrow the Islamic regime, did little to convince ordinary Iranians that their protests in fact disguised a revolution or insurrection. The trampling of rights and the law, *haq* and *hoqooq*, by their own Islamic government had resonated strongly among Iranians, a Shia people whose character is in part defined by a constant struggle—from the time of the Shia-Sunni split and the denial of the prophet's grandson's rightful place at the head of the Muslim nation—for the assertion of those rights.

As other protests erupted, the opposition leaders were emboldened to issue statements, openly challenge the government line while still calling for nonviolent protest, and even appear on the streets (or at funerals of the fallen) themselves, although the authorities often forcefully cut short such public appearances. Protests, generally peaceful, in fact seemed to occur spontaneously every time there was an occasion to gather on the streets of major cities, such as on *Qods* (Jerusalem Day) in September, or even at soccer games, where state television broadcasts mysteriously reverted to black and white (to avoid showing tens of thousands of green-wearing fans) and suffered the occasional loss of sound (whenever fans shouted political slogans instead of cheers for their teams). Wearing green, the color of Mir Hossein Mousavi's presidential campaign (and *the* color of Islam, which later became a symbol for opposition to the government of Ahmadinejad), had become de facto illegal in Iran, a supreme irony in a country where the green banner of the prophet and of Islam itself is a visible and daily reminder of the nature of the republic. Mousavi, a onetime staunch Islamist who had served as prime minister in the 1980s until the post was abolished, became the standard bearer of the reform movement in 2009, a movement still visibly Islamic not just because of the color it chose, but also because of its premise that Islam and democracy are fully compatible.

With every protest, and particularly the noisier ones or the ones where participants included the leaders of the opposition, the attention of the normally self-obsessed West was momentarily diverted East. Later allegations of rape and torture in Tehran's detention facilities in the immediate aftermath of the election made small headlines for the first time in weeks (although rape and torture of political prisoners had not been unknown in Iran since practically the dawn of its empire), and led some Iran experts and analysts, as well as some journalists, to conclude that the nascent summer revolution they had witnessed from afar (or up close, in the case of some reporters) was genuine and the days of clerical rule numbered, if not in months, then perhaps a few short years. Visible cracks in the leadership were analyzed ad nauseam; every word, gesture, or movement of top political figures and clerics was parsed for meaning, and the weakness of Iran (in the face of a peoples' unrest), once feared as a resurgent and dominant power in the Muslim Middle East, proclaimed as fact. But many Westerners, having viewed the first stirrings of unrest in June as the makings of a "color" or "velvet" revolution along Eastern European lines, fell back into the habit of viewing Iran and Iranians through a Western lens, passing judgment on everything from Supreme Leader Ayatollah Seyed Ali Khamenei's hold on power to the "meekness" of opposition leader Mousavi, according to one respected but highly disappointed journalist, who out of his entire life had spent only three or four weeks in Iran, one of them in June prowling the streets of Tehran and reporting with great flourish on the first great people's revolution of the twenty-first century. "Revolution"? *No.* Mir Hossein Mousavi *meek?* Yes, if the excitement of marching with a million people down Valiasr Avenue onto Azadi Boulevard should have, in the minds of hopeful Western journalists, led to two million marching on Khamenei's residence the next day, and perhaps three million a few days later, led by the heroic Mousavi waving a giant green banner, marching on Parliament or the presidential offices on Pasteur Avenue. Sorry, but neither Mousavi, as brave an Iranian politician as there has been in half a century, nor Iran itself, will ever conform to a foreign script or to its impatient timeline, much as some may want them to. And Ayatollah Khamenei's hold on power was neither as strong nor as weak as proclaimed: Khamenei and Mousavi were being Iranian to the core, acting as Iranians who understand Iran and as their fellow Iranians do, and in a way that has confounded non-Iranians for as long as Iran has mattered. *Allah is Great.*

The truth about the summer of 2009 is that there never really was a revolution, or even the beginnings of a revolution—green, Twitter, velvet, or otherwise—no matter how hard some, on both sides, tried to Tiananmen-ize the protests, ascribe sedition and insurrection to the opposition, or contort the unrest into analogies with the Iran of 1979. Putting a Western face on the unrest, one that viewed the teeming masses of Iranians as agitating for a liberal democracy and freedom from the rule of the mullahs, was never going to tell the whole story.

Initially, the Iranians who marched, protested, and shouted slogans were merely angry at the election results, leading even Ali Larijani, the conservative speaker of Parliament and a close ally of the Supreme Leader, to confess publicly that "the majority of Iranians don't believe the election," and some clerics to openly defy the regime, causing the first serious public rift in the leadership in the young history of the Islamic Republic. Anger is why Iranians came out onto the streets— young, old, bearded, clean-shaven, chador-clad, pious, secular, and Chanel-wearing fashionistas for all to see, to register their disapproval of what they believed to be a rigged vote, an insult to every Iranian who believed that the *one* truly democratic aspect of their system had been rudely violated. Islamic Democracy with a capital *D* had always been the goal of the reform movement, from well before the candidacy of Mousavi, a goal they believed was neither oxymoronic nor an impossibility. Along with millions of Iranians, including many conservatives who subscribed to the theory of power vested in the people, they now felt that that democracy had been subverted. In exercising their right to peaceful protest, a right guaranteed under the constitution, they kept democracy alive in Iran for another few days, but the government's subsequent brutal suppression of that right was an indication to those who protested of how horribly wrong the democratic experiment had gone.

We, Westerners and secular Iranians, may have wanted to impute to the protests something they were not—namely, a rejection of the Islamic regime altogether—but in doing so we inadvertently harmed the cause of the masses of Iranians we purported to be in sympathy with. Iranian exile organizations, with ready access to the Western media, joined in the frenzy of the Green Movement and the excitement of a brewing revolt; groups who had called for boycotting the vote were suddenly expressing solidarity with those who actually filled out a ballot. Nothing could have been more sickening to many of the Iranians who braved the batons and bullets of the *Basij* than to see Maryam Rajavi, head of the largely despised *Mujahedin-e-Khalq* (MEK), hold a press conference in Paris in the summer of 2009, in front of a large poster of the brutally murdered Neda Agha-Soltan as if to claim her for her group. (Rajavi couldn't, however, bring herself to wear green.) The Iranian state media, searching for evidence of foreign plots, or plots by hated exile groups, to convince the masses that what they had witnessed in June was not a stolen election but a foreign-inspired plan to overthrow their government, could not have engineered a better clue for its audience. In fact, the government quickly spun Neda's death as a planned and even rehearsed shooting by the opposition, by foreign-backed or exile groups (intimating that the Mujahedin were responsible) to discredit the Islamic Republic, even going as far as producing a documentary (broadcast on state television later in the year) on her death that purported to "prove" their case. As preposterous as that was, the government knew that at least some conspiracy-minded Iranians—and Iranians are nothing if not expert conspiracy theorists— would buy the story. Prince Reza Pahlavi, son of the last Shah and pretender to a throne that no longer exists, shed crocodile tears at his press conference in Washington, D.C., in the immediate aftermath of the election, comfortably distant from the burning streets of Tehran but available for all to see on YouTube. He was perhaps marginally less cynical than Mrs. Rajavi, but equally helpful to Mir Hossein Mousavi's enemies. His subsequent wearing of a green rubber wristband, symbol of Mousavi's opposition to Ahmadinejad but *not* to the Islamic Republic, only diluted the message that every green-wearing Iranian broadcast to the world. Pahlavi was now Green, but perhaps more with envy at what the children of Iran had managed to do in a few weeks than what he had been unable to for thirty years from his base in Washington.

The revolution may not be televised any longer, to paraphrase the great Gil Scott-Heron, but pirates seemed determined to hijack it anyway. A famous and well-meaning filmmaker, a self-appointed spokesman for Mousavi (who needed no spokesman as he was frequently able to deliver his messages, even filmed interviews, to the world via the Internet), spoke to the European Parliament a day before the eighteenth-of-Tir demonstrations. He warned the members that if nothing were done to confront Iran, it would presently be in possession of nuclear *weapons*, weapons that would be threateningly pointed at their home cities. Again, Tehran's propaganda machine could not have asked for a greater gift, one they could use to further marginalize Mousavi, who had actually proclaimed during his campaign that uranium enrichment would continue under his administration, and that Iran's nuclear policy would not change with a change of administrations. (The government has consistently labeled anyone who opposes nuclear development as unpatriotic if not an actual traitor, and indeed the nuclear program enjoys widespread support in Iran.) The same spokesman kept issuing various reports from Paris that conflicted with Mousavi's statements in Iran, who had insisted earlier that his positions would only be articulated from his headquarters in Tehran. In September 2009, just as President Ahmadinejad was again defending Iran's nuclear program at the United Nations, the filmmaker issued a statement claiming that the opposition was as concerned with Iran's nuclear program as was the West, thereby doing nothing for the cause of reform in Iran and only assisting the regime with its propaganda. We paid attention to all of these Green Iranians, we listened to those with the loudest voices, and we drew conclusions, but we also fed Iran's hungry propaganda machine, one that was determined to make Green not the symbol of Islamic freedom, but the color of counter-revolutionary insurrection.

As the summer of 2009 gave way to autumn, and the revolution that never was began to fade from fetishistic Western headlines, Iran was still undergoing turmoil and changes within, as faithfully reported by Iranian websites—some created in the aftermath of the election—but the nuclear question, one that for six years had been the preoccupation of most of the Western world, was sure to dominate headlines once again. And dominate it did, with a revelation in late September, while President Ahmadinejad was in New York City to address the UN General Assembly, that Iran had secretly built another nuclear facility in the desert near Qom. That dramatic revelation by President Barack Obama, Prime Minister Gordon Brown of the United Kingdom, and President Nicolas Sarkozy of France, on the sidelines of a G-20 conference in Pittsburgh, resulted in much speculation and mostly negative coverage of Iran and its nuclear ambitions, and added to Western suspicions that Iran was intent on developing weapons alongside its reactors, just as it also had oppressed its people and manufactured election results. But Iran countered, its propaganda and foreign policy machines in overdrive, comfortable in the knowledge that at least in regard to its nuclear rights it had the support of its people and, despite Western claims, had much of the world outside of Western Europe and the United States on its side.

If President Ahmadinejad's administration had been weakened by the events of the summer of 2009, it was a mistake to believe that Iran itself had, and anyone who really understood Iran recognized as much. For Iran, which embarked on a path of renewal as a great civilization and power, even empire, in the years following the revolution of 1979, was still very much united in its determination to continue, and no opposition leader would have suggested otherwise. Meanwhile,

Western sympathizers with Iran's Green Movement worried out loud that in any U.S. negotiations with Iran, negotiations President Obama had promised but hadn't quite started, great care had to be taken to avoid harming the cause of democracy or the opposition movement itself, for example, by legitimizing the government of President Ahmadinejad. But the opposition to the administration in Iran wanted no *farangi*, or foreign, help or involvement. The internal struggles in Iran were about the Ayatollahs' democracy, and they would not affect her relationship with the farangis, no matter what those farangis did or did not do. The battle in Iran was over her future, not her past, over what was democratic and what was not.

In the first decade of the twenty-first century, very few Iranians wanted a Persia defined for them by non-Persians, as it had been for so long preceding their Islamic Revolution of 1979. In the fall of 2009, perhaps the most perspicacious slogan of the Mousavi Green Movement was one completely ignored by both the Western media and most Iranian exiles, many of them agitating as best they could for the downfall of the entire regime. *"Na dolat'e coup d'état, na menat'e Amrika!"* Mousavi proclaimed, while green-wearing Iranians abroad joined former Iran-bashers such as former vice president Dick Cheney and Senator John McCain and countless right-wing talk-show hosts in demanding that President Obama offer overt support for the "pro-democracy" protesters on Iran's streets. "No to a coup d'état government," Mousavi's slogan said, and we heard that, but we did not hear the rest: "but no to an indebtedness to America." *Menat* is a Farsi word that is actually impossible to translate, and "indebtedness" is hardly the most accurate indication of its meaning. It can be a state of indebtedness or of begging a favor, of being in an uncomfortable state of *owing*. As far as most Iranians who did hear the message were concerned, though, Mousavi couldn't have been clearer in his sentiments. Iranians may have wanted sympathy from the West, but they did not want help, and they wanted to owe no one, in their quest for their own form of democracy.

For some observers, both Western and Iranian, the summer of 2009 was the beginning of the end of the Islamic Republic, as we know it. How could the fractures that appeared in June ever be healed? If it wasn't the presidential election itself (and elections are stolen all the time after all, even in the United States), then how could a political system survive street protests that wouldn't completely disappear; a great disaffection on the part of a large portion of the population, particularly the influential middle class; pressure from the West over foreign policy and the nuclear issue; and concern over the validity and credibility of the velayat-e-faqih, rule of the jurisprudent, or, in other words, the Supreme Leader himself? If what started out as a protest against a stolen vote then turned to mass disgust and anger over the government's reaction to those protests, even from conservatives opposed to Mousavi, then how could that government survive?

Looking at the unrest in Iran from a Western perspective, even a pop culture perspective, one might be forgiven for believing that the days of the Islamic system were numbered. After all, at no time in its history had the world's attention been so focused on its abuse of her citizens, or her citizens' fight for their basic human rights. In 2009, Jon Bon Jovi recorded a version of "Stand By Me" with an Iranian singer, in New Jersey–accented Farsi, to express solidarity with Iranians battling their government; U2 performed "Sunday, Bloody Sunday" bathed in green light—with Farsi words projected on multiple Jumbotrons but thankfully not issuing from Bono's lips—on its 2009 world tour, right before singing a song dedicated to Burmese dissident Aung San Suu Kyi (thereby lumping the Iranian protesters in with dissident citizens living under dictatorships everywhere); and Basij became a new code word for government thuggery and terror. But Iran suffered political fissures in 2009 precisely because the establishment (and almost everyone in the opposition could be considered a part of the establishment) had split so openly, not because dissidents had burst onto the scene.

Everyone on either side of the political spectrum, at least those inside Iran, had once been united in establishing the Islamic regime, and together they had led Iran's quest for independence and an independent political system. Everyone had worked within the system, quietly or openly, to reform it—those on the right to "reform" its democratic aspects to guarantee its future as a revolutionary state, and those on the left and in the opposition to reform its autocratic and dictatorial aspects to achieve what they saw as its original intent: an Islamic democracy that vested power in the people, and in consultative bodies (mimicking the early days of Islam) that would not legislate in direct contradiction of Islamic law. In the very beginning the two sides had agreed on everything, from the fight against anti-regime dissidents such as the Mujahedin-e-Khalq or against traitors within, to the U.S. Embassy seizure in 1979 and to relations with the West. The election of Hojjatoleslam (a Shia clerical title one rank below Ayatollah) Seyed Mohammad Khatami as president in 1997 (and his re-election in 2001) brought forth the idea that Iran's Islamic system *could* be reformed, that there were differing ideas of what an Islamic democracy might look like, and President Ahmadinejad's legitimate election in 2005 was a referendum on reform *of* such reform, or reform of the system against corruption and the perpetual rule of an established clerical elite, embodied by his opponent, Ayatollah Rafsanjani. Neither president was successful in pushing Iran forward politically, from a revolutionary state to a post-revolutionary state, and it is unlikely that a Mousavi win in 2009 would have had great success either. True reform, certainly of the kind we attributed to the demands of the protesters, would always be a Sisyphean task in Iran, a country where various factions and governmental bodies hold power, and disappointment with any regime that tried was virtually guaranteed up until now. Yes, up until now, but probably no longer.

At the end of 2009, a documentary aired on television in the United States and Great Britain on the life and death of Neda Agha-Soltan, the young woman whose murder on the streets of Tehran was witnessed by millions around the globe courtesy of cell phone camera footage uploaded to YouTube. Neda, her friends and family told the viewers, someone who became for many a symbol of the democracy movement, was disillusioned with life in Iran and would have jumped at an opportunity to emigrate if she had been presented with one. She was apparently none too keen on any of the candidates in the presidential election, and like many young, urban, middle-class Iranians, she felt that her future lay anywhere but in the land she called home. And yet she went out onto the streets to protest. A few days earlier she would have been happy to leave those streets altogether, but she continued to protest, even after the government threatened violence, until the moment she was shot in the heart and left to die on the pavement. Her actions were not those of someone who wanted nothing to do with her country any longer—which validates her martyrdom in the eyes of the movement—and perhaps she had never been quite as serious about emigrating either, but there were thousands, if not millions of Nedas (and not just in Tehran) who felt that the election and the government's response to their cries were insults they could no longer ignore. Importantly, these protesters galvanized the opposition leaders, Mousavi, Mehdi Karroubi, and Khatami, as much as those leaders galvanized their constituents. It was *democratic* action, and no Iranian could ignore it. Apathy among the middle class, evident in the turnout for the previous presidential election, which had brought Ahmadinejad to power, had turned into an activism unlike anything else Iran had witnessed in thirty years, and who—even young, urban youth dreaming of a better life in Los Angeles or London or Toronto— wouldn't want to be a part of *that*?

The government or regime may have viewed the Green Movement

and the citizen activism as a threat, just as governments everywhere, even in democracies, have always viewed such movements as threats, but the leaders of the opposition in Iran knew they could win more and more people to their side precisely because they were *not* a threat. The presence of many senior clerics on their side made it difficult for the regime to completely ignore their demands, and despite still widespread support for both the Supreme Leader Ayatollah Khamenei and President Ahmadinejad, particularly among the non-urban working classes, the message of democratic change, *Islamic* democratic change, resonated throughout the population. For according to pro-reform clerics such as Khatami, Karroubi, and even more senior Ayatollahs, Islamic democracy guarantees nothing less than power vested in the people, accountability of a government to those people, and Islam as the guide in the establishment of laws, laws that are designed, the pious believe, to protect the fundamental rights of the people. In a land of believers in Shia Islam, which through its clergy allows for wide interpretation of the faith and even its laws, Green was never going to fade away completely, no matter what.

To understand that the Green Movement is very much an establishment movement, it is important to note that the leaders of the opposition even had messages of support for the Basij on Basij Day in late 2009—yes, support for the militia charged with cracking down on them and their supporters, but also advice to them that their post-election behavior had been anti-Iranian and, of course, un-Islamic. No opposition leader in Iran can afford to ignore the Basij, who number as many as one million regime loyalists, but they believe these loyalists can be won over to their cause of democratic change. In late May 2009, right before the election, I told former president Khatami in Tehran that I had just met a former Basij who told me he was voting for Mousavi and for more freedom. "Last time, I personally filled out four hundred blank ballots for Ahmadinejad," he said to me, "but this time I'll do the same for Mousavi." Okay, maybe he didn't quite get the real message of democracy, but it *was* more democracy that he wanted. Khatami laughed, hopeful that his message of reform was finally trickling down (or across) even into the ranks of the military apparatus, and unconcerned, as yet, with the irony of the Basij's vow. Those in the opposition to the government in Iran, some of them like Khatami having called for reform for much longer than others, know that their calls for democratic change resonate among the population, not just because of its Islamic hue, but because democracy is not a new concept to Iranians—they've been fighting for it for over a hundred years. Their efforts have always met resistance, from the monarchy, from foreign powers intent on keeping Iran weak and dependent on them, and from some conservatives in the Islamic regime.

Democracy was not a concept imported wholesale from the West, nor was it ever the exclusive desire of the intellectual or upper-class elites of Iran; from the constitutional revolution of 1906 onward, Iranians of all stripes and from all classes have fought for the vote, for civil liberties, for the rule of law, and for a just and representative system of government, even as religious Iranians have always insisted on Islam, beneficent as they see it, as playing a role in their form of democracy. Democracy had been the stated goal of every leading Iranian politician in recent years, even President Ahmadinejad, the son of a blacksmith who, supporters claimed, could not have reached the highest levels of government without democratic institutions. Iran has fallen well short of democracy, of course, not just under Ahmadinejad but also under his more liberal predecessors. But the entry of Green into the political scene has ensured that whatever democratic reform occurs in the Ayatollahs' democracy, and reform *is* inevitable, it will occur sooner rather than later.

After a lull in the violence during the summer and in the mass protests that captured the world's imagination, at the very end of 2009, on what is known as Students' Day, Iranian youth once again took to their university campuses across the country and on neighboring streets to protest what they considered an illegitimate government and a dictatorial regime. Students' Day in 2009 became a particularly significant holiday to those opposed to the government of Ahmadinejad, for it is a commemoration of Vice President Richard Nixon's visit to Iran in 1953, only six months after a CIA-backed coup removed democratically elected Prime Minister Mohammad Mossadeq, and during which student demonstrators protesting the Shah's rule were shot and killed by government troops.

The parallels with 2009 were unmistakable to many activists, but some demonstrators went further than ever before in denouncing the government, and all of its leaders, even calling Mousavi an "excuse," something no one had dared to mention up until then. If Mousavi was an excuse to them, they offered no one else as a leader, but their calls had much greater impact than any previous student demonstration since the revolution in 1979. Leading clerics, Mousavi, and other opposition leaders (who were not really behind the Students' Day protests), and even Ayatollah Khamenei, paid close attention, for although the students had no charismatic leader like students did in the person of Khomeini in 1979, the regime could ill afford to ignore a unified youth population, one that numbers in the millions (more than 40 million Iranians are thirty or younger, and there are over 3.5 million university students across the country). In yet another unprecedented act, some students allegedly tore up pictures of Ayatollahs Khomeini and Khamenei during the Students' Day protests, and their actions were, again in an unprecedented move, repeatedly shown on state television. But those students were not Green, Mousavi claimed, stating that their act was a "wholly suspicious and anti-revolutionary gesture," and many in the opposition maintained that it was the state itself that organized the "great insult" to the Imam, as the founder of the Islamic Republic is known, in order to discredit them, especially as television stations repeatedly broadcast the sacrilegious images.

Whether the state staged the outrage against the Ayatollahs as propaganda to discredit the Greens, or whether it was provocateurs from opposition groups opposed to the theocracy who were responsible, or whether students tearing up pictures of the only two Supreme Leaders the republic had known did so spontaneously, the regime had to consider that discontent, now broadcast on national television, had perhaps finally boiled over. In the short term, the government could arrest, intimidate, and abuse the students who spoke out, but in the longer term unless the regime gave some ground, as Ayatollah Rafsanjani himself said in early December 2009 after a long period of silence, it might be faced with the question of whether an Islamic Republic was viable at all. "If the people of Iran want us," Rafsanjani had said to a group of students in Mashhad, "we [can] stay and govern; if not we [should] go." It was a powerful statement, for Ayatollah Khomeini had used the word "go" to great effect from the start of the Islamic Revolution with respect to the Shah. No matter what the Shah and his government did then to appease the opposition and street demonstrators, the unwavering but simple central demand of Khomeini and the Islamic revolutionaries—that the Shah must "go," *ou bayad bereh*—signaled the end of the monarchy well before the Shah's actual flight. Akbar Ganji, the dissident former revolutionary who went on a hunger strike during his imprisonment in 2005, repeated that demand of Ayatollah Khamenei, angering the establishment as he tried, with some effect, to equate the Shah's rule with that of the Supreme Leader. Rafsanjani and other powerful clerics, *and* the leaders of the opposition, though, were determined in 2009 to ensure that the possibility of them "going" or being asked to "go" would never come to pass.

Neither the Ayatollahs' democracy nor a Green democracy, still reliant on its *own* Ayatollahs, fits a Western definition of a democracy.

Maybe it will never reach a definition all Iranians can agree on, but
that is something that almost all Iranians *can* agree on. The events of
the summer of 2009 in Iran were, to be sure, an important, even vital
step in the development of democracy in the Islamic Republic, and
perhaps the best thing that could have happened to a young republic
struggling to identify itself, not just as far as pro-democracy groups
were concerned, but also as far as anyone who cares about the future
of the country, and the future of its relations with the outside world.
In that respect, the name of *all* Iranians is Green. In 2009 Islamic
Iran received the jolt it needed to end its thirty-year-long beginning,
and as unfortunate as the events of the summer and fall of 2009 were
for those who suffered and for the families of those who died, nothing
else, not even a legitimate Mousavi win at the ballot box, could have
provided the impetus for significant democratic change, even if that
change—which will always have a Persian and Shia hue, a particular
shade of Green, that is—might still seem far away.

DEMOCRACY, INTERRUPTED:

*It Takes a Thousand and One Villages
(and a Mullah or Two)*

*In the Kingdom of God, persons or groups govern on the basis
of divine laws.*

—Eighth-grade social teachings textbook,
Iranian public school system

A day after President Ahmadinejad gave a speech at the United Nations Durban Review Conference on racism, held in Geneva in April 2009, a speech that included a tirade against Israel and was viewed as particularly incendiary in the West and even in some quarters inside Iran, a friend of my father's, an aging former diplomat like him, was walking out of his apartment in Paris. When he entered the elevator, a longtime neighbor nodded and said hello. "Congratulations!" he added. Why, wondered my father's friend, the felicitation? "*Votre president!*" replied the neighbor. "Iran is the only country that dares challenge America and Israel, and is the only country in the world standing up for the Palestinians!"

A few months later, an Iranian ambassador from the current regime told me that after the post-election unrest began in Iran, a fellow ambassador from an Arab country said to him, "Congratulations!" Wondering why he was being congratulated in the middle of a brutal crackdown, while negative images of his country were broadcast on television twenty-four hours a day, the Arab ambassador replied to him, "Because what's happening in your country could never happen in mine." What he meant was that in his and many other Muslim countries, particularly Arab ones, a political opposition is not allowed to *exist*, let alone march on the streets. It is hard to imagine that anyone would be envious of Iran's political system, but as it is with Iran, one is often surprised.

Five months later, in October 2009, Iran appeared to have agreed in principle with a proposal by the West to resolve the nuclear crisis. Under the agreement Iran would send its stock of low-enriched uranium (a cause of concern because it could conceivably be further enriched into bomb-grade material) outside the country for conversion into fuel rods, which would be sent back to Iran and could only be used to power a reactor. Soon after Iran balked at giving a formal answer to the proposal, and while both conservatives and reformists decried Ahmadinejad's tentative agreement, my father, a former ambassador fired by the Islamic regime thirty years prior and not predisposed to sympathize with Tehran, asked me whether I thought Iran would, or should, accept the principle of the deal. I suggested that Iran was likely worried that the West might be setting a trap to get Iran's enriched uranium supply out of the country and then delay or refuse delivery of fuel back in until the Iranians agreed to Western terms. "They're right to worry!" he exclaimed. "Let's face it: Iran is doing the right thing in being careful. Why *should* they trust the West?"

To OUTSIDERS—even to many Iranians—President Ahmadinejad and his clique may appear to be unrepresentative of Iranians in general, a fringe element, particularly since his questionable re-election. But there have always been millions of Ahmadinejads in Iran, certainly in modern times: Iranians from sometimes humble backgrounds and from disparate towns and villages who have fought for equal access to power and to have their voices heard in its corridors, which until the twentieth century were restricted to a handful of elite families in the capital. (The last Shah's father himself came from a humble background, from a village in the north near the Caspian, and had he been successful in ridding Iran of an ineffectual dynasty, in a later age he might have chosen republicanism instead of coronation as his due.) There are differing ideologies among these Iranians, to be sure, as are there differences in social attitudes, but they have in common a particularly Shia resistance to despotism and a fierce determination to ensure that Iran never again becomes the weak and exploitable state it became after the empire. Ahmadinejad and his closest cohorts, perhaps inclined less to democratic principles than they often claim, also know that it was a nominal Iranian democracy, one that not only proclaimed independence from any greater power's influence but also gave the people a voice, that first allowed them access to the presidential office in 2005. Iran is theirs too, and they will, like their overwhelmingly deeply religious supporters, who still number in the millions, have a say in the future of the Islamic republic they call Iran.

IRAN IS the only country in the Middle East to have been a multi-ethnic nation-state, with the same name (in Farsi or Persian) and with identifiable borders, for millennia. Every other country in the region is less than a hundred years old, including Turkey, which was born out of the ashes of the Ottoman Empire. The only part of the region *not* ruled by the Ottomans was, of course, Iran. It is this sense of nationhood, this sense of having always been a distinct country, a distinct culture that grew out of many tribes and ethnicities, that forms the Iranian character. Persian ambition and Persian pride, the kind of pride that leads Iranians everywhere to defend their nation's nuclear program, have always been important. But there is a generational difference between the mullahs who rule Iran today (and who are unashamed of their backgrounds) and their sophisticated and Westernized predecessors like my father who eventually believed that they had to swallow that pride, even be subservient to greater powers, in order for Iran to be accepted into the family of modern nations. The Supreme Leader of Iran, an ethnic Turk from the Northeast provinces (whose only language other than Farsi is a Turkish dialect), is as much a Persian nationalist as he is a Grand Ayatollah, and as much a believer in the greatness of Iran as he is a believer in the truth of Shia Islam, or at least the truth as he sees it. He guides Iran's foreign policy, as did his predecessor, Ayatollah Khomeini, with as much a sense of Iran's place in the world and Iranian nationalism as a devotion to the prophet and his descendents, who were, after all, Arabs from the peninsula and not Cyrus's Persia. The roots of Islam in Iran are assuredly long and deep, but the roots of Persian nationalism are much deeper. Cyrus's Persian Empire, a glorious and benevolent one as far as Iranians are considered, gave way to successive Persias that suffered the ignominies of invasion and occupation, and only the occasional glory of greatness. By the beginning of the modern age of the twentieth century, Iran was still an independent nation-state, but "Persia," as it was known outside Iran, denoted a weak and backward country then, one ripe for exploitation.

IT WAS PERSIA, specifically a small village smack in the middle of the country, a *deh* by the name of Ardakan, into which my father was born. It was always "Iran" to its inhabitants and "Persia" to the rest of the world, but at the time it was more *Persia* than Iran—not the ancient Persia of glory and superpower but a feeble Persia—even to its citizens. Persia in the sense that, long without its empire, it was now dependent on foreign, specifically British and Russian, patronage to survive. Persian Ardakan, like thousands of other villages, went without running water and a sewer system, but it did have an ancient Persian air-conditioning system that was developed when Persia *was* still great: the *bad-geer* or "wind-catcher," using only the laws of physics mastered centuries ago, cooled the mud-brick homes located in a desert where summer temperatures easily surpassed 110 degrees. Born in the late 1920s into a landowning and religious family with clerics sprinkled among his ancestors, my father should have felt privileged, certainly as compared to the vast majority of other mostly illiterate Iranians, particularly outside of Tehran. But this was a time when Iran had embarked on a modernization program under the dictator Reza Shah, a barely literate army officer who had put an end to the weak Qajar dynasty and who equated progress with Westernization. It was with the West in mind that he insisted Iran be called by the name Iranians had always known it as, rather than the anglicized "Persia."

My father soon tired, even as a teenager, of what he saw as a backward rural setting (what he called, according to an older uncle, a *shit*-town because of the ubiquitous odor of sewage), a setting that also happened to be the home of a future president of Iran, Mohammad Khatami. My father tired of it despite the fact that his father had procured Ardakan's first automobile, the make long forgotten now, but a handsome machine in which he posed for photographs with local townspeople, both envious and admiring. (Even by automobile, though, Ardakan was hours away on unpaved roads from the nearest city, a fact that didn't stop the family chauffeur from establishing a side business, unbeknownst to my grandfather, in the transport of coffins securely strapped to the running boards.)

To his delight, my father, Nasser, and his older brother Mahmoud found an escape from their rural setting when they were sent to an exclusive boarding school in Tehran, Alborz (the Eton or Choate of Iran), and my father quickly and consciously lost his provincial accent, one that he has refused to employ since, even in the presence of President Khatami and other family, who unashamedly, in the age of a republic and a supposedly classless society, lapse into the instantly recognizable dialect in the company of fellow Ardakanis. The modernization begun under Reza Shah attracted the likes of my father, people who would later form the backbone of an Iranian middle class in a society that had been semi-feudal for as long as anyone could remember, but my father and my uncle's sojourn at school in Tehran, where modernization had its greatest (and perhaps at that time its only) impact, was short-lived. Expelled from Alborz for punching the headmaster in the chin in response to the fellow boxing my uncle's ears for some long-forgotten transgression, both boys were sent to Yazd, the larger ancient city thirty miles from Ardakan where their family now lived, and they were forced to complete their high school education away from the sophistication of Tehran.

Curiously, Yazd is at once one of the most religious and religiously tolerant cities in Iran. It has produced both the most liberal and the most hard-line clerics, military men, and politicians of the Islamic Republic era, as well as being home to large and vibrant Zoroastrian (and in my father's time Jewish) communities whose children played with, and remained friends with, their Muslim counterparts throughout their lives. It wasn't long, though, before my father was able to sit for the *concours*, the countrywide university entrance exam, and gain a place at Tehran University, coincidentally where my mother, Mansoureh, also was enrolled, and where her father, an Ayatollah and theologian, taught philosophy.

By that time, Reza Shah had been forced off the Peacock throne and into exile by the Allies of World War II—he had been a German and even Nazi sympathizer, partly because of his revulsion for the British and Russians, who had dominated his country for so many years, and partly because he admired German efficiency and technological progress—and the new young king, Mohammad Reza Pahlavi, looked to be vulnerable to pressure from pro-democracy Iranians. The democratic movement in Iran was not a new phenomenon; it had merely been suppressed and silenced during the reign of the Shah's father, who had also silenced clerical opposition to his secular ways. In 1906, in what is known as the constitutional revolution, pro-democracy forces had successfully forced the then Qajar king, Mozzafar al-Din Shah, to sign a decree establishing a *Majles*, or Parliament, the first of its kind in the region (and against the wishes of Russia, and to some degree Great Britain), whereby the absolute powers of the monarchy were curtailed and the Iranian people were given the vote. The Shah died shortly thereafter though, and his successor, Mohammad Ali Shah, a fan of Russia but no fan of democracy, attacked the Majles in 1908 with Cossack troops and suspended the nascent constitution. The revolution did not end there, though, and in a campaign of resistance against the Shah, the constitutionalists were successful in re-establishing the Majles and the rule of law in July 1909, forcing the abdication of Mohammad Ali Shah in favor of his thirteen-year-old son, Ahmad Mirza.

Curiously and ironically, two Americans played significant roles in the constitutional revolution and its aftermath: Howard Baskerville and William Morgan Shuster. Baskerville was a young Princeton graduate who went to Persia in 1907 as a teacher and missionary at the American School in Tabriz, a northern city that was a hotbed of revolutionary activity. Against the American consul's advice, he joined the constitutionalist revolutionary forces fighting the Shah's troops who had laid siege to the city, and he was killed, at the age of twenty-four, leading his students, who he had trained, into battle against the imperial army on April 19, 1909. He is buried in Tabriz, and Iranians, including the Islamic revolutionaries, recognize him as a martyr—in some ways he is the John Reed of Iran, his name forever associated with Iran's fight against the tyranny of dictatorship. (John Reed, made famous by Warren Beatty in his movie *Reds*, a portrayal of the young American fighting in the Russian Revolution, is the only American buried in Red Square.)

The other American, William Morgan Shuster, was a civil servant, lawyer, and financial expert hired by the government of Iran on the advice of U.S. President William Howard Taft—again, against the wishes of the imperial powers—to become Persia's treasurer-general in the immediate aftermath of the success of the constitutional revolution, a time when Persia was not only impotent but also essentially bankrupt owing to heavy Qajar indebtedness to both Britain and Russia. At that time the United States, powerful as she already was, had not, in the minds of much of the world, set her eyes on colonizing or exploiting less strong nations, at least not as the European powers had for more than two centuries. Immensely popular among Iranian nationalists who witnessed his dedication to building an independent nation, Shuster's tenure lasted less than a year. Against the wishes of the Majles, which had hired him, he was forced out of Iran by Russia, which opposed, along with Britain, his plans to bring financial autonomy to Persia. He wrote a book on his return to the United States, *The Strangling of Persia*, which is as damning of foreign interference in Iran's affairs as it is full of praise for Iran's quest for democracy. That was in 1912, more than a decade before my father was born. Shuster wholly believed in the Iranian constitution and wholeheartedly supported Iranian nationalists; in describing their vision of a "Mohammedan democracy" as having been thwarted by imperialist powers, he was also perhaps the first person to coin the phrase, linking Islam and democracy.

My FATHER was among the first group of Iranians from the outlying provinces to attend the university in Tehran—the college was founded in 1934, after all—but he was part of a trend to educate Iranians in a post-feudal society that continued up until the revolution of 1979, after which there was a veritable explosion in higher education, one of the priorities of the new Islamic regime. Well versed in the history of democracy in Iran, particularly the constitution of 1906, these college students, as well as high school students everywhere, saw an opportunity for a return to the Iranian democracy that the constitutionalists had envisioned at the turn of the century, with the appointment of Mohammad Mossadeq as prime minister in 1951—he had been an elected member of Parliament who was then voted to the premiership by the body—and with the presence of a weak Shah, the promise that Iran might finally become a constitutional democracy seemed ready to be fulfilled. But it was not to be. The history of the Mossadeq years, his battles with the Shah over authority, with Great Britain over oil nationalization, and finally with the United States over suspicions that he was a communist sympathizer or would allow Iran to fall into the Soviet sphere—a battle he was unaware of until his overthrow in a CIA plot—has been told often enough. Although the consequence of his overthrow and a return to the absolute monarchy is usually thought of as the genesis of anti-Americanism among Iranians, which is true to some extent, that doesn't tell the whole story.

For many Iranians, particularly those who had reaped the benefits of modernization and institutionalized higher education, the "Mossy" affair (as the British press, in their own peculiarly endearing way, was fond of calling Mossadeq) was one more, perhaps even final, nail in the coffin of Iranian self-determination and political freedom. This time, the strangler of Persia was Shuster's very own United States, but resentment of her never reached the level Iranians reserve for the British. Most Iranians who had once rejoiced in the return to constitutional democracy simply bowed their heads and moved on, no longer politically active, fatalistic about their ability to effect change in a country that seemed to always revert to dictatorship after a brief flirtation with democratic rule. My father, who had been doing his compulsory military service as a cavalry officer during the Mossadeq years and who had been an ardent supporter of him and Iranian constitutionality, not only decided that he could no longer be in opposition to the Shah, but also actually joined the government, sitting for the Foreign Service exam the first year it was offered to the public at large. He was one of a handful of candidates from a non-elite class accepted into the Foreign Ministry, a ministry that up until then had been closed to anyone from outside the very top elite families that dominated Iranian political life—families that did not include villagers, no matter their wealth and standing in the provinces. At the same time, his best friend from the army who had been a member of the now-outlawed communist Tudeh party was sent to prison on a two-year sentence for anti-Shah political activity, but as a measure of how Iranians had yet to adjust to what soon became an autocracy intolerant of dissent, my father visited his dissenter friend, Dr. Bazargan, in jail every Friday and signed his own name in the guest book. And next to his name, for employer, he wrote, "Ministry of Foreign Affairs, Tehran," not fearful of any consequence. Bazargan himself gave up political activism on his release and has since devoted himself to medicine, building a successful (and apolitical) medical practice in his native Mashhad and remaining friends until this day with his former army buddy who once worked for his jailer.

EVERY NOW and then Mossadeq's name comes up in conversations about Iran, whether among Iranians or among Americans. Curiously, the Islamic regime is ambivalent, if not actually hostile, to Mossadeq and what he represented, both because of the embarrassment of many mullahs' general collusion with the Shah (with few exceptions), and because ol' Mossy was in fact a strict 1906 constitutionalist (and monarchist), came from a prominent family, and was a secularist (albeit still a Muslim) who had allowed the communists to gain influence under his premiership. The Islamic regime is not, however, shy about invoking his name and legacy when it might be convenient. In 2005, only a few weeks after Ahmadinejad's surprise victory in his first presidential campaign, the new Iranian president traveled to New York to attend the UN General Assembly, in all probability his first trip outside of Iran in his forty-plus years of life (rumors that he spent time in Lebanon in the 1980s with the Revolutionary Guards cannot be confirmed, nor has he confirmed or denied them).

Ahmadinejad, a villager from a deeply religious family that had moved to the capital when he was still a boy, had drawn conclusions from the Mossadeq years (not having lived through them) that differed from those of his compatriots, and his antipathy to the monarchy under which he was about to be elevated from working to middle class, owing to his education, manifested itself in a devotion to Islam and Islamic principles. He was not part of the active resistance to the Shah (and unlike some of the clerics in power today had not served time in prison) until the revolution gathered steam, and when that happened, he, along with hundreds of thousands of fellow university students, many once villagers like himself, joined in the protests and demonstrations that quickly brought down the monarchy.

Ahmadinejad was not as confident a leader then as he is now, nor was he on sure ground as he made his first trip to the United States. Among his entourage was Ali Larijani, who had just been appointed as secretary of the Supreme National Security Council and chief nuclear negotiator to replace Hassan Rowhani, a mid-level cleric who was close to the defeated candidate Ayatollah Rafsanjani, and a middle-class Iranian who had changed his name from the somewhat aristocratic *Fereidoun* to the properly Islamic *Rowhani*, meaning "of faith." Larijani, actually a challenger to Ahmadinejad in the presidential election, had impeccable qualifications for the job: not only was he a former Revolutionary Guard but his father had been an Ayatollah; he was highly educated, including having earned a doctorate in Western philosophy; he was fiercely loyal to the Islamic system but was also urbane—and Ahmadinejad deferred to him on every occasion when the issue of Iran's nuclear program arose. The president had not yet denied the Holocaust nor had he uttered harsh words about Israel, so apart from curiosity about him as a person and what kind of leader he might be, the pressing issue of the day was Larijani's mandate, and it was he who patiently explained to the American media and to scholars who met with the Iranian entourage what Iran intended to do with its long-running but up until then slowly building nuclear energy program.

After Larijani and Ahmadinejad arrived in New York, Mohammad Javad Zarif, Iran's ambassador to the UN at the time, who arranged extracurricular activities for both men during their trip, threw a big party for Iranians living in the United States, or at least Iranians not openly hostile to the Islamic regime. During the Iranian delegation's last night on American soil, all three appeared before a crowd of some five hundred ostensibly friendly Iranian-Americans in the grand ball-room of the Hilton Hotel on Sixth Avenue in Manhattan. Ahmadinejad, still unaccustomed to the spotlight a president is perpetually under, gave a short speech, sticking to platitudes concerning the greatness of Iran and Iranians and his own humility, and left the podium to Larijani to explain Iran's nuclear program to an audience that perhaps had divided loyalties. Dr. Larijani, in a much better tailored suit than his president's standard issue, began by saying that Iran would never, *ever* give up its right to peaceful nuclear energy. But he then compared Iran's sovereignty over its nuclear fuel cycle, one that the administration of George W. Bush had declared unacceptable, to Iran's immensely popular nationalization of its oil industry under Mossadeq—a clever analogy that drew thunderous applause from the crowd. Dr. Larijani also recounted that he had told Jack Straw, the British foreign secretary, that Iranians still viewed Britain—which had decried its loss of control over Persia's oil under Mossadeq as a "threat to the security of the world"—with deep suspicion because of the one-sided oil concession of the last century, and had warned him that Britain should not repeat the same mistake when it came to nuclear power. But when the applause died down, a young woman in full black hijab—someone I had wondered about when I saw her outside, since she seemed to be the only guest who interpreted the hijab so literally, in New York City at that—stood up at her table and shouted, *"Agha'ye* Larijani!" She was visibly shaking. "How *dare* you," she continued, her voice strong but with a slight quiver of rage, "talk about Mossadeq when there isn't *even* a street in Tehran named after him." She stood waiting for his reply, as a few in the crowd applauded. Larijani seemed unperturbed but took a moment to gather his thoughts. "Mossadeq's place," he said gently, "is in every Iranian's heart"—rather than on a street sign, presumably an honor reserved for everyone from Imam Khomeini to martyrs of the Iran-Iraq War to Anwar Sadat's assassin. The woman, still shaking, turned and stormed out of the room, unescorted.

ALI LARIJANI may be a fierce nationalist, a loyal soldier of the Islamic regime, and even an apologist for many of its excesses, but he is a different political animal from Ahmadinejad, the president he once served. Although perhaps obliged to generally downplay Mossadeq's

significance in the development of Iranian democracy, he nonetheless sounded sincere in his laudatory remarks that night in New York.
Like many of those in the Iranian leadership, Larijani comes from a
clerical family, once its own class that sat happily beside the growing middle class of the Pahlavi era, far removed from the poor and
working class that made up the majority of Iran's population in the
earlier years of the twentieth century. Unlike Ahmadinejad and some
of his closest allies, he would have had the benefits of higher education, or the rigorous theological training his brother Sadeq, the head
of the judiciary, went through, under any government or system, and
his upward mobility would not have been so hard as Ahmadinejad's,
which was a struggle against the tide of class consciousness under
the monarchy and the enduring Persian class system. Larijani certainly would not have been elevated to the ranks of the elite as he
has been under the Islamic system, but he and other villagers, like
the landowning pistachio farmer Rafsanjani and dozens of others in
the leadership of the Islamic Republic, have a sense of history and
of the Iranian struggles for self-rule that an entire new breed of leaders like Ahmadinejad appear not to have, nor even particularly care
about. Larijani and the like joined the revolution of 1979 because they
were staunch believers in the struggle for democratic rule, in their
belief that Islam offered a more just political system than what Iran
had experienced under successive dynasties, and in a nationalistic
fervor whereby sentiment for a powerful and independent Iran was
a leading impetus for change.

Although their fervor led to excesses and outright abuses of human
rights in the early days of the revolution (and even well into its matu-
rity), leaders like Larijani who believed themselves to be inheritors of
causes such as those of the constitutionalists of 1906, or of Mossadeq
in the early 1950s, are markedly different from the clique that took the
election of 2009. The members of this clique, with no connections to

the clergy, except for their devotion to the most radical, least educated, most autocratic, and least respected of the Ayatollahs of Shia Islam, and hardly a connection to the revolutionaries and dissident thinkers of the Shah's days, rose to prominence in recent years. Their disdain for the old guard of the revolution, in their view a privileged and corrupt lot not unlike the Shah's men, is palpable and forms their political philosophy. That disdain does not go unreciprocated.

"Mongoloid," said one leading member of the old guard, himself the son of an Ayatollah and a noted reformist, for every name I mentioned in the Ahmadinejad clique. "Mongoloids, all of them." Sitting there in his home in North Tehran, sumptuously decorated with Persian antiques, he wasn't aware of the offensiveness of that term in the West. It isn't true of course—he meant that they were grossly unqualified for their jobs—for although the clique has no tolerance for the niceties of etiquette or even of democracy, most members are far from unintelligent. That their likes were shut out of power during the Shah's time because of their humble roots, and again shut out of real power after the revolution by a new privileged class, makes them hungry for revenge, but it does not make them stupid.

In mid-2009, before the election, I particularly wanted to visit one younger member who seemed quietly destined for greater things, Dr. Mohammad Hosseini, then the deputy minister of science and president of Payam'e Noor University, the open university of Iran offering degrees by correspondence as well as on campuses across the country. I had asked a friend of his for an introduction, and after being assured that Dr. Hosseini was expecting my call, I called him at his office one day.

"Baleh?"

"May I speak to Dr. Hosseini?" I said, after introducing myself.

"Give me a land line number," came the brusque reply. I frantically searched for the phone number for my friend's home, from where I was calling on my cell phone, now a victim of the technology that made memorization of phone numbers quaintly old-fashioned. I found the number on my computer and read it into the receiver.

"Hang up and I'll call you back."

I did as I was told, my eyebrows raised as I pressed the "end" button on my phone. Why on earth, I wondered, did the office of the president of one of the largest universities in the world concern itself with whether conversations emanating from that office might occur on a cell phone? The house phone rang.

"*Baleh*?" it was my turn to say.

"How can I help you?" asked the man on the other end of the line.

"I wanted to make an appointment to see Dr. Hosseini," I said. "I believe Dr. Hosseini is expecting me."

"Hold on."

The line went silent for a few minutes, and then Hosseini himself spoke.

"How about eight a.m. tomorrow, when I'll be at the ministry?" he asked, without the usual Persian banter of politesse, *ta'arouf,* and formalities. He then proceeded to give me the address and very basic directions.

"I'll find it," I replied, "and thank you very much." I hung up, still wondering if I was about to meet a deputy minister or an intelligence officer. He was probably both, I concluded. The next morning, I left plenty of time to get to the ministry building, one of the few that had been located in the northern extremes of the city and where many of its employees had to be bussed in from points south. I arrived early and watched the employees file into the building; getting out of cars, shared taxis, and government buses, many of them were women who kissed their young children goodbye before they continued on their way to their schools.

The ministry itself was a bustling place, with dozens of visitors waiting in the lobby to see this or that official, and I sat down and waited to be called to the minister's floor. A few minutes later I was on a jammed elevator, uncomfortably so because I was pressed into the body of a chador-clad but shapely young woman standing next to me, and headed for Dr. Hosseini's office. The assistant who greeted me in his outer office was gracious and exhibited none of the gruffness of the man who had answered his phone the previous day. I wondered if it was the same person, who face-to-face might exhibit, as almost all Iranians do, a different personality than when anonymous. But I didn't ask, and he didn't offer an introduction as he led me to the good doctor's office and an enormous sofa facing an equally enormous desk. The morning papers were laid out on the coffee table, and within seconds, the office tea man brought a tray of tea and biscuits. I perused the papers, all of them conservative, until Hosseini walked into the room, apologizing for his tardiness. We exchanged pleasantries, and then talked about the state of U.S.-Iran relations before I quizzed him on his specialty, science and education.

"My big question," I said, "is, why is there still no high-speed Internet access in Iran, at least not for the general public?" Under President Ahmadinejad, the government had restricted the speed of the late-to-arrive DSL connections, already burdened by ancient telephone wires, to a measly 128 kilobytes per second. "I mean," I continued, "doesn't that inhibit scientific progress?" Hosseini nodded and then launched into a statistical review of higher education in the Islamic Republic.

"We have over a million students," he said, "and they are among the best in their field, worldwide. The opportunities have never been better for anyone in Iran, and despite the sanctions imposed on us by America and the West, we are as advanced as any nation."

"But sir," I said, "surely if Internet access were faster and more readily available, our students could learn more, do more research more efficiently, and benefit from communication with the outside world."

"We Iranians," said Dr. Hosseini, "we have a different culture." He paused and smiled at me, like a patient professor about to explain the obvious to a dim-witted student. "We are a culture that likes human contact, not anonymous and disembodied communication."

"But . . ."

"You see," he interrupted, "we like to pay visits to each other, to drop in and chat with our friends and family, to see one another's faces. It's always been like that in Iran."

"Yes," I replied, "that's true." I was reminded of my father's village (which now has a university but lacked even a high school in my father's time), where neighbors and friends still drop by at any time of day, whether it is convenient for the host or not. With only dial-up Internet access at best, they tend not to e-mail ahead. This lack of privacy is perhaps one of the reasons why, way before the Internet was developed and even before home phones were common, people like my father, and I suspect Hosseini's family too, escaped to the big city. "But that doesn't explain why there are over forty million cell phones in Iran," I said, "and why texting is as popular here as it is in London or New York." Hosseini stared at me for a few moments, perhaps pondering the incessant ringing of his own cell phone, which he had to continually silence. "Iranians invented the postal system over two thousand years ago," I continued, "a rather impersonal communication system, but besides, the Internet isn't all about communication; it is also a valuable research and information tool."

"Of course," he said, nodding again. "And our students have full use of it." He was correct, in that university campuses tend to have fast connections, but when students go home, they are still plagued by glacial and intermittent dial-up access. "Neither rain nor sleet nor gloom of night" may have been Herodotus's description of what could not stop the Persian post from fulfilling its duties over two millennia ago, but he didn't reckon on the Ayatollahs of the twenty-first century, who can do so with a flick of the switch.

"I'm still not sure what the issue is," I told him, "given that you can block un-Islamic sites anyway, and that one measure of a country's progress these days is Internet penetration. We want to be an advanced country, don't we?"

"Of course," said Hosseini, "but we also must be mindful of our *culture*." It was perhaps serendipitous for him, anyway, that after the election of 2009 he would be appointed minister of culture and Islamic guidance, the head of a powerful ministry charged with precisely that—being mindful and protective of Iran's culture, guided by Islam. I wondered, when his appointment was announced, whether his views on culture, Iranian Shia culture, would influence ministry decisions on the arts. Would cinema be necessary at all, given that tradition in Iran dictated that stories be told orally? And face-to-face? Or would a press, let alone a free one, be necessary when Iranian villagers who at one time preferred to get their news from their neighbors, also face-to-face, might want *that* culture preserved?

MOHAMMAD HOSSEINI is not a mongoloid, as my reformist friend might insensitively insist, far from it, for he not only scored at the very top in his concours examination to enter university, but also struck me as a remarkably intelligent person in every way except for his somewhat inane explanation, one I can't imagine he himself believes, for the paucity of high-speed Internet access in his beloved country. Hosseini also displayed little of the *oghdeh*, the complexes, both superior and inferior, that Iranians seem to possess simultaneously and which defines much of their behavior. Oghdeh can be the hallmark of men like him and is a much used word in Iran, for although the envy Iranians once had for the privileged class manifested itself as an inferiority complex in the growing middle class during the Shah's time, oghdeh took on the characteristics of a distinct superiority complex among the new ruling class after the revolution. The matter of the Internet, though, is purely one of control, not culture, something Hosseini was loathe to admit. But in the cultural explanation he gave, he was not, as some urbanized Iranians with a heavy dose of the inferiority complex do, showing disdain either for the village mentality that was long the basis of Iranian social intercourse, or for the urban elite who might, like his students at Payam'e Noor, benefit from a more modern approach to communication. The Islamic Revolution was supposed to do away with class oghdeh, village versus big-city psychologies, and to a large degree it had succeeded. The Shah's version, one of fostering a large middle class, had also succeeded, but with their inferiority oghdeh intact, the once villagers who then made up much of the middle class sneered at their humble roots, whereas a new generation of once villagers, like Ahmadinejad and his cohorts, openly celebrated them.

In the election of 2009 that followed my meeting with Hosseini by a few weeks, the entire Iranian nation became embroiled in one big oghdeh-fest: the president and his followers claiming his representation of a silent majority, the non-urban working class, and his opponents claiming that an inept, even uneducated administration was resorting to fascist tactics and mob rule to remain in power at all costs. Even the Ayatollahs were split: the intellectual elite fell in with the opposition; the others, mostly the least published or venerated, with the populist president.

WHEN I LEFT his office, Dr. Hosseini, an intellectual himself in a now altogether different elite, in all probability dismissed me as another "West-toxified" Iranian, *gharbzadeh* in the Persian lexicon, and as one who had been seduced by the West into believing that its culture is inherently superior to that of Iran. West-toxification was a charge leveled at many of the middle-class Iranians at the time of the revolution, and although the term is hardly used today, the attitude of many on the far right of Iranian politics toward reformists and certainly liberals remains one of suspicion that they are more enamored of the West than they are of Persian tradition. Indeed, some view democracy, and certainly liberal democracy, as a Western notion that is or should be incompatible with Iranian culture. (Ironically, in one of President Ahmadinejad's more bizarre explanations of the 2009 election, in a speech he gave in Azerbaijan months later, he insisted that the turnout "signified the rule of full *liberal* democracy in Iran.")

But even the leading reformists are careful to distinguish between their views on democracy and Western notions, mindful of emphasizing the Islamic, in this case Shia, aspect of what Iranian democracy means. Shiism, born out of a sense of injustice perpetuated by tyrants, is central to the thought of the reformists who see power vested in the people but guided by the social system of Islam. Some might argue that the democratic achievements of the last century, all of them interrupted by either an iron fist or a foreign power, failed because they ignored Islam, which has been the state religion since the sixteenth century. In both the constitutionalist revolution of 1906 and the Mossadeq affair, Ayatollahs and other clerics fell on either side of the battle, pro- and anti-Shah, and even during the last Shah's reign (and his father's) there were clerics both dissident and compliant whenever the Pahlavis advanced social or democratic changes. Ayatollah Khomeini's promise of a pure Islamic democracy eliminated any ambiguity in terms of how the culture would be affected by democratic change, and most of the clergy as well as virtually all of the democratic movements in Iran supported his vision of a quintessentially Persian form of democratic rule, one that took into account the Shia nature of the Persians and their culture.

Naturally many argue, particularly today, that the Islamic democracy promised by the revolution never materialized, that whatever democratic institutions were created by the new constitution of 1979 are undermined by the authority of the valih-e-faqih, the Supreme Leader. But there are still many believers in the possibility of an Islamic democracy, including leaders of the opposition, backed by some of the senior Ayatollahs, such as Grand Ayatollah Yousef Sanei—known for his declaration that in Islam women and men have equal status—who claim that their vision in fact matches Khomeini's original intent, far more so, in their minds, than that of the current government's. It is a crucial point, for in Iran Khomeini is still widely revered as a savior, a latter-day Shia crusader for justice. Nothing that Mohammad Khatami and Mehdi Karroubi, and Grand Ayatollahs Hossein-Ali Montazeri and Sanei, among others, have articulated for the future of Iran is incompatible with democratic rule, even if most of the opposition clerics still cling to the concept of velayat-e-faqih and a Supreme Leader.

Ayatollah Montazeri, whose death and funeral in Qom in December 2009 sparked renewed mass demonstrations against the government, had the respect if not direct support of millions of Iranians, and clerics such as him who no longer believe in the absolute political authority of a Supreme Leader are in agreement with Grand Ayatollah Ali al-Sistani of Iraq (himself an Iranian), who prefers the clergy's role to be of guidance and not executive leadership. Montazeri, once Khomeini's handpicked heir, fell out with the founder of the Islamic Republic over the repression and violent suppression of dissent during the 1980s. He was under house arrest for years, and emerged a fierce critic of Ayatollah Khamenei's rule, finally ruling that the velayat-e-faqih itself was incompatible with Islamic democracy, a ruling few other Ayatollahs could support publicly even if they agreed with it. Sistani, the jurisprudent who is the most senior Ayatollah in Iraq, may have agreed with Montazeri on a limited role for the clergy in politics, but he is the de facto supreme leader of Iraq, not enshrined in the constitution, but effectively the one man who can derail any government initiative or law passed by Parliament. It is not without reason that the prime minister of Iraq visits him in Najaf as often as he can, to receive guidance but more important, approval for his programs. Anyone who has the ability to put millions of people on the street wields enormous power and influence, even as he might deny any political aspirations. And although Sistani has never met with an American official, or a general, no one doubts his enormous power. This suggests that whatever form of functioning democracy eventually takes hold in Iraq, it will be purely Islamic and probably Shia dominated.

SHIA ISLAM may have always been a part of the political equation in Iran, as it has been in Iraq despite the oppression during the Saddam Hussein years, but the clergy, and some Ayatollahs in particular, have also regularly exercised their power not in the advancement of democracy or even justice, but in the advancement of personal or church gain. My maternal grandfather was an Ayatollah, born in a village in Iraq to an Iraqi mother and Persian father, but he was apolitical most of his life, except when he refused to leave his home in protest against Reza Shah's banning of the turban in public life. During the reign of the last Shah, my grandfather's son, my uncle Nassir Assar, was appointed deputy prime minister in charge of *Oghaf*, the Iranian Religious Endowment and Pilgrimage Organization, but my grandfather wasn't proud; rather, he urged him to refuse the job. Oghaf was notorious among the clergy, for it was in charge of *vaqf*, or religious endowments, whereby land and other property were given to them for the maintenance of shrines or mosques or schools—in a measure of the importance of the church, the organization was second in wealth only to the National Oil Company. The Shah's intent was to exercise greater control over the administration of Oghaf's endowments. The clergy viewed this as interference in their affairs and a diminishing of their influence and power, and to be the point man for the Shah on a matter affecting the mullahs' pocketbooks was, in my grandfather's view, asking for trouble. *"Man een akhoundha ra meeshenasam,"* my mother tells me he said to Nassir—*"I know these mullahs."* He was prescient, for my uncle became a wanted man after the revolution, more because he had crossed the clergy than for his service to the Shah or even the prime minister, his friend from his Foreign Ministry days, Amir Abbas Hoveyda.

But during his tenure and throughout the Shah's days, neither my uncle nor his office were very successful in curtailing the power of the mullahs, either by monitoring their wealth or by any other means. The government may have controlled large sums of money set aside for charitable religious projects, but pious and wealthy Shias still gave generously and directly to their Ayatollahs or mosques in the form of *zakat*, or the alms that are mandated by Islam. And there have always been, throughout the villages, towns, and cities of Iran, pious and wealthy Shias. The middle class that my father represented, villagers tending pro-democratic and pro-modernization, may have abandoned tradition and the mosque, but there were always those, highly educated and not, in the villages and among immigrants to Tehran and other big cities who clung to the Persian way of doing things, ignoring the state and directly supporting the clergy. "Secularism," former president Khatami said in Berlin in 2005, "is the experience of the Western culture and thought. Insisting on spreading it to places where the underlying intellectual background, and the political and social reasons for its appearance are lacking, is clearly a mistake, regardless of being desirable or not." The Shah insisted; the Ayatollahs, and then the people, fought back. The *bazaaris*, merchants in the traditional bazaars of Iran's cities who have always been looked down on by the upper class and by the middle class aspiring to the upper, are perhaps the most glaring example of wealthy and pious Shias who always supported their

Ayatollahs, their revolution, and the Islamic system to this day. But there are many others in the new middle class, such as Dr. Hosseini and his boss, President Ahmadinejad, and many in direct opposition to them but still a part of the Islamic system, who, like my father and those before them, also came from disparate villages in a once agrarian society to form the backbone of a regime in the industrial age. And it is these people, from the smallest villages to the biggest cities, who fall into the reform, conservative, or pragmatist camps of Iranian politics, who will decide the future of the Ayatollahs' democracy.

OH YEAH?
KARDEEM VA SHOD!

*Persians consider themselves to be the superior race among
all nations. The exception in their eyes are the Medians who
worship the same deity. This as a Greek I don't believe, since
I know of Spartans who can be of equal gallantry to Persians.*

—HERODOTUS, 454 BC

When I was in college in the United States in the 1970s, before
the Iranian Revolution of 1979, I befriended a group of Iranian
students, a fast-growing contingent that reflected the expanding middle
class's ability to send its children off to faraway America to further
an education that was impossible in Iran, given the small number of
university places available at the time. Being the son of a diplomat
who served in many countries from the time of my birth, I had hardly
lived in Iran, and yet I was fascinated by these countrymen of mine,
who seemed at once both exotic and very familiar to me. We had no
shared childhood experiences, but I found their penchant for late-night
gambling, disco jaunts on the weekend, and sometimes incongruously
intense political discussions to be a refreshing diversion from the inter-
actions with my often earnest American friends and fellow students,

for whom the just-ended Vietnam War and resignation of Richard Nixon in the wake of Watergate meant some lost opportunities for youthful idealism. Nightly poker sessions among the affluent Iranians and sons of the powerful—a governor here, a general or police chief there—resulted in either supplemental income or deep debt. They also brought me face-to-face with my first SAVAK agent.

The Shah's secret police was ostensibly an intelligence organization trained by the CIA, but it was notorious for operating torture chambers in Iranian prisons and safe houses, an accusation the Shah repeatedly denied to foreign journalists, including Mike Wallace, who pressed him on the issue during a *60 Minutes* interview. SAVAK had always had a presence on any campus, in Iran or outside, where anti-government students might be encouraged to express their opinions. No one could be one hundred percent sure of who the SAVAK man (or woman) was on campus, whether he or she was merely a paid informant (and there were many of those) or an actual officer on assignment, but clues were bountiful. This particular person, I'll call him Masoud, was much older than the rest of us, he was clearly out of his league when it came to study (it was unclear that he was even pursuing a degree), his South Tehran street lingo and accent betrayed his underprivileged origins, and he was always more interested in where we stood in the political spectrum than in our college life, girls, or getting high— three priorities for most of us, though not necessarily in that order. He insinuated himself into every gathering at the cafeteria or other public place, and everyone whispered that he had to be *savaki*. I couldn't find anyone who actually liked him, but he somehow was able to join various Iranian cliques, and no one bothered, or dared, to tell him he wasn't welcome. He often asked me, casually while dealing cards, for example, whether I had recently been to any Confederation meetings, the "Confederation" being the largest organization of Iranian students abroad opposed to the ruling monarch. I knew he appeared at the meetings, because other friends had told me that he stood in the back of the room and was quiet, observing who showed up and what was being said. I wouldn't dream of attending a Confederation meeting, for I was conscious of what that could mean to my father, an Iranian ambassador at the time. I did, however, have friends of all stripes: Confederation members, some of whom were picked up by SAVAK when they returned home for summer vacation, and even tortured; *taghoutis* (those in the ruling monarchical establishment); and a slew of friends who were sympathetic to one opposition party or another, from Mujahedin to Fadayeen to straight Islamist.

One day Masoud warned me, in a creepy way that was his habit, to be careful of the people I associated with, for he had seen me in the company of students known for their dissident views (and for their dress, which consisted exclusively of U.S. Army surplus jackets shorn of their insignia paired with old jeans, a style they all took back to Tehran in 1979). I ignored him, for although I was confident by now that he had created a little file on me, it was unlikely he could pin anything on me in terms of my subversive views, which didn't really exist except in relation to *American* politics. I did imagine, however, him noting in my file that despite the Shah's preference for Republican administrations, the son of an Iranian ambassador was in fact an ardent and vocal supporter of the Democrat Jimmy Carter, on a campus a few blocks away from the White House no less.

BEFORE THE Islamic Revolution, few could imagine that the Shah would be overthrown one day—Iran had been a monarchy for over two thousand years, after all—and I would often tell my friends that I couldn't understand what they hoped to accomplish by agitating, abroad no less, for a change in a system that was unchangeable. "*Nemeesheh*," I used to say—"It can't be done." The United States supported the Shah unequivocally, and all one had to do was look around. "This country, with its size, its people, its power, and the fact that they easily stopped one democratic movement in its tracks in 1953 [the United States had not yet admitted CIA involvement, but all Iranians knew it]: this is not a country that will allow Iran to change," I would argue. "They like it just the way it is, with maybe a sprinkle of democracy thrown in because of Jimmy Carter's own preferences and his distaste for human rights abuses." I did not persuade my friends, most of whom grew more and more confident as the years went by and as we witnessed the revolution take hold from afar.

Masoud remained his nosy and annoying self almost to the end, but on the day of the revolution's success and the end of the monarchy, in February 1979, he disappeared for good. I often wondered what happened to him in the few months following Ayatollah Khomeini's triumph, whether he had returned to Iran and managed to ingratiate himself with Iran's new leaders (who needed spies, after all), many of them from similar unprivileged backgrounds, or whether he had returned and been jailed, or whether he had simply disappeared somewhere in America to reinvent himself. I didn't give him much thought in the years that ensued, as Iran went through purges of the *ancien régime*, reconstituted an intelligence service, and slowly began to move toward Islamic democracy. I didn't think about him, or about nemeesheh, not until the spring of 2009.

IN THAT SPRING, a month and a half before the fateful presidential election of 2009, I was in Yazd, my father's hometown and home to many of my relatives. It was a Friday, the Muslim day of rest, and I was looking forward to attending Friday prayers and hearing a sermon by Yazd's *Imam Jomeh,* or Friday prayer leader, an appointee of the Supreme Leader but the only one among Iran's Imams Jomeh who is not politically aligned to the conservatives. Although I have little interest in sermons, Iran's Friday prayers always include a political sermon that follows the religious one, and in the run-up to the election I was curious how Mohammad Sadoughi, the reformist Imam Jomeh, would square the speaking points from Ayatollah Khamenei with his own opinions. There was no question that he would be supporting the reform candidate in the upcoming election, Mir Hossein Mousavi (rather than Mehdi Karroubi, also a reformist but not in the Khatami political camp), while the Supreme Leader had already made clear his preference for Mahmoud Ahmadinejad. But as the Imams Jomeh and particularly the Supreme Leader were not supposed to show a preference for a candidate, and were certainly not supposed to encourage their flock to vote one way or another, political sermons in a campaign season promised to subtly show the divergent views on display in Iran, a country often considered intolerant of independent thought.

Sadoughi is married to Maryam Khatami, the former president's sister, and although he is not quite as liberal as she or her siblings, he is nonetheless a firm supporter of the reform movement started by Mohammad Khatami on his election in 1997. The morning of his sermon, his son, also Mohammad, called me at my hotel, suggesting we have tea together after which he would arrange to have me escorted to the mosque. When I met him in the lobby, he was, as is the Persian custom, bearing gifts for me, a visitor to his hometown, gifts of famous Yazdi sweets and pistachios.

"Let's go into the tearoom," I said, after thanking him profusely and insisting that I was an unworthy recipient of his family's largesse. I handed him a copy of my last book, one in which I had thanked him and his parents, in return. He seemed a bit more nervous than the last time I saw him, his eyes darting this way and that, and I wondered what was causing him concern. In his left hand he casually held a walkie-talkie, an item strictly forbidden in Iran except to the military, the Revolutionary Guards, and the security services—as his father's chief of staff he was never without it, and he used it to communicate with other staff, bodyguards, and Revolutionary Guardsmen who were assigned to protect the Imam Jomeh as part of their duties as guardians of the Islamic Revolution. We found an empty space in the vast tearoom, a traditional setup of two Persian-carpeted benches facing each other, and took our seats. He glanced around him, his eyes fixed on a group of four men who followed us into the room and sat down two tables away.

"Let's move to another table," he said, standing up. I followed suit, and we moved a few feet farther from the men. "They're following us," he whispered to me across a low coffee table, his eyes steadily watching the men over my shoulder.

"Really?" I asked. I slowly, and as casually as I could, turned my head and scanned the entire room, finally resting my eyes on the men, all with the same week-old stubble I was sporting but dressed identically in gray suits and white open-collared shirts. They didn't look back at me. I was excited, even proud for a moment, contemplating the fact that I was now an important enough person, at least in Iran, to warrant a government tail. "I should have guessed," I said, "that I might be under surveillance. I'm sorry."

"No, no," said Mohammad, "it's not *you* they're watching—it's me!" Embarrassed by my lack of required Persian diffidence and a little shocked, I turned to look at them again.

"Are you *sure*? Whatever for?" I said, when I turned back to face him. I don't think I hid my disappointment in not being the target of Iran's security forces and I may have even had a pout on my lips. But I suddenly thought of Masoud, the SAVAK man from my college days. Masoud had spied, we were sure, even on trusted families in the ruling establishment, some of whom he hung out with—no one, as far as the intelligence services or the Shah himself, thought that anyone was above reproach. Could it be that the Islamic Republic was no different in that regard?

"That's what Iran has come to," said Mohammad with a shrug.

"Are you sure?" I asked. I had not, in my years of traveling back and forth to Iran, experienced either surveillance (at least I didn't *think* I had) or the feeling that Iran was a police state, and I still didn't feel that way.

"I think so," he said. "They want to turn the country into a one-party state. The party of God." What Mohammad was saying made very little sense to me at the time. How could his family be under surveillance? The Sadoughis are protected by the Revolutionary Guards, after all—the most powerful and influential institution in the country, an institution that has its own intelligence division, which competes with and is often at odds with the government's own Ministry of Intelligence (known as MOIS). Furthermore, Mohammad was chief of staff of the representative of the Supreme Leader, the valih-e-faqih after all, the very raison d'être for the Islamic Republic and therefore the Guards themselves. Perhaps, I thought, it was the MOIS that wanted to keep tabs on the Sadoughis, just in case their reformist minds veered past reform and into revolution, but I also secretly wondered if Mohammad was just, as Persian ta'arouf would demand, trying to put my mind at ease and in fact they *were* monitoring my movements.

In the lead-up to what promised to be a hard-fought and even ugly presidential election, one that pitted extreme conservative thought embodied by Ahmadinejad against the liberal theology and progressive politics embodied by Mir Hossein Mousavi and his mentor, Mohammad Khatami, anything was possible. But the MOIS wasn't like the SAVAK, with spies on every street and in every living room, and Iran wasn't a one-party state anymore. Mohammad Sadoughi and myself, however, were relatives of Khatami (me by family marriage),

we both hailed from Ardakan, and we both were known for expressing our reformist views, so perhaps, I thought, it was just standard
practice to keep tabs on anyone with any political leanings, especially
at election time.

When I escorted Mohammad to the front door of the hotel after
our tea, I noticed the four men didn't follow, and an hour later, as I
was lingering in the lobby waiting for the car to take me to the Molla
Esmail Mosque, stepping outside now and then and walking back in, I
searched, as nonchalantly as I could, for any signs of a tail but couldn't
identify any suspicious persons. Well, in a nation where staring is not
considered rude and any unfamiliar face deserves a good long and hard
stare, perhaps everyone was suspicious. Everyone except the group
of elderly Italian and Japanese tourists who were happily oblivious
to the political machinations of the Islamic Republic. But I decided
that Mohammad might have been overly paranoid, and that as bad
as the Islamic Republic's security services could behave, they surely
still respected the regime's tolerance for opposing politics, even some
measure of dissent? No, nemeesheh! That was then.

Hojjatoleslam Mohammad Sadoughi, the Friday prayer leader
of Yazd, is by definition not only the representative of the Supreme
Leader of the Islamic Revolution for Yazd province in central Iran, but
also the host, at his sumptuously restored historic home in the ancient
city center, to the Supreme Leader whenever the hermitic Ayatollah
Ali Khamenei visits the hometown of his mother's family. Yazd, a city
known for its pre-Islamic Zoroastrian temples and grave sites, also
bears the distinction of being the only city in the world that could
boast, in the early days of the twenty-first century, that two of its native
sons, Mohammad Khatami and Moshe Katsav, simultaneously served
as the sitting presidents of two different countries: Iran and Israel.

Moshe Katsav's family emigrated to Israel when he was still a child; the once-vibrant Jewish community they left in Iran has been reduced to a fraction of its size in recent years. Khatami maintains close ties to his hometown as well as the nearby town of Ardakan, where he was born and where his mother still lives, and which just happens to be the site of a uranium mine that is on the list of targets for Israeli or U.S. long-range bombers or missiles.

Khatami's sister Maryam, Sadoughi's wife, hostess to the Supreme Leader at her home when he comes to stay, is a highly educated and erudite woman who, notwithstanding her black chador and obvious Islamic piety, holds reformist but even liberal political views. Like her husband, she is a strong supporter of her brother, who is politically the polar opposite of the Supreme Leader. In Iran, land of many paradoxes, there is, however, no incongruity in the Supreme Leader's representative's connection to and even support of a politician who holds often opposing political views to the valih-e-faqih, the ultimate authority in affairs of state. (The *velayat-e-faqih*, or rule of the jurisprudent, is an old Shia concept with differing interpretations over the ages; it was Ayatollah Khomeini who institutionalized it in Iran as the absolute authority and rule of a cleric over a Muslim nation, in the absence of the Shia Messiah.) Just as in Yazd, a deeply religious city that sacrificed many of its sons to the Iranian war with Iraq, there is no incongruity in Islamic fervor and fundamentalism combined with an unusual tolerance for other faiths, most notably Zoroastrianism, whose priests maintain an ancient fire temple in town that rivals any mosque as a popular sightseeing destination for Iranian and foreign tourists alike.

Only a few months before I arrived in Yazd, in April 2009, the Supreme Leader had been a guest in the Sadoughi residence while on an extended stay in the central Iranian province. On that trip, hard-line conservatives unhappy with a reformist cleric serving as their Imam Jomeh had intimated to the Supreme Leader that there might

be a cleric better suited to the task of disseminating conservative philosophy, but Ayatollah Khamenei had gone out of his way to praise
Sadoughi at public speeches, an indication that he sometimes liked to
keep the conservatives guessing and on their toes too.

ON FRIDAY MORNINGS, as the priests at the Zoroastrian temple in Yazd
go about keeping the embers alive, which they have done continuously
for over five hundred years (making it the longest fire in recorded history), Hojjatoleslam Sadoughi prepares to lead the prayers at the Molla
Esmail Mosque, named for a nineteenth-century mullah who, in this
city of contradictions, was actually a Jewish convert to Shia Islam. The
prayers themselves need no preparation—Sadoughi, like every Muslim
believer, has known the prayer by rote since childhood. The sermon,
however, and particularly the second half, which traditionally discusses
politics, does require some thought. Known for his moderate political
views, Sadoughi nevertheless is not one to advocate radical political
and social change; he is, after all, a believer in the Islamic system and
the ideals of the revolution that brought clerics like him, and before
him his father, to power. To make that clear, Sadoughi, who normally
walks with a cane, leans on a Kalashnikov automatic rifle, loaded,
while he delivers his sermons, just like every other Friday prayer leader
in Iran. On the Friday I attended mosque, President Ahmadinejad had
recently given what many in the West described as an incendiary and
virulently anti-Zionist speech to a UN conference on racism held in
Geneva. It was also the eve of the anniversary of the failed 1980 U.S.
mission to rescue American hostages held in Tehran. Both those events
featured heavily in the political segment of the prayer leader's sermon,
delivered to a large audience of men of all ages. Tabas (where U.S.
helicopters were destroyed and American servicemen died), Sadoughi
reminded his audience (some of whom weren't born at that time),

resulted from the student takeover of the U.S. Embassy in Tehran, a "den of spies" as he described it, and the failure of the rescue mission signified Iran's resilience in the face of decades of American interference and malevolent designs. So far, his words could have ushered forth from the Supreme Leader's mouth, although most Iranians in the leadership, including almost all the "liberal" reformists, agree with that characterization of American-Iranian relations. The United States, he then conceded, had elected a new president, Barack Obama, who had promised change, and Iran was simply waiting to witness real deeds that might signify change beyond the new rhetoric emanating from the White House (something he repeated wistfully to me later that night in his office).

His sermon presented a somewhat softer line than the Supreme Leader would take, but it was not completely off message. The Leader himself, after all, had said, with respect to President Obama's New Year message to Iran and Iranians, one in which Obama had praised Iranian culture, that "if the U.S. changes, then Iran will change too." Obama's optimistic words about the future of U.S.-Iran relations, "it is a future where the old divisions are overcome," were met cautiously by Iranian authorities. But Iranians, and mullahs in particular, are masters of rhetoric, and from their perspective it is not Iran that has the clenched fist (for Iran has never in their minds threatened the United States) that President Obama had spoken of in his inaugural address, but rather the United States, with its threats of military action and with its troops and navy surrounding Iran, to say nothing of the unilateral sanctions and the other pressures the United States has brought to bear on the Islamic Republic. To paraphrase Jerry McGuire in the 1996 movie of the same name, what Sadoughi and the other clerics seemed to be saying to President Obama in the early days of his presidency was that you can't out-rhetoric the masters of rhetoric, so "show us the *rials*."

Moving on, Sadoughi then described Israel in far less inflammatory language than Ahmadinejad used at the conference in Geneva a few days earlier. Sadoughi nonetheless defended the Iranian president he is opposed to, and chided the Western participants at the conference (parroting the pragmatist and centrist former president Ayatollah Hashemi Rafsanjani, who made a similar speech at prayers that day in Tehran), who "allegedly are against racism and are defenders of free speech," for their hypocrisy in walking out on the Iranian president's talk, thereby insulting not only him but the "Iranian nation." The Friday prayer leader will not stray too far from the Supreme Leader's stated views (and his instructions on the content of his weekly address, which are faxed to Imams Jomeh offices across the country the night before), but Sadoughi's description of the Ahmadinejad imbroglio before the election controversy is a perfect example of Western lack of understanding of the Iranian psyche. Whether we like it or not, the majority of Iranians, both conservative and liberal, indeed most in the Muslim world, generally agree with the sentiments Ahmadinejad has often expressed regarding Israel (except perhaps for his frequent questioning of the Holocaust), but most would prefer that he express them in more polite language, if at all. This was a subject of fierce debate in the presidential campaign a few weeks later. (The length of Iranian presidential campaigns is limited by law to four weeks, but they can begin unofficially a few weeks earlier.) Indeed, a day after Ahmadinejad returned to Iran from Geneva, Sadeq Kharrazi, a senior official in the Khatami administration and a staunch reformist (and main author of the 2003 offer to the Bush administration to enter into negotiations), wrote on his website that what Ahmadinejad had said was nothing new and merely an affirmation of the Islamic Republic's thirty-year stance toward Israel. He admonished Ahmadinejad instead for attending the conference in the first place (and the Foreign Ministry for its ill advice), thereby embarrassing Iran as the only country that sent its head of state to a lower-level meeting, and for subjecting Iran to wide ridicule with his choice of venue and words.

Beyond relatively respectful criticism of Ahmadinejad, though, privately some ordinarily judicious and influential Iranians whispered to me that they were becoming more and more convinced that Ahmadinejad had to be an Israeli agent, perhaps a sleeper Mossad man recruited long ago and activated before he became president. Why? Apart from the obvious benefit to Israel of almost all of his unnecessary rhetoric, from the Holocaust to belligerent cartographic questions, they said, his speech at the UN conference was a gift to Israeli public relations. Before the conference, Israel was under severe criticism from even its allies in the West (and certainly the media) for the siege of Gaza, and Ahmadinejad in one fell swoop removed the issue of Gaza from the Middle East discourse, for the time being anyway, something Israeli propaganda had been unable to do. A collective sigh of relief, some Iranians suggested, must have been audible in Jerusalem and Tel Aviv.

Not satisfied with merely having given the obligatory reading of the days' events from the point of view of the clergy (and the Supreme Leader), Sadoughi also found time before leading the prayers to criticize the government, in this case for failing to ensure that Iranian pilgrims traveling to Iraq were adequately warned or protected from danger, for a large number of them were killed the day before in a suicide bombing near Baghdad. (Hundreds of Iranians—the most pious Shia Iranians, who form the backbone of support for the Islamic Republic—have been killed in Iraq since the 2003 U.S.-led invasion, usually by roadside bombs or suicide bombers, a fact rarely mentioned when Iran is accused of being behind some of those suicide attacks or the manufacturer and exporter of the improvised explosive devices, or IEDs.) And never missing an opportunity to criticize the United States too, Sadoughi mocked the invasion of Iraq "in the name of bringing freedom to the Iraqis." However, unlike past Friday prayers and prayers in Tehran, there were no chants of "Death to America" or "Death to Israel" at the end of his speech, not even half-hearted ones. Yazd, it seems, had moved on.

A city smack dab in the middle of Iran on the ancient silk route, Yazd is a place where Iranian politesse takes on extreme forms (and even comical ones, such as when I was boarding my flight from Tehran and a bottleneck was created at the aircraft doors, not because of the large crowd squeezing in, but because men with heavy Yazdi accents simply refused to board ahead of their companions, much to the bemusement of a large group of tourists). As a reminder of the political conflicts that exist in Iran, but that were less obvious in the days before the presidential election, a number of hard-liners (thankfully in the minority that day) attending the Friday prayers approached Sadoughi as he made his way to his car after his sermon and they demanded to know, rather rudely, why he hadn't defended the president more forcefully. Sadoughi, not one to be intimidated, responded that he had disagreed with Ahmadinejad's decision to attend the conference at all, and as such, any defense of him was perhaps too generous on his part. With that, he hurried into his waiting car, asked me if I wanted to join him on a trip to Ardakan (which I politely declined), and sped off with his guards. I was directed to another waiting car, driven by a university professor who was a friend of the family's, and I sat in the passenger seat. A Revolutionary Guardsman jumped in the back for a ride to the Imam Jomeh's compound, and he casually threw the Kalashnikov rifle on the seat next to him. It was the safest ride in town, I thought, but I still wondered if MOIS agents were following somewhere behind.

THAT SPRING DAY in Yazd had been one of not only affirmation but also discomfit. Affirmation that despite the sometimes heavy and clenched fist of the theocracy, to borrow President Obama's phrase, Iran's experiment in democracy, or at least an *Islamic* democracy, was still alive and well. The Supreme Leader supported a cleric openly in disagreement with his government. The cleric had fearlessly confronted the government's supporters, and the upcoming presidential election still promised to affirm that the republican aspect of the Islamic Republic was as powerful as the theological one.

At the same time, it was discomfiting because there were signs that the state apparatus under President Ahmadinejad, an apparatus created and supported by the more radical and extreme clerics, was becoming more onerous. It wasn't just young Mohammad Sadoughi's unease in the morning during our tea, but his later afternoon confession to me that he had had doubts about his seminary training in Qom. The only son of an Imam Jomeh, the grandson of an Ayatollah who was martyred in his presence (assassinated by a suicide bomber at the Molla Esmail Mosque in the early days of the revolution), he had felt an obligation to enter the clergy from an early age. He had faithfully studied at a seminary while also studying at university, but he told me that during the presidency of Ahmadinejad (ironically, a layman after successive mullah presidents), the "*hezbollahi*" contingent had been bullying seminary teachers and students alike to "follow their line," and they were squeezing out the independent thinkers and intimidating students who wished to further their study of Islamic law and theology but not necessarily politics. In Iran, *Hezbollah*, or "Party of God," now known in the West more as the name of the Shia political and military organization in Lebanon (itself a creation of the Islamic Republic), has always meant, particularly when used as *hezbollahi* (Hezbollah-like, or belonging to Hezbollah), a person with a certain kind of radical Islamic philosophy, a political philosophy that some in the Shia clerical community, whether "quietist" (for non-involvement in politics) or just moderate, are at odds with. (It is another paradox that while in Iran many use the term "hezbollahi" disparagingly, even those who do, tend to support Lebanese Hezbollah in their goals and tactics.)

DESPITE MY SLIGHT discomfort at hearing a pessimistic view of a resurgent authoritarianism under the presidency of Ahmadinejad, and about his brand of politics having penetrated the mosques and seminaries, I nonetheless remained optimistic as I headed back to Tehran that fine late spring day. Ahmadinejad, after all, had been elected with a large majority in 2005, and if he, like our very own President Bush, had tried to stifle dissent, even resort to extra-legal methods during his presidency, then the voters who had put him in office would either reward or punish him on June 12, depending on their opinion of his record. Not that I was particularly optimistic that punishment would be his fate, for six weeks before the election the opposition appeared to be in disarray. But like the 2004 election in the United States, if the voters returned Ahmadinejad to the address on Pasteur Avenue (the presidential compound), then at least the democratic process worked, even if I wasn't happy with the results.

At the home of Sadeq Kharrazi one evening a few days later, I tried to understand why, with so much talk about the failure of Ahmadinejad to provide even modest economic benefits to his base, the working class, the opposition was not yet able to mount any serious challenge to him. Sadeq explained, in the very Persian way of dealing with hard numbers rather than percentages when it came to political support, how Ahmadinejad still had a lock on the presidency. "He has ten to twelve million solid supporters—there can be no doubt about that. If twenty-five million go to the polls [and six weeks before the election it appeared that the turnout would be low because of general apathy toward the opposition candidates], then in a multi-candidate field he has the majority. As it is now, we will be guests of Mr. Ahmadinejad for another four years." Sadeq was a strong supporter and close confidant of former president Khatami; he and other reformists had urged Khatami to run again as the only candidate who stood a chance of defeating Ahmadinejad, something Khatami reluctantly agreed to in February 2009, only to back out a month later when Mousavi announced his own candidacy.

Khatami had been put in an awkward position: he had, from the year before, when reformists and opponents of Ahmadinejad prevailed on him to run, maintained that the best reform candidate would be the former prime minister Mousavi, and that if he would run, then Khatami would see no reason to be in the race himself. Mousavi had consistently refused to run for office, and as far as the reformists were concerned, he had taken himself out of consideration by the time Khatami announced his candidacy. The day Mousavi changed his mind and announced his candidacy, after Khatami had already begun campaigning, some of Khatami's supporters felt betrayed, but there seemed to be a method to the madness. Khatami told me that he had had a meeting with Mousavi before he bowed out, wanting to make sure that Mousavi intended to stay in the race and not drop out at the last minute as a strategy to put pressure on Ahmadinejad right up until the end, a strategy that could have been brilliant but also carried risks. Pressuring Ahmadinejad with multiple challengers who could appeal to different constituencies, only to have all those challengers unite before the vote, could have drawn support away from the incumbent, but it also could fracture the opposition irreparably, particularly if rival reform candidates turned on each other, as candidates do in American primaries, in order to court support. Mousavi assured Khatami that he indeed was in the race to win, and he felt that if Khatami withdrew and supported him, he would have a strong chance of defeating Ahmadinejad.

Rumors flew around Tehran as the news of Mousavi's candidacy and Khatami's withdrawal was made public. One rumor that gained favor was that the Supreme Leader—uncomfortable with Khatami's popularity and his early campaign successes, indicating that he very well might defeat the Leader's protégé Ahmadinejad—had prevailed on Khatami to withdraw. That was untrue, for although the Supreme Leader didn't personally approve of another Khatami presidency (much as he didn't approve of another Rafsanjani presidency in 2005), he had not yet, in early 2009, jumped into the fray of factional politics; he continued to maintain a position of indifference, at least publicly and even to the candidates, when it came to who might challenge the sitting president. The other rumor, which was likelier true but which circulated only among certain political operatives, was that Ali Larijani, the speaker of Parliament and a close associate of the Supreme Leader, had pressured Mousavi to run in the knowledge that if he accepted, Khatami would knock himself out of the race. Larijani, who had commented that Khatami's candidacy was "a good thing" when it was announced, had also seen signs that Khatami might actually win and sensed that the top leadership of the Revolutionary Guards and other hard-line conservatives were threatening to prevent another Khatami presidency at all costs (which presumably meant manipulating the vote, or worse, if necessary).

Conservatives were worried about Khatami for many reasons, but mostly, and ironically, because of the precedent that Ahmadinejad had set with respect to the power of the presidency. Until Ahmadinejad was elected, no Iranian president had actually acted with the authority of a president, in other words, acted as the "decider," as George Bush was once fond of saying. Khatami had Ahmadinejad to thank for showing that a president could do very much what he wanted (with some limits, of course) without too much regard for the opinions of the Supreme Leader, who was forced, on occasion, to publicly distance himself from some of the president's more outlandish ideas and proclamations. And

Khatami had expressed the view that if he were to become president again, he would, like a left-wing (and saner) version of Ahmadinejad, be far less cautious in ensuring that Ayatollah Khamenei was on board for every decision, big or small, or that he would even be consulted beforehand on certain matters of state, as Khatami had always done in the past. No more Mr. Nice Guy, in other words—not when it came to wielding power and authority.

For the conservatives who worried that an invigorated Khatami might be difficult to control, a simple solution to avoiding a potential crisis was to convince Mousavi, also a reformist but a far less polarizing figure than Khatami, to run instead. Besides, as a relative unknown (he had been retired from politics for twenty years), Mousavi would face an uphill battle in the race. The Supreme Leader and other conservatives would have little issue with a Mousavi campaign, and would probably tolerate a Mousavi presidency knowing that it would be weak, certainly much weaker than a Khatami presidency, in the face of a conservative-dominated Parliament and powerful conservative clerics. It was, if true, a brilliant move on the Supreme Leader's part to get rid of Khatami, but then again everyone, it seems, seriously misjudged Mir Hossein Mousavi.

"Don't worry, Hooman," said a friend, and former senior member of the leadership, to me one late night in his Tehran home. "If Ahmadinejad wins, he'll be impeached within eighteen months." Reformists and conservative opponents of Mahmoud Ahmadinejad were already sharpening the knives weeks before the election, expecting that the incumbent president stood a good chance of winning. Of course, Ali Larijani, the speaker of Parliament, would have to be on board for impeachment, for the impeachment of a president rests solely with the Majles. He was known to despise Ahmadinejad personally; it was Ahmadinejad who had had him removed as secretary of the Supreme National Security Council and as chief nuclear negotiator, but Larijani would also have to convince his mentor, Ayatollah Khamenei, that impeachment was the best course of action. Presumably Larijani, who had presidential ambitions himself, would have a vested interest in seeing his nemesis disappear from the political scene. He had run for Parliament from Qom (not where he's from), after all, with the full backing of the clerical elite, positioning himself to make a bid for the presidency once Ahmadinejad was out of the way. If Ahmadinejad could be impeached, Larijani would be in the best position to win the snap election that would have to be called under the constitution. But, nemeesheh, I thought. Impeachment had never happened, and even if there were those who wanted to rid Iran of Ahmadinejad and his clique, there was no guarantee that he would go quietly, or that he wouldn't take down a good number of the elite with him by exposing the many files he kept on various members of the Iranian leadership. Nemeesheh.

Except a few months later, after the disputed election and during one demonstration against the Ahmadinejad government (at Friday prayers presided over by Ayatollah Rafsanjani), both of Larijani's sons were arrested and taken to Kahrizak, the infamous detention facility that Ayatollah Khamenei subsequently closed because of abuses, including the torture of prisoners and the rape of detainees of both sexes, that had taken place there. Larijani's sons were held for a little over twenty-four hours, and as such were among the luckier prisoners, but a friend who saw them on their release said to me that they did not look the same as when they stood outside Tehran University listening to Ayatollah Rafsanjani over loudspeakers. They had been standing outside the grounds because they couldn't get into the venue, and were rounded up along with dozens of other men and women and carted off to prison. (One of those taken was Mohsen Ruholamini, son of former Revolutionary Guardsman Abdol-Hossein Ruholamini, a senior advisor to conservative candidate Mohsen Rezai. Mohsen Ruholamini was tortured to death at the facility, leading to shock and disgust in conservative quarters.) I wasn't sure what to make of the story, even though I trusted my friend implicitly. Then, a few weeks later, an Iranian diplomat who was trying to convince me that the mass arrests in Iran were part of the democratic process, and indeed showed that Iran was a true democracy because it applied the law equally, said to me in frustration, "Did you know that *even* Larijani's sons were arrested?" Indeed, I replied, I *had* heard, and thank you for confirming it on behalf of the government.

Larijani himself, perhaps, unlike the diplomat, a believer in the kind of democracy that can distinguish between sons of the revolution and regime-change agitators, told the same friend who had informed me of the arrests that he would take care of Ahmadinejad in his own good time. *"Khar-o-madar'esh ro yekee meekonam"* were apparently the words he used—"I will fuck his mother and his sister." Nemeesheh? We'll see. But before the election, or at least before it became apparent that Ahmadinejad was vulnerable, reformist foes of Ahmadinejad were less than optimistic about their chances of unseating him, and strategies for dealing with a *post*-Ahmadinejad win were already being discussed.

I WAS SITTING with former president Khatami in his office one day, before the official four-week campaign began, trying to understand how the reformists were going to mount a serious challenge with Mousavi as their standard-bearer.

"He doesn't have much charisma," I commented, "and we know Ahmadinejad does."

"Mir Hossein Mousavi will have to win this *himself*," said Khatami, in a sort of acknowledgement of Mousavi's weakness. "I can only help so much, but he'll have to be the one to convince voters. I will do everything I can, of course."

"Well, he better get going," I said, "because from everything I've seen around the country, there's a lot of apathy about him and even the whole election process."

"If a *mowj* [wave] of support doesn't materialize, or if we can't create that wave, then we're in trouble, but we'll see in the next few weeks," said Khatami, not quite optimistic but still not completely dejected. (It was the first time I heard the word "mowj" in reference to the opposition's strategy, a word that later morphed into "Green Wave" and then finally into "Green Movement.") I wondered if Khatami was a little resentful that Mousavi, clearly the less popular and less charismatic politician, had deprived him of the chance of another presidency, but he assured me that he was happier not running, and I believed him.

"Isn't Karroubi [Mehdi Karroubi, the liberal cleric who ran in the 2005 race as well] acting a little like a spoiler?" I wondered out loud. I knew that Khatami had good relations with Karroubi, and I had assumed he had tried to persuade him to throw his support behind Mousavi so that the reformists could present a unified challenge to Ahmadinejad. In Iranian elections, if no one candidate receives more than 50 percent of the vote, then a run-off is scheduled between the top-two candidates, and Karroubi, who had drawn more than five million votes in the last election and who had many liberal and young supporters, could very well prevent Mousavi from achieving a plurality, assuming the mowj even occurred. "Aren't you going to convince him to drop out?"

"He's a *Lor*," said Khatami, laughing. "He does what he likes, and he genuinely thinks he can win. We just have to concentrate on our campaign." Karroubi is indeed a Lor, from Lorestan province, and the Lor characteristics that are famous throughout Iran are sheer stubbornness and fearlessness. As confirmation of that, after the election,

I heard that a Lor was arrested outside the British Embassy in Tehran; he had traveled there from Khorramabad, the big city in Lorestan, and was asking if the embassy was where he could request asylum. "Come with us and *we'll* show you where you can request asylum," said a group of security officials, who promptly removed him to Evin prison. A few days later, when he was finally allowed to make a phone call, he called his brother in Khorramabad. "Are you already calling from *London*?" asked the brother, oblivious to the improbability of what his brother had set out to do, particularly under the tense post-election atmosphere. Nemeesheh? Maybe not in this case, but the Lor didn't believe it, and Karroubi, it seems, has never believed in nemeesheh either. But more about him later.

ANOTHER FEW WEEKS in Tehran, another afternoon tea with Khatami. At his offices in Jamaran this time, in the ersatz Greco-Roman villa once owned by Houshang Ansari, one of the wealthiest ministers in the Shah's entourage (who also made the Forbes list in exile). The Islamic government had confiscated the villa after the revolution as part of a program to retrieve assets believed to have been obtained illicitly, through corruption, bribes, or "exploitation" of the people. (Part of a series of villas that make up the Khomeini compound, this villa was given to Khatami after his presidency to use as offices for his Dialogue among Civilisations organization.) Astonishingly vulgar architecturally, it serves as a reminder of the excesses of the *nouveau riche* in pre-revolutionary days (excesses that Beverly Hills residents have, to their dismay, now had firsthand experience with), but the visible decay also serves to illustrate the Islamic regime's disdain for such displays of wealth and decadence. The furniture, left over from the Shah's days, is still Louis Quinze reproduction, a favorite then among the upper class and seemingly still in vogue in government offices and private homes throughout Iran. The overall effect of entering the compound, though, walking over cracked concrete pathways, past a long-empty and paint-deprived swimming pool, and up to the peeling stucco by the massive front doors, is not quite the same as entering Grey Gardens, the famously decrepit mansion of New York socialites Edith Beale and her daughter, but sometimes I think it's getting close.

It was a few days before the big kick-off event of the Mousavi campaign, and already campaign posters were appearing on the streets of Tehran, posters of Mousavi *with* Khatami, both in profile. Taking no chances with the charisma factor, the Mousavi campaign was using Khatami's familiar face to ensure that everyone knew a vote for Mousavi was a vote for Khatami. In hindsight this was a risky tactic given that the one person the hard-liners despised more than anyone else in the hierarchy of revolutionaries was Khatami. Khatami was a little more optimistic at this tea, though, and felt that the mowj he had described to me might even take form at the event he was due to attend in a few days—a big rally at Azadi arena, with the main attractions being him and Zahra Rahnavard, Mousavi's wife, who had taken the unprecedented step of joining her husband on the campaign trail. I promised that I would not only attend but also bring Ann Curry and an NBC news crew, who were in Tehran at the time filming a *Dateline* special on an Iran most Westerners knew little about. The Azadi sporting complex, on the outskirts of the huge metropolis, comprises a soccer stadium with a basketball or sports arena adjacent to it; the campaign had been denied permission for a rally in the stadium, comparable to NFL or European soccer stadiums in capacity, so it had settled for the arena, comparable to Madison Square Garden. No one knew how many people would attend, and advance publicity was minimal, given that state-controlled television and radio rarely gave the opposition airtime.

On the afternoon of the rally, I made my way to the arena, in one of two minibuses (to accommodate the NBC crew and their equipment) and with VIP parking passes in hand (courtesy of Khatami's office). A long line of cars was gathered at the gate, waiting to be let into the parking lots.

"It's full," said a policeman standing guard, as we snaked our way forward. I jumped out to show our passes. "It's full, you can't go in." Cars behind us started to honk, and frustrated drivers piled out of their cars.

"We have passes," I insisted, "and we're here with a news crew." Ali Arouzi, the Tehran bureau chief for NBC News showed another policeman his permission slip from the Ministry of Culture and Islamic Guidance to film at the rally. The officer gave it a perfunctory glance and shrugged.

"You'll have to wait," said yet another policeman. I called the cell phone number of one of the Mousavi campaign managers and told him we were stuck outside, and he promised he would send someone to rescue us. Twenty minutes later, we were in, and the outdoor parking lot, a good walk from the arena was, not surprisingly, virtually empty. Iranian bureaucracy, I thought, never fails to impress (or disappoint). At the time I didn't think the cops were being difficult because they had orders to be that way, in the hope of limiting the audience size; I thought they were being difficult just for the sake of being difficult, as cops throughout the world can be on occasion.

Streams of pedestrians were walking along the path to the stadium, however, which was predictable given that Iranians are naturally undeterred by rules and regulations, and I wondered where they had parked. Probably by the side of the highway, I thought, parked and double-parked, if past rallies and gatherings of any sort were any indication.

During the long drive to the arena, I had questioned the driver of my minibus as to his political preferences, and specifically if he intended to vote.

"*Na, baba!*" he had said to me with a grunt. "Why should I? It doesn't make any difference anyway: *they* decide for us, and *they* run the country anyway." He was in his fifties, I guessed, and I asked if he had any children who thought otherwise. "You know kids—of course they want me to vote, but it won't make a difference."

"Are you satisfied with Ahmadinejad, then?" I asked. He grunted again, and looked at me.

"It's not a question of being satisfied with *him*," he said. He smiled and then said, "*Shomaha deletoon khosheh!*"—"You people are wishful thinkers!" I left him standing outside the vehicle after we had parked, unloaded the equipment, and began our walk to the arena, and I wondered if a mowj might change his mind somehow. He didn't want to join us at the rally, but if the mowj appeared, he would hear its roar, even in the parking area a good distance away.

When we arrived at the arena, I was surprised to find it completely full, with many people lingering outside, in the hallways, and by the doors. Khatami and Rahnavard hadn't arrived yet, and Mousavi himself wasn't scheduled to show; he had flown to Esfahan to participate in a rally there, a city that was going to be hard to break away from Ahmadinejad's grip. The two NBC camera crews set off separately, wandering into the crowd in the arena and ignoring the media center set up in the middle of the floor, while I tried to make my way to the VIP enclosure where I would be able to see Khatami and his aides. I never made it. It was far too crowded to even get close to the doors, and cell phones were useless, as the deafening noise of the boisterous crowd drowned out everyone's ringtone. I ended up wandering too, walking outside occasionally to get some fresh air and to talk to people who had come to show their support for the main challenger to President Ahmadinejad, almost all of them wearing some green, the color of the Mousavi campaign. I was more curious about the older folk who had made the trek to Azadi, as it was assumed that, like the Obama campaign in the United States, younger voters would be most enthusiastic for change, particularly change that in Iran's case involved reform and a more liberal government and society. One older white-haired man standing outside by the main entrance had a green scarf wrapped around his neck, despite the ninety-degree weather. "You're for Mousavi?" I asked, "or would you prefer Khatami?" Khatami had entered the arena a few minutes earlier to a rousing reception and loud chants of *"Khatami! Khatami!"* that could be clearly heard outdoors.

"Let me tell you who and what I'm going to vote *against*," he replied. "I'm voting against Hezbollah and Hamas, and the Palestinians." He was one of those Iranians, evident from a toothless grin framed by an unshaven chin, shabby clothes, and scuffed and well-worn shoes, who was unhappy with the emphasis the government had put in the last four years on bringing Iran's oil revenues not to the common man's dinner table, as Ahmadinejad had promised in his 2005 campaign, but to causes beyond its borders. It was a curious moment, I thought, and I scribbled his words in my notebook. The working class was suffering under a groaning economy, but few, at least among the poor, expressed dissatisfaction with the economy in these terms. The old man's words didn't, however, really resonate for me until much later, during the summer protests against election fraud, when other Iranians, in the thousands, virtually repeated the words "No to Palestine and Lebanon" as a new slogan. I wondered if he was among them, and if he was, if he ended up in prison like many other nameless Iranians. I recognized, however, that it would be a mistake, as some Western observers did during the post-election demonstrations, to equate the old man's expression of frustration with his government's fiscal priorities with a general lack of Iranian sympathy for the Palestinian cause, to believe that the government was philosophically out of step with its people on the issues of Palestine and Hezbollah. Iranians by and large still morally supported the underdogs in their battles and disputes with the Israelis, even liberal and young Iranians I spoke to who couldn't abide the regime in almost any other way.

After the rally ended, a large crowd mingled outside, reluctant to call it a day. A sea of green, many were carrying posters and flyers, and trucks were handing out free bottles of water. Was this the mowj, the wave? It certainly appeared to be, or at least the beginnings of a wave. The arena had been filled, no, *over*filled, beyond capacity, there was excitement in the air, and the youth, who make up the majority of Iran's population, were energized, passionate, and involved. Iranian or Islamic democracy is visibly different from American democracy, but Khatami and Rahnavard were treated like rock stars that afternoon, and I couldn't help but think of the similarities between this Mousavi rally and the Obama rallies in the United States a year before, something even the American news crew admitted had surprised them. Ahmadinejad bore more similarities to George Bush than either would admit, and his popularity at the end of four years was probably where Bush's was at the end of his first term, but for the first time in months, it seemed the Iranian opposition might have, for reasons not yet clear even to themselves, a campaign strategy that mirrored Obama's in 2008 more than John Kerry's in 2004.

The independent Iranian press, already enthused (and even surprised) by the inclusion of a female in the campaign, heretofore unheard of in the strictly Islamic state, had begun to compare Zahra Rahnavard to Michelle Obama (something the Western media quickly picked up). When I saw her in her office a few days later, in response to being asked what she thought of sometimes being referred to as the Michelle Obama of Iran, she replied, "No, *Michelle* is the Zahra Rahnavard of America." Persian pride, oghdeh (complexes), and *gholov* (exaggeration) all rolled into one sentence. Nemeesheh. It isn't possible. Not just Rahnavard's elevation of her importance on the world stage, but also the kind of wholesale attitudinal change in Iran that Obama's election had brought to the United States—it isn't possible, is it? The twenty-two thousand who had poured into Azadi on May 25 thought it was. And the tens of thousands who showed up in Esfahan that same day to hear Zahra's husband speak thought it was. When I spoke on the phone later that night to a senior official close to Mousavi, his words were, *"Emrooz yakh'e Esfahan'o sheekoondeem"*—"Today, we broke the ice in Esfahan." *Nemeesheh? Kardeem va shod.* We did it, and it was possible. The Green Wave had taken shape, and the nemeeshehs were falling, one by one.

On the drive back from Azadi after the rally, I asked my skeptical driver what he thought of the crowds, which he had seen leave the arena, and if he had heard their cheers and shouts earlier.

"I didn't think there would be this many people," he said.

"And what do you think, do you think you might be persuaded to vote?" I asked him.

"Perhaps," he said, after a long pause. "I'm still not convinced it will make any difference, but perhaps. We'll see."

We passed a giant poster of Ayatollah Rafsanjani, one of many sprouting up all over town. Next to his image were the words "If the majority don't vote, the minority will rule." Nemeesheh? My driver paid no attention, but the turnout for the election was an astonishing 85 percent. Kardeem va shod.

AYATOLLAH Ali Akbar Hashemi Rafsanjani, widely recognized as the second most powerful man in Iran, had presided, only a few days before, over Friday prayers at Tehran University, the venue for the capital's weekly Sabbath ceremonies (which needn't be held in an actual mosque, for anywhere a sermon is delivered and communal prayers are said is by definition a mosque). I had been present, in the press box only a few feet away from his stage, and had watched him repeat the mantra on his posters, tightly holding on to his Kalashnikov rifle. He and Ali Larijani, who, unarmed, had delivered a speech before Rafsanjani's sermon, encouraged the crowd and the millions listening on radio or watching on television to participate in the election, both of them Ahmadinejad antagonists who knew the larger the turnout, the more likely the president's defeat. But Rafsanjani and Larijani also recognized that democracy, even as narrowly defined as in conservative circles, required the people to believe that their vote meant something. Conservatives, who dominate the Friday crowds, and listeners elsewhere needed no persuasion; they are far less skeptical of the democratic process as defined in the Islamic Republic. But a large population of young, and apathetic citizens most certainly did. For many of them this is because the Guardian Council, *Shora-ye Negahban'e Ghanoon'e Assasi*, the governmental body made up of six clerics appointed by the Supreme Leader and six jurists appointed by Parliament from a list approved by the head of the judiciary (another Supreme Leader appointee), approves candidates running for high office, thereby eliminating any possibility of someone radically different or less than strictly Islamic, or *Islamist*, from ever assuming office, a fact that every opponent of the Islamic system raises when it comes to discussion of Islamic democracy. It is also the unsaid part of the equation when someone, like my apathetic minibus driver, declares that voting is irrelevant and that it makes no difference who the candidates are. But there were still, in 2009, millions of Iranians who came to believe that despite the Guardian Council's reluctance to countenance divergent political views, certain candidates within the system *could* overcome the obstacle and, if not present radical change, present enough of a change to alter their lives and the future of the country.

Just like in America, where most candidates for political office, despite their personal views, must present themselves as mainstream to survive the nominating process, so it is in Iran. Although there is no prohibition on radicalism in American politics, reality trumps theory, and no American candidate for high office could, for example, run as an atheist or a communist, let alone socialist or a Muslim—that is, not if he or she wanted to be taken seriously by the mainstream media, which, as Dennis Kucinich and Ralph Nader effectively complain every four years, is the genteel and subtler American version of Iran's Guardian Council. Sure, Iranians may have been disappointed by Khatami's failure to deliver a far more democratic society in his eight years as president, or by the conservatives' blocking of much of his agenda, but in May 2009 many Iranians were convinced that the differences between a Khatami-like presidency, which both Mousavi and Karroubi were promising, and even to some extent the conservative Rezai, and an Ahmadinejad presidency, which they had experienced for four years, were real and significant.

As ELECTION DAY approached, excitement continued to build. The previous presidential election, in 2005, had a turnout of approximately 60 percent, which was low by Iran's standards (and high by American) and was considered a contributing cause to Rafsanjani's defeat against the relatively unknown Ahmadinejad. Perhaps the low turnout was also a reason why Rafsanjani felt compelled not to openly endorse a candidate in the 2009 race, but to spend his energies and money to encourage greater voter participation. In 2005 Rafsanjani had failed to energize the youth and the liberals who should have been turned off by Ahmadinejad's conservative values and tired revolutionary rhetoric, but this time it seemed different. For many Iranians, less was at stake in the last election, with the relatively prosperous, peaceful, and stable Khatami years just ending—socially liberal years marked by increased cooperation and trade with the West. In 2005 many voters deemed it unlikely that what seemed to be the beginnings of a post-revolutionary era would be affected too much by a change in administration, even with a conservative candidate promising to bring back the revolution of 1979. Street parties, which appeared forced back then (pretty young girls on roller blades, holding up posters of the septuagenarian Rafsanjani), this time, four years later, erupted spontaneously every night, especially in the northern and wealthier parts of Tehran, and a tailgate atmosphere, minus the drunkenness, invaded major intersections and some of the boulevards, not just of Tehran, but even in more conservative cities like Esfahan and Yazd. Mousavi was also nearing seventy, but he looked younger, his image in silhouette on campaign posters even stronger (and evocative of the iconic Obama poster), and of course there was his wife, Zahra, who many young women could readily identify with. But even Ahmadinejad supporters, or those paid to adorn their cars with Ahmadinejad posters, joined in the carnival atmosphere; heavily outnumbered, they nonetheless smiled and waved—their gelled hair, pushed-back scarves, and hip clothes incongruously clashing with the photos of their candidate—as they drove slowly past a sea of green, at least on the occasions I was caught in street-party traffic jams.

On one hot evening, the driver of my car shook his head as we passed a particularly noisy party. "This is bad," he said, looking out the open window at boys and girls, adorned in green and dancing, a few on the hoods of their double-parked cars.

"Why?" I asked, wondering what could be bad about a vibrant civil society being excited about the prospects for effecting democratic change.

"*They're* not going to like this," he said.

Masoud again, I thought to myself; Iranian paranoia of a security apparatus that watches everything, and everyone. Yes, the government was aware of the raucous atmosphere on the streets of Tehran and other major cities, but government agents couldn't be watching and listening like the SAVAK of the old days, ready to pounce when they felt they might lose control. Iranians didn't even have the vote back in the Shah's days, or at least not any kind of vote that really mattered. A whole generation had grown up with the vote in the Islamic Republic, and electioneering had never been an issue in the past, so what could be "bad" about this campaign? And who were "they"? Ahmadinejad could be voted out, so it couldn't be *his* campaign that mattered. The security services, or the Revolutionary Guards? They had not interfered in past elections, at least not on a scale that would make a huge difference, although, yes, they had tried—dirty tactics, even some ballot tampering. But Khatami had won, twice, against the Supreme Leader's favorite candidate, and everyone had accepted the outcomes. The Supreme Leader himself had been, back then, if not completely gracious in accepting Khatami's wins, then not quite churlish either. What were "they" going to do? Were they photographing the kids partying? Were they going to arrest some of them, now or maybe later? Of course not, I thought. Nemeesheh. My driver was paranoid, I concluded, one of those older Iranians who could never accept things as they were and had to ascribe a hidden hand to every political situation. It wasn't just the Twelfth Imam of Shia Islam who was hidden from the faithful for centuries since his occultation; it was also always some powerful force, the British, the Americans, or members of their own leadership, which prevented Iranians from controlling their own destiny. "They." And nothing could be done about it: nemeesheh.

A HIDDEN HAND. *Posht-e-pardeh*, or behind the curtain. Iranians for at least two centuries had very little faith in their ability to decide anything for themselves, a notion that grew out of inordinate foreign influence in Persia when it was at its weakest, and subsequent dictatorial governments that countenanced no political debate whatsoever. There are Iranians, supporters of or sympathizers with the Pahlavi monarchy, who believe that it was President Jimmy Carter's decisions first to insist that the Shah pay more attention to human rights and second to abandon the Shah in the face of a people's revolt that led to the revolution and all the woes of life under a theocracy. And then there are Iranians, onetime revolutionaries and supporters of the Islamic regime, who insist that it was Jimmy Carter who tried his utmost to save the Shah and, once the revolution succeeded, to restore him or his dynasty to the throne. Others will say it was the British, the British who at one time held great sway over Persia but who had lost influence in the wake of American ascendancy after World War II, who engineered the fall of the Shah, the U.S. Embassy takeover, and the subsequent breaking of relations between the United States and Iran, all so that they could once again be *the* influential and dominant power in Persia (they never could quite bring themselves to call it "Iran").

Otherwise sophisticated, well-traveled, and highly educated Iranians will repeat these theories over tea, at dinner parties, over a *vafour*, or opium pipe, and whenever the favorite topic of conversation for most Iranians, politics, comes up. The revolution of 1979 was supposed to put an end to foreign or hidden hands; it was supposed to create a system, a third and uniquely Iranian, Shia system to counter the communism of the East and the liberal democracy of the West. Many Iranians believe that the revolution was successful—not only the many die-hard supporters of the velayat-e-faqih, those who enthusiastically shout "Death to America!" on command, but also those who believe, like Khatami, Mousavi, and Karroubi, that the experiment isn't over, that Islamic democracy hasn't matured quite yet, and that reform is needed in order to reach the utopia of a new political order in the Islamic world.

Nemeesheh? There have been lots of nemeeshehs in Iranian history, as many since the revolution of 1979 as before. An *Islamic* revolution? Nemeesheh. Storm the U.S. Embassy and take American diplomats hostage, against every international convention? Nemeesheh! "America cannot do a damn thing," Khomeini said, once he endorsed hostage taking as statecraft. Nemeesheh! Uneducated and unsophisticated mullahs eliminate their technocrat, intellectual leftist allies in a struggle for power? Nemeesheh. Fight a war against an invading Saddam Hussein, armed and financed by all the Arabs and by the West, at Iran's weakest moment, and force him to sue for peace? Nemeesheh! Elect a president, Khatami, against the wishes of the Supreme Leader? Nemeesheh. Not even Khatami thought that was possible, not until it actually happened. Elect a president, the unknown Ahmadinejad, running against Rafsanjani, the second most powerful man in Iran? Nemeesheh! A long-forgotten sixty-seven-year-old politician successfully challenge the incumbent Ahmadinejad for the presidency four years later? Nemeesheh! Prevent that politician from winning, at all costs? Nemeesheh! Oh yeah? Kardeem va shod.

THAT IS A friend's favored expression when it comes to anything to do with Iran, an expression that I can't help but think of almost daily when I'm in Iran. Someone educated in the West but who has lived in Iran for most of the post-revolutionary years, my friend has seen everything that there is to be seen (and much of what is not). He has witnessed countless instances of nemeesheh but, more important, countless instances of kardeem va shod. Explaining Iran's post-revolutionary zeitgeist, he once said to me, "*Meegan madar-zan'o nemeesheh kard. Ma kardeem va shod*"—"They say you can't screw your mother-in-law. Oh yeah? I *did*, and it was possible."

WHERE I SAT IN BABYLON

*We're prepared to give our precious lives for four reasons: God,
our nation, family, and our friends.*

> —Iranian rapper Hichkas, in his song
> "Bunch of Soldiers"

During the Arab League summit in early 2008, when Libyan
President Muammar Qaddafi's turn came at the lectern, he
launched into a fiery criticism—a rant, really—of his fellow Arabs,
specifically on the issue of Palestine and Israel. "Whatever happened
to the [Palestinian] cause we had before 1967?" he asked. "Were we
lying to ourselves or to the world?" he continued. "How can you say
that Israel must return to the pre-1967 borders? Does Palestine consist
only of the West Bank and Gaza? If so," he said with an air of disgust,
"it means that the Israelis did not occupy it in 1948. They left it to
you for twenty years, so why didn't you establish a Palestinian state?
Wasn't Gaza part of Egypt, and the West Bank part of Jordan?" Qaddafi
seemed particularly angry at Arab acquiescence to a two-state solution to the long-running Middle East crisis, a solution that would give
Palestinians a state, yes, but the exact one, he pointed out, they could
have easily had all the way back in 1967 if only the Arabs had given
them the land they then controlled. The heads of state and sheikhs

in the room all smiled, or in some cases laughed, uncomfortably. All except Manouchehr Mottaki, the foreign minister of Iran, whose country had been invited—very unusually—that year as an observer, and who remained stone-faced while he listened through headphones (for very few Iranians speak or understand Arabic). The smiles of the Arab leaders for the cameras betrayed their view of Qaddafi, known as well in the Arab world as in the West (at least among the ruling elites) for a certain, shall we say, wackiness, as well as their discomfort with the truth of what their wacky, often clownish cousin was saying, words that were being broadcast to millions of their citizens. Citizens who, according to polls in 2006 and 2007, were far more enamored of the leaders Sheikh Hassan Nasrallah of Hezbollah and Mahmoud Ahmadinejad of Iran, perversely both Shias, than of their own smiling, Sunni, pro-Western, and well-fed, if not corpulent, leaders.

As in years past, the Arab League summit was convened partly to address the single most important issue facing the Arab (and Muslim) world over the past sixty years, namely, what was once the *Arab*-Israeli and is now the Palestinian-Israeli conflict. The two nations Qaddafi mentioned by name as having held Palestinian territory, Jordan and Egypt, are also the two Arab countries that have made peace with Israel and have diplomatic relations with the Jewish state, a point not lost on the television audience. Jordan, for one, having a large Palestinian population, is particularly wary of that audience—and is at best ambivalent about Arab overtures to Israel—so much so that Israelis driving into Jordan by car are given Jordanian license plates by Jordanian officials right at the border to affix over their Israeli ones— you know, just in case.

In 2008, though, the country most vehemently supporting the Palestinian cause and the only nation still vociferously denouncing Israel, *Persian* but not Arab Iran, had pointedly been invited to the summit, and Al Jazeera television cameras often slyly panned upward to Mottaki's face in the gallery—serious, frowning, head cocked at times, his expression one of intent listening. Iran was present not because the Arab states both fear her and revile her, which they do, but because there is a recognition that today, unlike any time in the past, there will never be peace between the Arabs and the Israelis without the Persians, and that Persia, or Iran, once an empire that ruled over every inch of territory that each head of state represented, was, alarmingly to most, a resurgent and potentially dangerous power.

Qaddafi's point that the Arabs have essentially abandoned the greater Palestinian cause (even Syria, who most recognize would be willing to make a deal with Israel as long as it would guarantee a return of the Golan Heights to its sovereignty) was both an approving nod to Iran and a seamless introduction to the next topic in his fractured harangue of a speech: Iran itself. Qaddafi quickly warmed to the subject, both in recognition of the country's uncommon presence at an Arab meeting and as a warning to his fellow Arabs of the futility and dangers in confronting it. "By no means," he admonished the audience, "is it in our interest to turn Iran against us." He continued on the subject, moving on to address the issue of the Persian Gulf and disputes between Iran and the United Arab Emirates over two strategic islands. "Eighty percent of the people of the Gulf are *Iranians*," he said, painting a broader stroke than necessary, but to the undoubted delight of the stern Mottaki, who, however, continued to show no emotion. "The ruling families are Arab, but the rest are Iranian. The entire people are Iranian," he said, an exaggeration to be sure, but a point not lost on the Iranians and some of the Arab audience back home. The sheikhs no longer smiled, but looked away glumly. "Iran cannot be avoided," Qaddafi carried on unambiguously, perhaps even shockingly taking Iran's side against his fellow Arabs. "Iran is a Muslim neighbor and it is not in our interest to become enemies." Reminiscent of a speech a year earlier, when he stated bizarrely that "we are all Shias," in his first major tilt toward Iran, it was also almost an admission of defeat by an Arab nationalist leader not known for his meekness, and the men in the room knew it. Qaddafi's speech, as easy as it may be to dismiss as the ranting of a now older revolutionary, highlighted what many in the Muslim Middle East feel and already recognize: the Persians are ascendant as the region's predominant power and the Arab leaders no longer represent pan-Muslim or even pan-Arab interests. In early May 2008, Iranian-backed Hezbollah of Lebanon stunned America, Saudi Arabia, and the beleaguered and hapless U.S.-supported government of Lebanon by taking over Beirut in a matter of hours. It was a counter-coup that caused the Saudi ambassador to flee Lebanon, a flight Tehran publicly mocked, and the Iranian daily *Kayhan* (the mouthpiece for Iran's Supreme Leader) trumpeted: "In the power struggle in the Middle East, there are only two sides: Iran and the United States." Indeed.

It's NOT a very well-known fact that Lebanese Hezbollah leader Nasrallah holds the official title "Representative of the Supreme Leader of the Islamic Revolution in Lebanon," that Leader being none other than Iran's Ayatollah Ali Khamenei. (Despite the Iranian penchant for mangling English translations of Iranian words and expressions, it was not an error of omission that the name of the country was left off both the Supreme Leader's title and the name of the country's elite military force, the Revolutionary Guards. The Supreme Leader is the Leader *of the Islamic Revolution*, and the ideological military force is the *Corps of the Guardians of the Islamic Revolution*, not "Republic," known and sometimes feared in the West simply as the "Revolutionary Guards." The Islamic Revolution, started, controlled, and maintained by Iranians, knows no national boundaries, as the late Ayatollah Khomeini once said.)

While Arab nations struggle over how to come to terms with Israel, and how to solve the Palestinian problem without offending the United States, the "other side," as *Kayhan* put it, Iran, views the issue in simple terms: support a people their fellow Arabs have abandoned in their tilt to the West, and the masses will once again view a resurgent Persian empire as the supreme (and even benevolent) power in the region, whether peace comes between Israel and the Palestinians or not.

But more ominously, at least for many Westerners and certainly the Arabs, Iran's ambitions do not stop in the Middle East. Iran believes, and many of its top officials, both conservative and in the opposition, have told me this, that it can become the real bulwark against what it sees as U.S. hegemony across the globe, by appealing not only to friendly governments but also to the masses of people in the Third World—and not just the Muslim Third World. Arab Muslims may share their distrust of the United States and the West and praise Iran for its stand against Israel, but Iranian leaders recognize that in the long term the Shia-Sunni split will be difficult to completely overcome in Arab countries. However, the leaders think Iran's anti-imperialist message will be easier to sell in non-Arab Muslim lands, and certainly in non-Muslim but still revolutionary lands. Iran also believes that the key to the longevity of the Islamic regime is its ability to win friends and influence people, while at the same time dominate and instill a certain amount of fear where necessary, just as the ancient kings of Persia—Cyrus, Darius, and Xerxes, whose name alone inspired dread—once did to great effect.

IN SEPTEMBER 2008, during his trip to New York to attend the opening of the UN General Assembly, President Ahmadinejad had his usual meetings with American think-tank scholars and peace activists and interviews with the U.S. media, and he again also held a lavish dinner, this time for nearly a thousand Iranian-Americans (who are by and large opposed to his policies and philosophies). A gift bag, brought from Tehran on his jet, was distributed to his guests as they departed the Hyatt hotel ballroom in midtown Manhattan. On the bag, in large, fanciful lettering, was the word "Persia," as part of an Iranian tourist board promotion, but perhaps the first use of the word by Iranian officialdom since the Islamic Revolution of 1979. Persia, apart from being a Western word that the late Shah's father banished from use, conjures up images of a kingdom ruled by lay monarchs without regard for the primacy of Islam, images that have been anathema to the Islamic regime for a long time. In the immediate aftermath of the Islamic Revolution, authorities went to great lengths to scrub Iran of its pre-Islamic history, in actions ranging from the deletion of that history from school textbooks to the government neglect of historic sites, and in some ways rewrote history to reflect their view that Iran's glory came only during its Islamic phase.

The Iranian government today, however, has finally decided that the ancient empire of kings, non-Islamic ones at that, is a fitting image for Iran's new role in the world. Projected on one wall during that dinner with Ahmadinejad in 2008 was a huge map of the Persian Gulf with the words "Persian Gulf Forever!" printed on it (a reference to the allergic reactions, across the Iranian political spectrum and among all expatriates, to the idea of renaming it the "Arabian Gulf" or just "The Gulf," as the BBC is wont to do). But more interestingly, the flag of Iran was superimposed not only on the country itself, whose borders any Iranian would instantly recognize, but on the entire Arabian Peninsula to the south, a not-so-subtle indication of what Iran views as its dominion. *Persia* and the *Persian* Gulf.

WHERE HAS THIS renewed desire for influence and power come from? In a post-Soviet and unipolar world—that is, a world without

competing political ideologies—most developing countries are generally satisfied to be given a leg up by the West. They are satisfied with
the quid pro quo of the alliance in which they reap the benefits, most
often economic, in return for their allegiance (or as some would argue,
subservience). The handful of countries that have resisted Western
domination—Cuba, for example—have done so out of revolutionary
political commitments, but no non-superpower country has set out an
agenda that so clearly challenges American supremacy as has Iran,
which is intent on becoming a superpower in its own right within
a generation. And Iran has the audacity to view itself as a potential
superpower very simply because Iranians have always felt it is their
natural place in the world. They were an empire that controlled half
the world's known geography, and their Islamic view holds that Iranian
Shias are the natural and true defenders of the faith.

While it may seem counterintuitive that Iran, a still relatively weak
country militarily and even economically despite its massive oil and
gas reserves, could imagine itself as an empire to rival the great powers, Iranians, especially the ambitious post-revolutionary generation,
don't think so. "A billion and a half Muslims have woken up," a deputy
foreign minister in Ahmadinejad's first administration said to me. And
Iran sees itself as the hope for Muslims and non-Muslim people everywhere who imagine themselves, or in fact are, the oppressed majority,
but it also sees itself as their leader, much in the way that Iran's ancient
kings saw themselves as the rightful supreme leaders of and guides to
various tribes and smaller kingdoms across the globe. "All the kings
who sit upon thrones throughout the world, from the Upper Sea to the
Lower Sea, who live in the districts far-off, the kings of the West, who
dwell in tents, all of them, brought their weighty tribute before me,"
reads an inscription on the Cyrus Cylinder in the British Museum,
"and kissed my feet where I sat in Babylon." In the biblical book of
Isaiah, the coming of Cyrus is predicted, confirming for Persians of

the time and Iranians today that Yahweh (God) chose the Persian king to liberate Babylon. You can't get any more "supreme" than that. The Iranian leadership also sees itself as analogous to the early Soviets, who viewed themselves as the hope for socialists and communists, as well as the working class, everywhere. Iranian leaders will unapologetically claim that within another generation they will have extended Iranian influence, and even Iranian leadership on vital world matters, to all corners of the globe.

Go ahead, laugh. I do too, along with some other Iranians who are used to the gholov, the grandiose hyperbole common to Iranian discourse. I laughed at a joke making the rounds of Tehran in 2009, after yet another military parade and another exaggerated technological accomplishment by its navy, which along with the Revolutionary Guard naval division, is charged with protecting the *Persian* Gulf from Arabs and Westerners alike. Ali and Asghar, the joke went, are two unemployed youths (like many of their contemporaries) in Tehran, and while looking for work one day they stumble on an ad for the Iranian navy in the back of a newspaper. "Let's go join!" says Ali. "We have a *navy*?" asks Asghar. "With *ships*?" "Come on, let's go and sign up," says Ali, "of *course* we have a navy." The two boys show up at the recruitment office and are called in for their preliminary interview. "So," says the officer, looking at their birth certificates and taking a pencil to paper, "can you swim?" "See!" whispers Asghar to Ali, "I told you these motherfuckers don't have any *ships*."

Yes, it's true that the Iranian navy is hardly prepared to rule the waves (although it does have ships, and even domestically produced submarines, which I, for one, would be hesitant to board), but to dismiss Iranian ambitions, and the Iranian leadership's determination to achieve its goals, would be a mistake. Underestimating Iran and Iranians has been the one constant factor in Western opinion for the last thirty years, and in recent years, *inflating* the danger of Iran has become fashionable in some quarters. The Supreme Leaders of Iran, past, present, and future, may not measure up to Cyrus and the "tribute" he commanded, their armies will never be on par with those of the kings of ancient Persia, but nor will Iran be the meek and toothless nation of its more recent past. The truth of Iran's ambitions and its potential lies, as it always does, somewhere in the middle.

As A YOUNG CHILD I would sometimes see my father, when he was a diplomat under the last Shah, come home angry and frustrated. Often, I would glean from conversations I overheard that it was because he had had to deal with an issue that day that he felt strongly about, but one in which the United States had made the decision for Iran, or an issue that the Shah had shown a particular weakness in when it came to Iran's national interests. Ironically, as my father became a senior diplomat, ambassador to Japan, he no longer talked about work at home, mainly, as I discovered, because the Iranian government had thoroughly wired the homes it provided for senior officials (and undoubtedly it continues to do so). The Shah had actually started to believe, for a moment in the 1970s, that he had risen above a dependence on America and the West, evidenced in his lecturing tone when discussing their profligate ways in interviews, particularly during the oil crises. (Pro-monarchy conspiracy theorists still claim that the British and the Americans engineered the Islamic Revolution as payback to the newly bumptious Pahlavi.) Ayatollah Khomeini didn't buy it, this independent-minded king who had visions of himself as the heir to Cyrus the Great's legacy, but some of the Shah's men did, until he began calling on the American ambassador to Tehran for advice when Khomeini's revolution showed signs of taking hold. I don't think my father ever bought it fully either, for he still grew visibly agitated by issues of foreign policy, the corruption of the Iranian elite, and the

Shah's tendency to bend to the will of American presidents; when
the revolution came, my father was hesitant only because of his great
dislike of organized religion and the politicized clergy, not because of
a great love for the Shah's regime.

When I talk to my father today, and tell him stories about my
meetings with current Iranian ambassadors and other officials, I see
in him an envy, not for their positions or jobs, but for the way they
behave and for their ability to act completely in the interests of their
country, without regard for whether a greater power might object. And
he, like so many of the old guard who detest the rule of the mullahs,
expresses an (often reluctant) admiration for a government that has
been able to accomplish so much in terms of its influence and power
on the world stage. To the astonishment of those like my father though,
it took what they considered the un- or under-educated, the provincial
and unsophisticated, those who never succumbed to the temptations
or the conventions of Western society, to turn Iranian dreams of past
glory into realistic ones for the future. And sometimes even those most
opposed to the likes of Ahmadinejad can reluctantly admire him for his
in-your-face *por-roo'ee*, cheekiness or impudence, in the face of foreign
attempts to control Iran or its development.

In late 2009, a few days after the International Atomic Energy
Agency, or IAEA, issued a resolution demanding that Iran halt construction of its newly revealed uranium enrichment site near the holy
city of Qom, Ahmadinejad declared that Iran not only would refuse to
do so, but would build an additional *ten* enrichment sites (the United
States has only one, believe it or not, in Kentucky) on a much larger
scale than the one under sanction. He added, just in case anyone
was wondering, that he was *not* bluffing. He may not have thought
he was bluffing, but his statement was classic gholov, bluster that
drew an admiring remark from even my mother. "You have to like how
he sometimes deals with the West," she said with a slight grimace,

"as *loathsome* as he is." And in the Muslim and developing world, Ahmadinejad and his government know, despite their falling in stature because of the 2009 election, that standing up to the parvenu West in that manner wins the hearts and minds of those, proud of their long histories and cultures, who would like to see their own leaders display a similar stance on their own nations' rights.

ALTHOUGH Ayatollah Khomeini first broached the idea of an expansionist Iran, it was only after his death that Iran formulated such a policy. Khomeini's concept was that since Islam knows no borders, then an Islamic Iran needn't either. His goal was to spread the revolution to Muslim lands, starting with Shia Muslim lands such as Lebanon and Iraq, and since other Islamic revolutions would be under his guidance, Iran would become the dominant power in the region. Khomeini's plans were no secret to Arab leaders—he spoke quite openly about them—and when Saddam Hussein attacked Iran shortly after the revolution, every Arab country save Syria (and a hapless Levant) rushed to Iraq's support, militarily and financially. King Hussein of Jordan even flew to Baghdad, inspected Saddam's troops, and declared his undying allegiance to the latest Arab invader of Persia. Because of the length of the war—a brutal one that was fought in trenches and by the Iraqis with poison gas, cost almost a million lives, and ended exactly where it started, that is, with no changes to either border—Khomeini's plans were essentially on hold, with the exception of Lebanon, where Iran still had the ability to influence its politics through support of Shia groups, specifically the Iranian-created Hezbollah. After the war ended and after Khomeini's death, however, Iran, along with rebuilding its military capability, which it felt it needed to do indigenously because of sanctions against it and because the United States was arming its neighbors, turned its gaze outward.

First President Rafsanjani, in office from 1989 to 1997, began the process of repairing relations with Arab states. They were less nervous about Iran after the stalemate of Iran's war with Iraq, but it was important to reassure them about Iran's future intentions, which were no longer to export the revolution per se but were defined by a far more subtle expansion of influence. President Rafsanjani also made attempts to expand Iran's reach into the Far East and into Africa, but it was under President Khatami that Iran, having rebuilt its economy, its military, and developed a nuclear program unbeknownst to the world, put its plans into practice for domination of the Middle East and influence across the globe.

Khatami was actually very popular among Arab and even European leaders, but they didn't for one moment believe, despite their willingness to see a thaw in relations, that the president of Iran actually set foreign policy. The president does have influence in the direction of foreign policy—by default he sits on the Supreme National Security Council—and the reformists and pragmatists are able to steer the tone of that policy, even affect its strategy, as much as the hard-liners. But virtually no one, in the leadership, the opposition, or even among the population at large, believes that Iran should pull back from an aggressive move to expand its influence and reclaim the mantle of a regional superpower. In the wake of widespread opposition to President Ahmadinejad, his domestic economic policies, and his belligerent foreign policy rhetoric, some politicians, and particularly supporters of reformists, believe that Iran needs to concentrate on the home front—much as in hard times American politicians tend to criticize foreign entanglements or an aggressive foreign policy—but few believe Iran should do so at the expense of losing the valuable economic and strategic benefits of spreading its influence across the world.

PRESIDENT KHATAMI'S outreach to the world took him on state visits to African, Asian, and South American countries. Ahmadinejad continued that outreach enthusiastically by taking trips to Africa, Asia, South and Central America, India, Pakistan, Sri Lanka, Central Asia, and most of the Arab countries, building ties and cementing friendships, friendships that usually resulted in increased Iranian influence wherever his plane landed. In addition, confidants of the Supreme Leader, government officials and leaders of governmental bodies such as Ayatollah Rafsanjani, Ali Larijani, and Ali Akbar Velayati (foreign policy advisor to Ayatollah Khamenei and foreign minister for sixteen years), and even the mayor of Tehran made notable international trips and appearances, mostly since 2005, that have garnered hardly any coverage in the West, yet all those trips have been significant in Iran's expansion of its influence and power. President Ahmadinejad, no hero to Arab governments, who are wary of his belligerent tone and naked ambition, was personally invited to the *haj* by the king of Saudi Arabia in 2007, and in the first week of June 2008, Rafsanjani, who regularly meets with foreign ambassadors and dignitaries in his role as chairman of the Expediency Council and the Assembly of Experts, was also personally invited by the king to attend a Muslim conference in Riyadh, an invitation he accepted.

Iran's foreign policy has many tentacles and its reach is expanding, but its head sits in Tehran, surveying the landscape of foreign lands like no Iranian king has dared in the last two or three hundred years. When my father was an ambassador, Iran had embassies throughout the world, but not in countries that the Shah didn't view as strategically important to him, or where Iran was irrelevant. Within Africa, for example, Iran had small embassies in North Africa, a tiny one in Ethiopia (only because Ethiopia had an emperor, and the Shah, no surprise, *liked* emperors), Kenya, and South Africa. Under the Islamic regime, over time Iran has built embassies in every single African nation. African leaders regularly make the trek to Tehran on state visits, and Iranian presidents (starting with Rafsanjani) regularly reciprocate on tours of the continent. Iran knows that its money, its oil, and its technology will win friends in Africa (where many countries have a Muslim population) and elsewhere, but it also knows that the key to influence and safeguarding its interests is in close personal contacts with governments and the people. It may seem unimportant that Iran exports automobiles to Senegal (and has even built an assembly plant there), for example, or that it sends a trade delegation to Gabon, but when it comes time to count Iran's friends at the UN, or when Iran claims that over one hundred countries support its nuclear program, it is not exaggerating.

In my father's time, Central and South America (and the Caribbean) were thought of as too far from Iran to be significant; they were in America's backyard after all, and America, Iran's patron, didn't need Iran's input in the region. Today, Iran has tractor, automobile, and bicycle factories, housing developments, and a bank in Venezuela; construction operations in Nicaragua; and an embassy in every country (except the small Caribbean nations). And, of course, wherever there are Muslims (and Muslims are everywhere, including in South America), Iran is there to provide moral and financial support, even without an official embassy or consular office. A measure of Iran's importance to the developing world was revealed in the summer of 2008, when I was in Tehran and Bolivia's Evo Morales paid his first visit to the Iranian capital. Apart from the natural empathy La Paz and Tehran share as revolutionary governments, and their mutual distrust of the *Yanqui*, Morales announced that the sole Bolivian embassy in the Middle East, long based in Cairo, America's ally, would be packing up and moving to Tehran, the center of state-sponsored anti-Americanism. To Bolivia, there was far more value to having close ties with Iran, potentially the regional superpower but importantly a wealthy and technologically advanced patron, than with Egypt, once the center of the middle eastern world but now less and less relevant to the world outside of its immediate neighborhood.

"IF HE ATTACKS Iran, in two minutes Bush is dead. We are Muslims. I am Hezbollah. We are Muslims, and we will defend our countries at any time they are attacked." This not-uncommon sentiment was heard many times among avid supporters of Iran, such as members of Hezbollah. But this statement, made to Telemundo, the Spanish-language American network in 2007, was not made by a Lebanese citizen in Beirut or Tripoli, not even a disaffected man somewhere in the Middle East. It was uttered in Spanish by Mustafa Khalil Meri, a young Arab Muslim that Telemundo interviewed in Ciudad del Este, *Paraguay*. Ciudad del Este, the city at the center of the largely lawless area intersecting Paraguay, Brazil, and Argentina, known as the Tri-border region, is home to a generation or two of Lebanese immigrants. Hezbollah, with the support of and as proxies of Iran, has set up shop in the Tri-border region, mainly to further the interests of Iran, not Lebanon, which can hardly be described as having special interests beyond its own fragile borders. And there is nothing the countries whose borders Hezbollah operatives move across with ease, whether smuggling arms, equipment, or cash, or the United States, can do about it. Thirty years ago, it wouldn't have even occurred to Iranian government officials, not in their wildest dreams, that a small, unknown section of South America might be ripe for exploitation, or for creating a base for Iranian interests. Senior, well-traveled, and highly sophisticated officials in their well-tailored Western suits probably would have had trouble even identifying some of these South American countries on a map, let alone be able to describe their strategic importance to Iran. And yet in the spring of 2009, Avigdor Lieberman, a new right-wing foreign minister of Israel, undertook a tour of South America, a visit characterized by Israeli officials specifically as "an attempt by Israel to ward off Iran's strengthening economic and diplomatic presence in the region."

They presumably also meant, but didn't want to say, *military* and *intelligence* presence. It is not surprising that Israel should take a keen interest in Iran's influence in Latin America given that Israel believes Iran to be behind the 1994 bombing of the Argentine Jewish Mutual Association, something Iran vehemently denies. However, Israel is also aware that when it comes to the struggle for dominance in the Middle East, economically and militarily, whoever has a longer global reach will have the advantage.

The United States, which should be far more concerned with Iran than its much smaller ally Israel is, has not completely ignored Iran's foray into its own hemisphere, but it is unsure of what to do, or even what can be done, about it. In January 2009, in testimony to the Senate Armed Services Committee, Defense Secretary Robert Gates said, "I'm concerned about the level of, frankly, subversive activity the Iranians are carrying on in a number of places in Latin America, particularly South America and Central America. They're opening a lot of offices and a lot of fronts behind which they interfere with what is going on in some of these countries." That description of Iranian activity in the region, "subversive" no less, would surprise most Latin Americans, given that the "offices" and "fronts" that Iran has opened have been mainly embassies, factories producing goods, banks, and direct airline service to the Middle East that bypasses the United States and Europe—sort of like what the United States has traditionally done wherever it has seen a market for export, import, and manufacturing. What Robert Gates didn't want to say, evidently, was that Iran's growing influence in the region, to say nothing of its already outsized influence in the Middle East, was a threat to American political and economic interests. Forget GM, Bechtel, Schwinn, and American bases; welcome

Khodro, Kayson, and the *Sepah*. Catholic and socialist-leaning Latin America, oddly in some ways religiously and ideologically close to political Shiism, is one place where Iran is trying to lay the foundation for future influence and global relevance, if not renewed empire.

Secretary of State Hillary Clinton echoed Gates's warning in December 2009, after Iran had advanced its relations further, despite domestic upheaval, in the intervening ten months. "We can only say," Clinton said in reference to Latin American–Iranian ties, "that it is a really bad idea for the countries involved." She accused Iran of being the "major supporter, promoter and exporter of terrorism in the world," an argument not likely to convince any of the Latin American nations enjoying cordial relations, if not close ties, with the Islamic Republic, but she also warned that "if people want to flirt with Iran, they should take a look at what the consequences might well be for them. And we hope that they will think twice." Hillary's warning, some might say threat, was unusual in that Iranian relations with countries such as Bolivia and Venezuela had not been viewed until then with the kind of alarm that would warrant her choice of language. (Needless to say, Hugo Chavez of Venezuela lambasted the speech as U.S. "interference" in the internal affairs of his country.) American concerns, though, had little effect, for the president of another unlikely South American country keen on "flirting" with Iran, Guyana, showed up in Tehran in January 2010. Bharrat Jagdeo was granted a special audience with Supreme Leader Khamenei, where he remarked that Guyana welcomed Iran's active presence in Latin America as well as in the Caribbean region. I can almost guarantee that most Iranians would not be able to tell you where Guyana is, let alone *what* it is.

Hezbollah setting up bases in the region, supported by Iran, could naturally be viewed as a military threat—whether in Paraguay, whose foreign minister Alejandro Hamed Franco was banned from entering the United States or even flying an American-flagged airline because of his alleged ties to the organization, or in countries like Venezuela where they can operate freely—but the real question is how much of a threat. Does Iran ever want to attack the United States or U.S. interests using its proxy, or does the implied threat of direct retaliation for an attack against itself or its interests suffice? It's far more likely that Iran, following the Cold War playbook but with a twenty-first-century twist, and imagining itself, as unlikely as it seems, as a power to eventually rival the United States, positions itself not with armies and missiles on the borders of the United States and its allies, but with proxies able to engage in asymmetrical warfare should the need arise. That may be a practical consideration on the part of Iran at a time when it considers itself threatened over the nuclear issue. However, other factors also play into Iran's move into Latin America, Africa, and even Asia, and they have to do with both its self-image and its economic development rather than any notions of asymmetrical warfare with the world's greatest superpower.

AFTER THE overthrow of the Shah, one of the first things the new revolutionary government of Iran did was to define itself as neither in the Western nor in the Eastern (Soviet) camp. The Iranian foreign ministry, a beautiful compound of art deco buildings with Persian flourishes set in park-like grounds in downtown Tehran, has a number of entrances, but the original building, one that houses the offices of the minister and many of his deputies, has two entrances through which all visitors must pass. Over the tall and heavy wooden doors are traditional blue Persian tiles, floral in design, with the Farsi words for "Islamic Republic of Iran" and "Ministry of Foreign Affairs" written into them. Underneath, in smaller letters, is also written, "*Na gharbi, na sharghi; Jomhouri-e-Eslami*"—"Neither Western, nor Eastern; Islamic Republic." Self-image. This is Iran's way of reminding the world, and indeed itself, that Iran is an independent nation that bows in no direction, a country that is neither the liberal democracy of the capitalist West nor the onetime atheist communist of the East. Rather, it is a state that has defined its own political system, unique in the world today, and is a sovereign entity.

Ayatollah Khomeini, in a speech to military officers just days before the revolution, said, "The foreign hands must be cut off from this nation. How much should America loot this country? How much Britain and other powers? We must resurrect ourselves, wake up, and take back our freedom. . . . We want an independent army, not a servant." No Iranian politician, from the hard-line conservatives who rule to the leftist liberals, even those in jail, would disagree with Khomeini's sentiments today. *You are either with us or against us?* How about neither? How about, we have the balls to say neither, and the balls to *mean* it. Sitting in New York, Washington, or a European capital, it is easy to imagine Iran as an isolated, forlorn place with a delusional government. But stand in the main hall of Imam Khomeini airport in Tehran and look up at the flat-screen flight monitors. There are planes arriving from every corner of the world, every day, and planes taking off for every corner of the world, including Caracas, every day. Except from and to the United States, of course. All of these planes are transporting passengers and goods, and from that vantage point Iran doesn't seem so isolated. IKA, as the airport is known by International Air Transport Association, or IATA, codes, is not José Martí in Havana, nor is it Sunan International in Pyongyang. Iran imagines itself as not just a power to be reckoned with, but as an influential player whereby it figures into almost every other nation's political and economic calculations.

PRESIDENT AHMADINEJAD, perhaps overly given to the Persian penchant for gholov, often says things that appear to be nonsensical, particularly when he refers to the world's problems as soon being solved by the Mahdi, or missing Imam, the Messiah of Shia Islam (who, according to him, will reappear on earth with Jesus by his side not just soon but near Qom, in Iran). But his words about Iran's ambitions and its place in the world are merely a cruder expression of what most of the country's leadership, and even much of the population, actually believe. In October 2008, regarding Iran's role in the world, he said, "The mission of the Iranian nation differs with its mission 30 years ago. Our mission is now global and we believe that only the scientists and Ulema in Islamic Iran can play a pivotal role in guiding humanity in the right path. Therefore we should be well-prepared and accountable in dealing with the needs of the world." Huh? Prepared to deal with the needs of the *world*? Some Iranians might say, particularly after the post-election unrest and upheaval, that Iran might want to deal with the needs of *Iran* before worrying about the world, but Ahmadinejad was expressing a view shared by the entire leadership that envisions Iran leading a new Muslim enlightenment. Of course, Ahmadinejad's view of what Islamic enlightenment means is diametrically opposed to the view of many of the reform-minded clerics and certainly the political opposition to him. However, Ahmadinejad's personal views on Islam are not that relevant in the long term, for unlike the senior clerics who no matter what office they hold at one time or another are *always* in the leadership, when his term as president is up, he will, like most U.S. presidents, lose much of whatever influence he has over the direction of Iran's domestic and foreign policy, if not completely fade into oblivion. As long as there is an Islamic republic in Iran, and as long as the Ayatollahs maintain their support among the people, it is they and not lay politicians who will decide Iran's role in "guiding humanity."

IN THE MEANTIME, Ahmadinejad as president has done more to win hearts and minds across the globe than any previous Iranian head of state. Despite deep unpopularity at home, he continues to be popular abroad (outside the West, of course), among those who are either reflexively anti-American, generally anti-imperialist, or living under autocratic if not dictatorial regimes—which means most of the population of the world outside the developed countries. When Ahmadinejad visited Malaysia in 2007, he was treated to smiling throngs of people— men, women, and children—lining the streets by the tens of thousands and waving his portrait at his motorcade. Even in developed countries, however, Iran is popular among those who have more sympathy for the Palestinians than the Israelis, those who believe U.S. hegemony needs to be confronted, and those who root for the underdog in every fight.

We are sometimes blinded by our misunderstanding of terrorism, particularly terrorism directed at Israel. The West considers Iran to be a state sponsor of terrorism and therefore only one step removed from evil (or evil itself, according to one U.S. administration), but the majority of the planet's population does not view what Iran is accused of, support for Hezbollah and Hamas, as terror sponsorship. While our televisions and newspapers show an act of terror against innocent Israelis, TV sets around the world show the daily misery of Palestinians suffering in refugee camps or in Gaza under a blockade. Hamas, viewers of those TV sets are reminded, won an election demanded by the United States, only to be vilified and deemed unacceptable leaders for the Palestinians by Israel and most Western countries after their victory. Iran and Syria are virtually the only two countries that continue to support Hamas, and insist that the Palestinian organization must be included in any peace process, a fact that makes both countries popular among the masses in the Muslim and Third World but unpopular among the leaders of Arab countries reliant on, and therefore reluctant to annoy, the United States.

Although Iran supports Hamas morally and economically, and is accused of supporting it militarily, it hasn't cut off relations with the Palestinian Authority, headed by Mahmoud Abbas. The Palestinian embassy in Tehran, on the site of the old Israeli embassy, is still an outpost of the Palestinian Authority, which means Fatah, the West's allies, and Abbas appoints the ambassador. Hamas has an office and official representative in Tehran, though, and Iran has continued to court both parties, indicative of its wanting to play a role, so far denied it, in the peace process.

In early 2005, before President Khatami left office, I saw him one day at his office at Sa'adabad Palace in northern Tehran. The nuclear issue was then, as it is now, the primary concern of the West, and although Iran had suspended uranium enrichment while waiting for the West to deliver its proposals for a package of incentives, there was still much concern in the United States regarding the possibility of Iran joining the nuclear club. "I know," Khatami said to me, smiling broadly, "they say we're going to build a bomb and then hand it over to terrorists!" I explained to him that most Americans were concerned with Iran's anti-Israeli stance and its support for Palestinian groups known to have engaged in terror, but not necessarily concerned with Iran attacking the United States. "Our position on the Palestinians and Israel is very clear," he said, turning serious. "Iran will fully support whatever the Palestinians decide." And although it appeared that his successor Ahmadinejad held a different view with his constant baiting of Israel, including his denials of the Holocaust, on at least two occasions his boss, the Supreme Leader, publicly repeated exactly what Khatami said to me, almost word for word, after particularly troubling Ahmadinejad outbursts. Ahmadinejad's statements seemed to indicate, at least to those uninitiated in the ways of Persians, that Iran might independently seek to destroy Israel, something Iran has been at pains to deny while at the same time keeping up a steady flow of anti-Israeli invective. But the official Iranian position of supporting whatever the Palestinians decide means supporting Hamas as well as maintaining relations with the Palestinian Authority, and that, whether we like it or not, is perfectly logical to the millions of hearts and minds who give a damn.

In the case of Hezbollah, based in Lebanon, Iran's support for it is, again, extremely popular across the Muslim world. Israelis and many Westerners may view Hezbollah, a creation of the Islamic Republic, as a terrorist group, and it does consider Israel a mortal enemy, but unlike Hamas, Hezbollah is neither seeking to gain land at Israel's expense (with the exception of the disputed Shebaa Farms) nor looking to help the Palestinians do so. A Shia group that is far more interested in power in Lebanon, Hezbollah has committed terrorist acts, including against Westerners in Beirut, but it has fought to expel foreigners, including an occupying Israeli army, and as such is viewed, rightly or wrongly, as a freedom movement that has twice defeated the most powerful army in the Middle East. Sheikh Hassan Nasrallah is popular among Shia and Sunni alike, and among Iranian leaders, conservative and reformist (one of the most liberal reformists I know in Tehran, a man who despises Ahmadinejad and the hard-line clerics who support him, is a close personal friend of Nasrallah's, and he entertains him at his home whenever Nasrallah quietly visits Tehran).

Iranian citizens by and large support Hezbollah, perhaps more than they support the Palestinians, but in recent harder economic times some have begun to question the amount of Persian treasure devoted to a non-Persian cause. The leaders of Iran are unconcerned, though, mainly because they never make public the amount of money that goes to Hezbollah or Hamas (and in fact they deny they contribute militarily). They also know that whatever grumblings their overt financial support may cause, Iranians are still generally predisposed to support anti-Israeli groups over Israel itself. The hearts and minds Iran wins across the globe are, at any rate, paramount to its long-term ambitions of becoming a power to be reckoned with, and this means not only securing its legacy as the guardians of a resurgent Islamic Persian empire but also ensuring its longevity as those guardians. The election of 2009 in Iran, but more particularly the bloody aftermath beamed to televisions across the world, may have given pause, but many in the Muslim and Third World resent Western interference in their countries to such an extent that *anything* the West supports, even its questioning of the Iranian government's legitimacy in the wake of the 2009 election, is viewed suspiciously.

THERE HAVE BEEN missteps, or perhaps better described as premature steps, along the way toward a revived Iranian empire. Iran is quick to acknowledge these missteps, but the reactions of its Arab neighbors betray their fear of Iranian dominance. In February 2009, Bahrain, home to the U.S. Fifth Fleet and a staunch ally of the West, in a fit of apoplexy, broke off negotiations with Iran over a proposed gas-export deal. Bahrain is one of those tiny kingdoms in the Persian Gulf that Qaddafi referred to a year earlier as being Persian in everything but its rulers, and it is in fact the one Persian Gulf Arab nation that has a majority Shia population that views itself as oppressed by the Sunni leadership. That leadership was apoplectic not over terms of the gas deal, but over remarks made by cleric Ali Akbar Nateq-Nouri, speaker of Parliament at one time, presidential candidate, and close confidant of Supreme Leader Ayatollah Khamenei. Nateq-Nouri had been quoted as saying that Bahrain was Iran's fourteenth province until 1970, the year of Bahrain's independence, a statement perhaps uncomfortably reminiscent of Saddam Hussein's claim right before and after he invaded Kuwait that that country was in fact nothing more than Iraq's Province 19. Although Iran did rule Bahrain in the seventeenth century, when the second Persian Empire, a Shia one, was at the height of its glory, some Iranian hard-liners believe that Iran still holds sovereignty, at least emotional sovereignty, over the island. The Iranian government quickly distanced itself from Nateq-Nouri's statement, insisting that Iran had no territorial ambitions on Bahrain, but the suspicion remains that Bahrain would be one of the lower-hanging fruits ripe for an eager Persian picking.

In Central and South America, there have been missteps too—not necessarily premature steps, but instances where Iran's appetite may have been larger than its stomach. Having had no experience in imperialism for over four hundred years, and with economic problems of its own, Iran can be thought of as being on a learning curve. In Nicaragua, after Daniel Ortega's victory in the presidential elections, Iran opened an embassy and began courting the anti-American government. But the announced aid and multi-million-dollar economic projects have yet to materialize. With little obvious in common with Latin American nations other than revolutionary zeal combined with anti-imperialism, Iran recognizes that it will have to do more to win hearts and minds than merely promise to pour its oil riches into the region. Yet even so Iran has made strides in Paraguay with its proxy Hezbollah, and soared in Venezuela under Hugo Chavez, a leader perhaps more disdainful of the United States than even some of the Ayatollahs. At the Venirauto factory in Maracay, Iranian automobiles are being built, sometimes one at a time for lack of parts or for other reasons, for a Venezuelan market apparently desperate to have them, based on the number of inquiries it receives from potential customers and the almost equal number of requests for cars it turns down.

At one point in 2008 it seemed that every foreign reporter based in Caracas, perhaps curious about the IranAir flights landing at the airport, made the trek to Calabozo, ground zero in Iran's economic ties to the region, and filed reports about the worrisome growing presence of Iran in America's backyard. The BBC even broadcast a special report on the phenomenon on Radio 4, and interviewed Iranian project managers and Venezuelans involved in everything from construction to maize-processing plants. Maria Cristina Rodriguez, a worker from President Chavez's United Socialist Party and a resident, was quoted as being proud of Calabozo's association with Iran. "For the first time our young people are being trained properly," she told the BBC, pointing out that her father owned a Veniran tractor, one assembled at an Iranian-built factory with Iranian parts. In Calabozo, apart from the tractor factory and agricultural engineering, Iranian engineers and specialists are building thousands of low-income housing apartments, and a twenty-seven-hundred-unit apartment complex going up in Venezuela's dusty southern plains is not too far from the Iranian club, yes, the *Iranian* Club, where the engineers from the contracting firm and other Iranian specialists based in the area spend their free time playing pool, socializing, and eating halal *abgousht* and other Persian food (expertly prepared by Venezuelan cooks) with other Iranians. It is oddly reminiscent of the British clubs in far-off colonies that were symbols of Great Britain's imperial reach, but tropical cocktails are unlikely to be invented at the Iranian club in Calabozo. No alcohol please: we're *Persian*. But Iran's bank in Caracas, Banco Internacional de Desarrollo, or BID, which was inaugurated to facilitate Iranian economic development in the region (such as in Calabozo), has fallen under U.S. sanctions and has undergone intense scrutiny for possible links to Iran's attempts to circumvent those sanctions as well as sanctions against the purchase of weaponry. The bank cannot, just like its domestic banks Iran has learned, gain access to the U.S. monetary system, which hinders it immensely. Yes, it's a learning curve, and one that does not come without setbacks.

Iran has benefited from elections in Latin America that have brought left-wing and intuitively anti-imperialist presidents to power, most notably in Venezuela, but it wasn't about to squander an opportunity in South America's largest nation, Brazil. The election of Luiz Inácio Lula da Silva, better known simply as Lula, has allowed Iran to forge closer ties with his country, a country whose economic and military clout surpasses that of all other nations in the region. While not a country in need of Iranian technology or aid, it is a country that could offer long-term benefits to Iran, whether it be through joint economic development projects, a dramatic increase in trade, or cooperation on nuclear energy projects. Perhaps more important, Brazil's support for Iran in the international arena (particularly at the UN) is vital, for it is seen, despite its leftist government and unlike Venezuela or Nicaragua, as a Western-style democracy with no overt anti-American agenda.

Iran's investment in Brazil paid off dramatically in 2009 when the overwhelmingly popular President Lula rushed to Ahmadinejad's and Iran's defense, even using Ahmadinejad's language in comparing the protesters on the streets of Tehran who believed his re-election to be fraudulent to fans of a losing soccer team, and describing them as "poor losers." That may have been good enough for Ahmadinejad, who craved international legitimacy in the aftermath of the elections, but Lula went further than that. At the UN General Assembly in New York only a few months after the election, Lula met with Ahmadinejad, was filmed smiling with him and slapping his back, and gave an interview in which he strongly defended Iran's nuclear program, including its right to enrich uranium. He also invited Ahmadinejad to Brazil for a state visit later in the year, an invitation Ahmadinejad immediately accepted, expecting a reciprocal visit by Lula to Tehran, which will do even more for Iran's standing in the world, particularly with respect to its nuclear program.

Brazil's cozy relationship with Iran did not go unnoticed by Israel—already concerned with Iranian influence in the region—and President Shimon Peres quickly scheduled a visit to Brasilia only two weeks before Ahmadinejad's to "discuss the Iranian infiltration into South America," according to the Israeli government. In the game of winning hearts and minds, Israel appeared to be playing catch-up everywhere outside of Europe and the United States. Nonetheless, Lula warmly received Ahmadinejad in Brazil (with a bear hug, no less, that a Brazilian friend of mine deemed "embarrassing"), and the Iranian president and his delegation of over ninety cabinet members, advisors, and Iranian businessmen signed a number of agreements with their Brazilian counterparts that could not have made either the United States or Israel very happy.

IN 1964 my family was posted to North Africa. Before that, my brother and I had attended the American School in New Delhi, India, a big, well-equipped institution populated with children of Americans assigned to the large U.S. Embassy nearby, and a handful of non-American "diplobrats" like ourselves. We had, in my short life to that point, lived in London (only months after I was born), then San Francisco, and then Tehran for a short time, where we also attended the American school—a smaller school, which indicated to me that India had to be more important than Iran. While in India, I vividly remember the day in 1963 (or the next day, given the time difference) that President John Kennedy was shot. My parents grieved along with their American friends—it seemed the whole world grieved—and I remember walking with my young American schoolmates, arms over each other's shoulders, in silence, aware that something had gone horribly wrong but something that we didn't really understand.

America was a supreme nation to me, so the assassination of its president was of vital significance, and India was big and majestic—significant to a world that knew Gandhi and Nehru—but what about Iran? None of my mostly American classmates in India had any awareness of Iran, and in the segregated diplomatic community where we lived, I knew no Indians except for workers who spoke little or no English. (*Pani-lau'o*—"Bring me water"—was the one useful phrase I quickly learned.) So being a young child with no awareness of Iran's great history, and its having little international significance ten years after the fall of Mossadeq, I identified more with America than I did with the country of my birth, the country that had sent my father to serve in Delhi. I was—like many of my countrymen, even in Iran—unaware that 1963 was also the year that Ayatollah Khomeini was arrested and later sent into exile for advocating an Iran different from the one the Shah imagined, and an Iran that, if nothing else, might become a source of inspiration for the world's Muslims, tens of millions of whom lived at that time in India.

We were to go to Rabat, Morocco, next, my father told us one day, and although I knew where that was, I didn't give it much thought other than to wonder what the American school might be like in that kingdom. At the last minute, however, even as our household goods were already on their way to Rabat, my father was diverted to the embassy in Tunis, Tunisia, a country I had no awareness of (and one that had been independent for only as long as I had been alive). Rabat, Tunis—it didn't make too much difference to a seven-year-old, but when we settled in and started at the American Cooperative School of Tunis in 1964, basically a few classrooms (and no high school) in a nondescript one-story building by the side of the Tunis-Carthage road, I realized we were in a much smaller country that just *had* to be less important than Iran. I recognized also that we were now in a Muslim country, where Arabic and French were the two languages spoken, but it seemed to my young mind a country sorely in need of development. Tunis was, for Americans and foreigners, a country with Peace Corps volunteers (some of whom served as substitute teachers at my school), an outpost of the Ford Foundation, and an Iranian Embassy that was essentially a two-man operation with very little to do. The Peace Corps, which I understood even as a child, did not go forth into developed nations.

Toward the end of our stay, politics intruded on our lives in a way I hadn't imagined, and in a completely different way than the Kennedy assassination did in 1963. At the start of the Six-Day War in 1967, between Israel and its neighbors, small mobs of angry Tunisians attacked American institutions, and the American school evacuated its students—I remember hurriedly piling into my father's Volkswagen with a bunch of classmates, Iranians helping Americans—and we were home for the duration, all six days of it. This was an Arab versus Israeli war, and Tunisians were Arabs and Americans stand-ins for Israelis. But where did Iran fit in? Nowhere, as far as I could tell, but that troubled me, for I identified somewhat with the Muslim Tunisians who prayed like my mother did every day, but also with my American friends, some whose fathers were in the U.S. military and had already been on tours in Vietnam. If *they* were under attack, then *I* was under attack, right? Yes and no. Iran, a non-Arab country, had no dog in the fight, I knew, but sympathies had to be with fellow Muslims, even as the Shah had to bend over backward to avoid displeasing America, his patron.

If Tunisians were angry that their pro-Western government under President Habib Bourguiba didn't express enough support for Arabs fighting Jews, or that it didn't send troops fast enough to help its fellow Arabs, they were lashing out at Americans, who I thought had been sent there to *help* them. It was the first time that I became aware of foreign policy, American foreign policy, and of the fact that my country, Iran, didn't seem to have one of its own. Unlike neighbor Libya, where the United States once had an air base, Tunisia remained essentially in the Western camp and under the iron fist of its dictator presidents and Western-trained intelligence services, but now, more than forty years later, Tunisians have no doubts where Iran stands when it comes to foreign policy, and about its independence from East and West. Iran's embassy in Tunis is no longer a two-man operation, the children of its diplomats do not attend the American school, and its presidents and foreign ministers visit their Muslim counterparts in North Africa regularly. It is not that Tunis always agrees with Iran, or that Tunis stands with Iran against the West; it is that Tunis cannot, as Qaddafi once implied, afford to ignore or more specifically *antagonize* Iran. Iran has already largely won, after all, the hearts and minds of its people.

GUESS WHO'S COMING TO DINNER?

Iran and America in the Age of Obama

Cutting ties with America is among our basic policies. However, we have never said that the relations will remain severed forever. . . . Undoubtedly, the day the relations with America prove beneficial for the Iranian nation, I will be the first one to approve of that.

   —Supreme Leader Ayatollah Ali Khamenei,
    Yazd, March 1, 2008

For the USA, preservation of dominance over others is important.

   —Twelfth-grade social science textbook,
    Iranian public school system

In February 2007, when I was sitting with former president Khatami in his office in North Tehran, he asked me about Barack Obama. Iranians were just beginning to hear about this new force in American politics and had grown deeply curious of him.

"He could be the next president," I said, "but you know, his middle name is Hussein, and that won't go over well with many Americans." Khatami was surprised to hear of Obama's Muslim connection.

"*Ajab!* Really?" he said on hearing the news, with a big smile. The idea that a black man might be taken seriously in a run for his party's nomination was surprising enough to the Iranian leadership and to most ordinary Iranians, but a black man with a Muslim middle name, the name of the prophet's grandson and a Shiite saint no less, was almost too much to consider. Khatami, I felt, was humoring me when I spoke earnestly of Obama, as if he didn't want to dash my hopes, but his expression gave away what he and all other Iranians I saw that winter really thought: *it will never happen.*

The Iranian revolution had been a revolution of the oppressed, and because of that, Iranian revolutionaries, still very much in charge, had a soft spot for African-Americans. The sentiments that led Ayatollah Khomeini and those revolutionaries to release all of the African-American hostages at the U.S. embassy in Tehran within a week or so of the takeover in 1979 had not died, despite the decades of animosity between U.S. administrations—its black officials included—and Iran. A year and a half later, in early September 2008, I was back in Khatami's offices in Jamaran, Tehran, and he, along with most Iranians, was contemplating an African-American president in America.

"Do you think he can make it?" he asked me, still unconvinced.

"He is our next president," I replied, "despite his name and his color."

All of Iran had followed the American presidential primaries and watched the two political conventions on satellite television, but there was still astonishment that Obama might actually win the presidency. Iranians harbored a fatalistic disbelief that a majority of Americans would actually vote for him, no matter what the polls said (which, not surprisingly, echoed what was being said in some quarters in the United States too). For conspiracy-minded Iranians, no matter their education or sophistication (such as President Ahmadinejad, who is educated but decidedly unsophisticated), the idea that he would be *allowed* to become president was itself preposterous, no matter the vote. Hindsight allows us to consider that President Ahmadinejad, who expressed doubts as to whether Obama would be allowed to ascend to the highest office in the United States, knows a thing or two about *allowing* candidates a well-deserved victory. Iranians by and large once had a great admiration for America, a country that until the coup of 1953 had shown benevolence toward their country—even protecting its sovereignty from partial Soviet occupation in the aftermath of World War II—while other great powers had sought to bring it to its knees. Iranians continued to admire the very concept of America even after the CIA-sponsored coup that returned the Shah to power, but had lost faith that America's promise was real, even more so during the eight years that George W. Bush was in office—most Iranians, like many of their American counterparts, believed his election was stolen—an era marked by American eagerness to utilize its military strength to accomplish foreign policy goals.

The "Death to America" that Americans see and hear Iranians chant, and the burning of American flags at every anti-imperialist rally in Tehran, are deceptive indications of Iranians' feelings toward America. The chanters and burners are sincere, but they are sincere in their dislike and even hatred of American foreign policy, not of America itself or Americans. Never in history has an abbreviation,

"American foreign policy" to just "America," caused so much misunderstanding, but Iranians who chant and burn flags are always amazed when they are told exactly how Americans regard their theatrical displays of anger. "What about Americans who burned their own flag in their protests?" some will ask, referring to the Vietnam War era when images of American protests filled television screens. "Those people were also protesting their foreign policy." Sure, one says, but that was forty years ago. Some Iranians, it seems, are forever caught in the past. Their numbers are dwindling, however, and fewer and fewer Iranians feel the urge to burn an American flag or wish death on it, even though they will, using a common Farsi expression, wish death on *themselves* a few times a day whenever horror strikes them. Or wish death to *potatoes*, as they did en masse during their own presidential campaign when Ahmadinejad, in what was seen as a cynical and desperate attempt to gain votes, gave out free spuds to poor families. "Death to" has never meant anything more than disapproval, and although disapproval of American policy toward Iran (and other weaker countries) has long been a predominant sentiment among Iranians, weariness with thirty years of blaming America for its problems was beginning to show as the George Bush years were coming to an end.

Despite doubts expressed by many Iranians that America might vote for a black man with a Muslim name as opposed to a white Christian war hero, some Iranians contracted Obama fever anyway, just as their American (and European) counterparts did. After the Democratic convention had finally confirmed to them that at least most Democrats, a large enough population, would be voting for a black man with a Muslim name as opposed to a white woman with all the right credentials, Tehran was filled with rumors, some preposterous and some only marginally less so. In Tehran in September 2008, I was surprised to learn from ordinarily sane and wise Iranians that not only was Obama a black man with a Muslim middle name, but he was in fact Iranian (with presumably Shia roots). Persians, as is their wont with those they admire, had begun to claim Obama as their own. What I have to think began as a joke, that Obama's family had Persian ancestry and was originally from the city of Bushehr (on the Persian Gulf, and once a major trading post with Africa), was fast becoming accepted by some as either possibly or definitively true. *Kayhan*, the ultra-conservative newspaper and media organ of the Supreme Leader, published the information, implying that Obama's original family name was *Ab-ba-ma*, meaning "water with us." This convinced many that the story had merit, but it is likely that *Kayhan* picked it up from a satiric website that had first floated the notion. Although it is within the realm of possibility that Obama has Persian ancestors, just as I and everyone else on the planet certainly have African ones, the fact that Iranians *wanted* to believe it was a sign of how keen they were to have an American hero, one who might reverse the decades-long antagonism between their two governments. Most Iranians, even those reflexively anti-American, have grown tired of not just rhetoric, but the antagonism itself. Superstitious Iranians, a large group in a country where Shia superstition plays a big role, also parsed his names, both Barack and Obama, for any signs of virtue. "Barack" can mean auspicious in Farsi, and "Obama" can be read to mean "he's with us" (sounds much better than "water with us," whatever that means), so many believed, and probably still do, that President Obama was meant to ascend to the presidency if only to put Iranian-American relations on the right track.

The Iranian government was wary before the election, neither wanting to appear to be pouring cold water on the idea that the United States might actually change, nor wanting to champion an American candidate no matter his color or even Muslim connection. But in conversations with Iranian authorities, it was clear that they were preparing for the worst, the worst being either the McCain "Bomb, Bomb, Iran!" presidency or an Obama presidency that would be difficult to

demonize. (A number of officials, however, told me that neither scenario was a probability, because if McCain won, he wouldn't dare
attack Iran, and if Obama won, he would not be the friend to Iran
that many hoped he would.) Nonetheless, the Iranian government,
which generally tries to stay away from appearing to endorse, and
therefore interfere, in the elections of any foreign country, couldn't
resist the temptation in 2008. The night before the U.S. election, state
radio, always reflecting the government's view, broadcast a commen-
tary in favor of Obama, highly ironic in light of the Iranian election of
June 12, 2009, saying, "Obama entered the race under the slogan of
change. The American people expect their government to put aside
neo-conservative policy of unilateralism and return to dialogue in their
dealings with the international community."

When Obama won the election, President Ahmadinejad, wanting to
get out front with an overture of his own, sent the president-elect a congratulatory note, unprecedented in the thirty-year history of the Islamic
Republic. It was an exceedingly clever bit of *ta'arouf*—the defining
Persian characteristic that can include not just exaggerated politesse
and self-deprecation but also one-upmanship and manipulation—for
if Obama responded positively, then Ahmadinejad would claim that it
was *Iran* that had quite reasonably *first* reached out to a former foe, and
if Obama did not respond, then Ahmadinejad could claim (as he later
did) that not only was the American president a boor, but the United
States was in fact insincere in its desire for change. The hard-line
daily *Kayhan* in fact, on the Wednesday after the U.S. election and
in preparation for the latter, had already run the headline "A Shift in
the White House—He Returns in the Cloak of a Dove" (*aan baz dar
lebass'e kabootar amad*). Employing the flowery and obfuscating language Persians love, it implied that any U.S. president, "he" (although
"aan" is not gender-specific), is ever a hawk, never a dove. Rudeness
is unforgivable in Iranian and indeed in Middle Eastern culture, and

either Obama's reputation or his strategy was sure to suffer, if even only slightly, no matter how he dealt with Ahmadinejad's letter. The president-elect's first detailed discussion of Iran (and one that didn't acknowledge the congratulatory note) came in December 2008, in an appearance on NBC's *Meet the Press*. In response to what his strategy for Iran might be, he suggested one of "carrots and sticks" to induce Iran to change its behavior, a wince-inducing phrase to almost all Iranians. Carrots and sticks, as former secretary of state James Baker once innocently told Ali G on his mock television talk show, may be tools of diplomacy, particularly in the arsenal of a superpower, but the language is insulting to a nation that simply does not consider itself inferior to the United States and, perhaps more important, is not particularly intimidated by the United States.

Sticks? In the summer of 2006, the day after the UN Security Council, under American guidance and prompting, passed its first resolution demanding that Iran suspend uranium enrichment, I was sitting in deputy ambassador Mehdi Danesh-Yazdi's office at the Iranian Mission in New York.

"Do the Americans think we're *afraid?*" he asked me. "We're a generation that has seen the most horrific war, we've had bombs and poison gas rained down on our heads, we've watched as our brothers have died in our arms, and the Americans think we're *afraid* of them, or of a UN resolution?" Danesh-Yazdi, as gentle and progressive an Iranian official as there was, was not being hostile or engaging in bluster; he was merely suggesting, as he always did, that Americans misunderstood the Iranian psyche and made policy decisions that could only lead to more misunderstanding, on the part of *both* sides.

Predictably, though, the Iranian response to Obama's first foray into U.S.-Iran relations was laced with ta'arouf. The Foreign Ministry also made it abundantly clear that the very concept of "carrot and sticks" will not work with a country like Iran. (Ministry officials would likely

have asked, like Ali G, "What if we don't want any carrots?" Iranians
do not see themselves as a naughty child or much worse, a donkey that
requires discipline if it does not do as it is told, and rewards if it does.)
But even before Obama's *Meet the Press* appearance, many conservative
Iranians had their suspicions of him confirmed when he repeated some
of his campaign slogans at his first press conference after the election.
"Iran's development of a nuclear weapon . . . is unacceptable," he had
said, and "Iran's support of terrorist organizations . . . is something that
has to cease." Ali Larijani, the conservative speaker of Parliament and
a political rival of Mr. Ahmadinejad's, but a pragmatist who has long
advocated negotiations, even conciliatory ones, with the West, was the
first to condemn the remarks, saying, "What is expected is a change
in strategy, not the repetition of objections to Iran's nuclear program
which will be taking a step in the wrong direction," and "Obama must
know that the change that he talks about is not simply a superficial
changing of colors or tactics." A rather harsh reaction, it would seem
to most Americans, given that Senator Obama had just been elected
president and had hardly any time to formulate an Iran policy, let alone
a response, if there was to be one, to President Ahmadinejad and his
letter. So why the strenuous objections to these throwaway statements?
And why did the Saudi stock market then immediately suffer a steep
decline, a decline the Saudis attributed to Mr. Obama's pronounce-
ments on Iran? It had to do with ta'arouf, and the way Iranians, and
to some degree Arabs, parse every word for nuance.

Ta'arouf has many forms, including supreme politesse that can
sometimes mask darker or even sinister sentiments, but its use (and
Iranians cannot help themselves in employing it) means that signals
are constantly being sent with layers of language. Messages received
in return that do not allow for ta'arouf are resented, and even rejected.
Barack Obama's oft-repeated proclamation during the campaign that
his offer to negotiate with the Iranian leadership meant he would meet

with them "at a time and place" of *his* "choosing" was viewed as insulting in Tehran because the language implied that America was the superior party that could dictate terms to an inferior Iran. Negotiations, the
Iranians believe, are a matter of mutual consent between parties that
at a minimum require some measure of respect (a word Iranians are
perhaps excessively fond of) toward one's adversary. And Obama's proclamation at his press conference that Iran's "development of a nuclear
weapon is unacceptable" was straightforward enough but offensive to
some Iranians on two levels: it implied first that Iranians were lying
about their nuclear program (and that the Supreme Leader, who had
issued a fatwa against the development and use of a nuclear weapon,
was a supreme *liar*), and second, that the United States had the moral
superiority to decide for the rest of the world what is "acceptable" and
"unacceptable." (That Israeli possession of nuclear weapons was evidently still "acceptable" to the United States grated even further, and
not just on Iranians.)

The Saudi stock market reaction was one of worry: that a new
president of the United States might simply continue familiar U.S.
policy and language toward Iran that the Arabs, at least, understood
didn't work with the Persians. "Iran's support of terrorist organizations," another seemingly straightforward statement and a fact that
President-elect Obama believed "must cease," was presumably a reference to Hezbollah and Hamas, neither of which, despite U.S. insistence, are considered terrorist organizations by the vast majority of
the people of the Muslim world. In any case, the Iranians were under
no illusion that President Obama would remove, with a wave of his
hand, Hamas and Hezbollah from the list of terrorist organizations
or Iran from the list of state sponsors of terrorism, for that was to be
negotiated as far as they were concerned (and something they actually
offered to do in 2003).

U.S. politicians have often been blissfully unaware of both the

psychological makeup of Iranian leaders and what motivates them, if
not Iranian culture as a whole. During the almost two-year-long process for the UN Security Council to implement three sets of sanctions
against Iran, the Iranians made it clear, to use former UN ambassador Javad Zarif's words, that they were "allergic" to a certain kind of
language—the language of threats and intimidation, and a language
bereft of ta'arouf. President Obama's messages, in his very early days
as president-elect, didn't come back to haunt him, but he quickly
came to understand how language was going to affect the future of
Iranian-American relations.

As it happened, Obama's first real outreach to Iran (and the Muslim
world in general) didn't come until his inauguration, which included
his famous "unclenched fist" remark. Many Iranians reacted positively,
except for those who saw it as rhetoric unmatched by deeds. The
Iranian propaganda machine, now recognizing a delicate mission, once
again went into overdrive. It pointed out to its audience that a nation
with armies on either border of Iran and a navy in its waters, a nation
that had imposed debilitating sanctions on a smaller and weaker country, and a nation that repeatedly refused to take the option of military
assault on their nation "off the table" could hardly be described as
extending a "hand," whereas a nation, Iran, that had not threatened
another in centuries, and one that merely defended its independence
and its rights, could hardly be described as presenting a "clenched
fist." Westerners may have been delighted with President Obama's
address, and it was an admirable one, but it gave Iranians who don't
see their country as a threat to the United States an excuse to play
victim once again.

The man supposedly from Bushehr, however, still hadn't lost his
overall appeal with average Iranians. Many in Iran ascribed his Iran
statements both before and after his inauguration to naiveté, or to the
indebtedness of all American administrations to the Israeli lobby, the

American Israel Public Affairs Committee, something that is assumed
as fact throughout the Middle East. But with Obama, Barack *Hussein*,
they still hoped that he might be the one president who could break
free of AIPAC, and apply an unbiased strategy to the Muslim world.

In March, two short months into his presidency and with Iran high
on his foreign policy agenda, Obama took the further unusual step of
sending an open message to the Iranian people *and* the Islamic government, which the United States still had not formally recognized since
breaking off relations in 1980. As Iranians prepared for the *Norooz* celebration, the Persian New Year (equivalent to Christmas, Hanukkah,
Kwanzaa, and New Year's all rolled into one), Obama recorded a
video message congratulating Iranians and the *Islamic Republic* of
Iran, his use of the country's full name extending it de facto recognition. But President Obama's message, which was warmly applauded
by Iranian-Americans and by many Iranians unaccustomed to congratulatory notes from American presidents, again gave Iran's government a golden opportunity to criticize American attitudes toward it.
Ahmadinejad may still have been sulking because his own congratulatory note to Obama had gone unanswered and unmentioned for almost
five months, but it wasn't left to him to react to the Norooz greeting,
even if he wanted to. In the video, Obama praised Iranian culture and
history, but he also suggested that Iran would have to behave according
to Western standards, according to *Western* determination of what is
good behavior, before it could take its rightful place among the family
of nations. It took a full day, evidence of the seriousness with which
Iran's leadership took Obama's message, but at the end of Supreme
Leader Ayatollah Ali Khamenei's long speech in Mashhad the day after
America's message was aired, he said, "If you change, our behavior
will change too. If you do not change, our nation will not change, as it
has only become more and more experienced, patient, and powerful
in the past thirty years."

The fact that the Supreme Leader himself responded showed the concern the government had with Obama's popularity, but his words rang true for many Iranians. Not only had Khamenei acknowledged, for the first time really, that Iran might change (something hitherto deemed unnecessary as Iran's behavior, we were always told, was exemplary and faultless), but he tapped into the Iranian superiority/inferiority complex, one that causes Iranians to view themselves as victims of a more powerful West while still enormously proud of their culture and sometimes too confident in an innate superiority.

The complexes Iranians suffer from have deep roots, all the way back to Shia Islam itself, multiple foreign invasions of their country, and the lost glory of the Persian Empire. Iranians may believe in their superiority because of a long history as a cultured, sophisticated nation with definable and ancient borders in a region where no other country has existed as a nation-state for longer than a hundred years, but they can simultaneously feel inferior because of the West's obvious technological, educational, and economic advantages, to say nothing of the sheer military might it possesses. Those most loudly proclaiming Iranian superiority and Iran's ability to be independent from Western influence, though, are not immune from a pronounced inferiority complex. Ali Kordan, the archconservative interior minister in Ahmadinejad's first administration, was impeached by the Parliament in 2008 for his solecistic claim and boast that he had received his degree not from a competent Iranian institution, but from "London's Oxford University," proof enough of the superiority/inferiority complexes at work even in the most ardent revolutionaries.

The Supreme Leader, well aware that a new era had dawned in the United States, had in fact already given a speech before Obama's message in which he prepared his people (and himself) for the inevitability of restoring relations with the United States. In his speech in Mashhad, however, he put the onus on the American president to make

THE AYATOLLAHS' DEMOCRACY   173

the changes necessary to bring that about. The truth is that Iran has long wished for a real détente with the United States, including recognition of Iran's legitimacy as a sovereign nation with its own concerns and interests, but, above all, with mutual respect and recognition of Iran's rights under international law. In February 2009—a mere month after Obama took office—Iran's Deputy Foreign Minister Reza Salari, on a trip to Mexico to determine why Iran's influence and trade with a country sharing a long border with the United States hadn't reached the levels it had in South America, said to reporters, "After President Obama, we think that the tone has changed in America. We want to be patient, give them some more time to thoroughly investigate and see for themselves what are the real solutions for the ambiguities and the crisis." Coming from the foreign ministry of a hard-line Ahmadinejad administration, it didn't sound like Iran was shying away from a potential thaw in relations with its archenemy. (Granted, for those Iranians who *don't* wish for détente, hard-line clerics such as Mesbah-Yazdi and some hard-liners in the Revolutionary Guards who believe relations with America, *any* America, will lead to Iran's weakening, Obama is their biggest nightmare, mainly because he is more likely than any other American president to deliver what Iran craves, and insists on having, in its relations with the United States.)

Every Iranian leader has articulated détente under the umbrella of mutual respect, from liberal reformers to some hard-line conservatives, and the leadership has always recognized that the Iranian people overwhelmingly want relations with the United States anyway. Firebrand President Ahmadinejad, perhaps the most hard-line and conservative of Iran's presidents since the early days of the revolution, actually went further than any other Iranian leader in attempting an outreach to America. His letters, to both President Bush and President Obama, were evidence of that, given that even President Khatami, who perhaps most desired détente with the United States, wasn't allowed by the Supreme Leader to extend a hand to either President Bill Clinton, who once waited outside the men's room at the UN—after Khatami delivered a speech—for a presumably washed one, or President Bush, who pre-empted an Iranian hand by inducting Khatami's government into the "axis of evil."

It was under former president Khatami that Iran had made the greatest effort to bridge its gap in relations with the United States, an effort spearheaded by Khatami himself but often undermined by hard-liners "on both sides," as he once said to me. Iranian politics has always, perhaps counterintuitively, favored Republican administrations over Democratic ones, stretching all the way back to the early days of the Shah's rule. It was a Republican administration (Eisenhower) that restored the Shah to his throne in 1953 after a Democratic one (Truman) refused British entreaties to stage a coup to remove the troublesome Mossadeq. Moreover, the Shah worried about Democratic presidents, who had, in his mind, a more emotional stance on the issue of human rights in its client states and allies. President Kennedy, although publicly a supporter of the Shah, also pressured him on human rights (and on implementing his "White Revolution," a plan to reform a still somewhat feudal Iran), but Lyndon Johnson, consumed as he was by the Vietnam War, was simply happy to have an Iran that could be reliably trusted to be in the "American camp."

Richard Nixon and Henry Kissinger, eager to overlook any human rights abuses by America's friends, perhaps did more for the Shah than any other administration, arming him to the teeth and granting him great latitude in raising oil prices, which in turn allowed him to proudly and vaingloriously build the fourth largest army in the world. President Ford merely continued Nixon's policy, but Jimmy Carter, who made human rights central to his campaign for the presidency, rang alarm bells in Tehran when he won the election in 1976. It was left to Ardeshir Zahedi, Iran's urbane ambassador to Washington and the Shah's once son-in-law, to ensure that the Carter administration didn't lose sight of the fact that Iran was America's closest ally in the region after Israel (with which Iran also had diplomatic and even good relations), and to downplay to the extent that he could any discussions of SAVAK, political prisoners, or human rights in general. But Jimmy Carter nonetheless pressed the Shah on human rights, particularly on the issue of political prisoners and SAVAK, despite his praise for him (and his famous declaration that Iran was an "island of stability," just as a revolution was taking form on New Year's Eve 1978). The Shah obliged to some extent, leading many Iranian supporters of his to declare, to this day, that the Islamic Revolution was Carter's fault if not his actual plan (along with the Sandinista victory in Nicaragua).

One might be forgiven for thinking that the Islamic revolutionary government that took over from the Shah's would feel somewhat indebted to Carter and fear no threat from him, but that was not the case. Quite the opposite, for although it recognized that Carter's pressing of the human rights issue weakened the Shah, it didn't trust the Democrats, who it saw, paradoxically as the Shah did, as members of a party that vacillated too often when it came to foreign relations. (And the fact that the revolution was about to embark on a killing spree, eliminating not just high-ranking members of the *ancien régime* but any political opposition to it, may have had something to do with the Islamic revolutionaries' concern with an American administration known to speak up on human rights.) With Republicans, Iranian politicians have always felt, they know where they stand and can adjust their policies accordingly, whereas with Democrats they have always felt unsure of how an administration might react to them and their policies, foreign *and* domestic. When Democrats are in power, the reasoning goes, U.S. support for or opposition to undemocratic regimes might change on a whim. President Obama's dilemma in formulating an Iran policy, and Iran's dilemma in how to deal with a Democratic administration, particularly after the June 2009 election and its bloody aftermath, were only compounded by Iran's suspicion of Democrats, although the new U.S. administration may have been less than aware of prevailing Iranian attitudes and long-standing paranoia toward the Democratic party.

Whether or not one chooses to believe the conspiracy theories surrounding the hostage crisis, a failed 1980 "October Surprise," or a Reagan November counter-surprise, there can be no doubt that Khomeini's government took full advantage of Ronald Reagan's defeat of Jimmy Carter in 1980 (helped as it was by the continuing hostage crisis). First, there were the Iran-Contra arms deals and then Reagan's subsequent emphasis on Afghanistan rather than Iran, even after Iranian client Hezbollah blew up the Marine barracks in Beirut, killing more than two hundred American soldiers. Reagan was preoccupied with his own "Evil Empire," and Iran with its war with Iraq, but the Reagan and George H. W. Bush years were marked less by outright hostility (albeit with the occasional flare-up, such as the 1998 incident where an IranAir passenger jet was shot down in the Persian Gulf by a navy ship, the USS *Vincennes*; the navy declared it an accident but Iranians considered it a deliberate act) than by a general disinterest in Iran by the U.S. administrations. It was under President Clinton that Iran once again became a prominent (if not center-stage) foreign policy issue when the new Democratic president revived publicly the U.S. policy of regime change in Iran, although admittedly in a somewhat halfhearted fashion; but Iran took careful notice.

Western interest in Iran, beyond unenthusiastic regime-change notions, grew dramatically after the election of Mohammad Khatami as its first reform president. The Clinton administration, looking for ways to jump-start a potential thaw in relations with its adversary, went as far as effectively apologizing for U.S. involvement in the 1953 coup (in a speech by Secretary of State Madeleine Albright), an apology and recognition that Iran had always demanded, but subsequently Bill Clinton referred to the Iranian leadership as "unelected," a word that gives the Iranian leadership an allergic reaction. Khatami, who had prevailed on the Supreme Leader to allow him latitude in exploring re-establishment of ties with what he saw as a willing U.S. administration, was effectively thwarted by one word, and distrust of the Democratic American administration and its intentions only intensified in Tehran.

The election of George W. Bush to the U.S. presidency, partly on a campaign promise to reduce American adventurism abroad, was greeted by the Iranian leadership with a shrug. They did think, however, that Republicans might be more inclined to deal with an "unelected" leader, and so Khatami was permitted to continue his efforts to bring about a slow thaw, if nothing else, in relations with the United States. The 9/11 tragedy was, as far as Iran was concerned, a perfect opportunity to move more quickly toward a rapprochement, something that Iran craved at the time. Khatami was the first Muslim leader to condemn the act, and the first to send his condolences to America, acts the Supreme Leader supported. Furthermore, Iranian authorities, usually quick to organize anti-American rallies with a seemingly unlimited supply of quick-burning American flags, allowed candlelight vigils, *without* flags, in Tehran for the victims of the terrorist attacks. That Al-Qaeda was responsible for the 9/11 attacks was helpful, given that Iran considered it an enemy as much as the West did, and that Afghanistan was soon to become the target of American wrath was almost a godsend, for other than Saddam Hussein's Baath Party, Iran loathed no other political group or party in the world more than the Taliban. Iran had been supporting the Northern Alliance in its war against the Taliban for years, had hosted some four million Afghan refugees in its territory, and had almost gone to war with Afghanistan in 1998. The Taliban had killed nine of Iran's diplomats then at its consulate in the northern city of Mazar-e-Sharif, an act of war as far as Iran was concerned. Cooler heads, including Khatami's and Khamenei's, ultimately prevailed but not until Iran amassed its troops on the border, ready to strike. The decision to not enter the "graveyard of empires" was a wise one in hindsight, for three years later America conveniently vanquished the foe on Iran's eastern border.

In 2001, though, Iran made it a policy to overtly support the American war against Afghanistan once it became apparent that the United States was intent on driving out the Taliban, to be replaced by Iran's allies, the Northern Alliance. There were practical considerations, not least of which was that Iranian assistance would, in the mind of Khatami and his administration, be rewarded by a Republican administration that might be receptive to restoring relations on a pragmatic basis, if nothing else. After 9/11 Bush proclaimed, "You're either with us, or with the terrorists." Iran was clearly "with us" on this one, even though it resented Bush's formulation of an either/or world. Early indications were that the U.S. administration appreciated Iran's offers to help in the war against the Taliban (and later on was very helpful, some in the Bush administration even say indispensable, in the attempts to form a new government in Afghanistan under Hamid Karzai).

President Khatami believed he was in a strong position in early January 2002, and his strategy of limited engagement seemed to be paying off. The seesawing Clinton days were over; a decisive Republican administration had taken over and had so far shown a willingness to deal with an adversary with shared interests. Even the hard-liners in Tehran were unable to persuade the Supreme Leader that Khatami, their bête noir, was weakening Iran, or worse, the revolution and its ideals, by collaborating with the United States. No one was under any illusion that U.S.-Iran ties would normalize immediately, and hard-liners thought that they could derail things at any time. But for

the moment, Khatami and his reformist allies were in control and had
the Supreme Leader's backing for baby steps along a path to détente.
Until, that is, George Bush's State of the Union address at the end of
the month, when for some inexplicable reason (other than an alleged
intention to someday march on Tehran), he placed Iran, along with
Iraq and North Korea, in an "axis of evil" and condemned it as an
enemy to be confronted by the United States (this just after ousting the
Taliban of Afghanistan, who would have undoubtedly been included
in said axis had they survived the initial American onslaught). And,
as if to pour salt on the wound, he resurrected Clinton's "unelected
leaders" terminology. On that day, Khatami told me later, he knew he
was dead—dead as in unable to alter the trajectory of U.S.-Iranian
relations, and dead as in his reformist ideals and plans were sure to be
crushed by the opposition, which had been waiting for such a moment
to declare any deals with the United States as fraught with deception
and double-dealing, and anathema to the Islamic Republic.

Beyond U.S.-Iranian relations, though, *all* ideas of reform were
tarred with the same feathers. Now, the prevailing attitude was that
any reform would weaken Iran. Khatami's credibility with conservatives sank to a new low. Hard-liners in Tehran rejoiced, for Bush had
proved their point that America was an untrustworthy, hegemonic
beast. Hard-liners (or neo-conservatives) rejoiced in Washington too,
but the reform movement in Iran and all who had championed a new
era in Iranian foreign policy, particularly as it applied to the United
States, took a blow from which it was going to be hard, if not impossible, to recover. Khatami was deterred but he pressed on, and he and
his top aides were successful in persuading Ayatollah Khamenei to
try one more approach with the Republican administration, one that
in 2003 appeared to be readying itself to remove Iran's *other* arch-foe,
Saddam Hussein.

Iran had a number of back-channel communication lines open

with the Bush administration, one of which was through Mohammad Javad Zarif, Iran's popular ambassador to the United Nations. Zarif had been instrumental in working with the U.S. administration on its Afghanistan efforts, and he never neglected to pay a visit to the Supreme Leader's office as well as to the president on his almost monthly trips back to Tehran. But it was there in Tehran, through the Swiss ambassador to Iran (who represented U.S. interests in the absence of diplomatic relations), that Khatami's administration decided to directly approach the White House, with an offer to meet and negotiate all areas of concern, including Iran's support for groups such as Hezbollah and its opposition to Israel as well as its nuclear program.

Sadeq Kharrazi, who was Iran's ambassador to Paris at the time and a nephew of Kamal Kharrazi, the foreign minister, was the main author of the now-infamous "letter to the Bush administration." The Swiss ambassador to Iran delivered the letter to U.S. officials, but the U.S. president ignored it and the White House rejected his conveying of the message as "interference" in the affairs of the United States. Some in the Bush administration even considered the letter a forgery, arguing that lacking a letterhead, the faxed document could not have been issued by the Iranian government, thus implying that the Swiss ambassador, extraordinary and plenipotentiary as his diplomatic title went, was also an *extraordinary* patsy.

Kharrazi was also a close advisor to Khatami (and remains so today), but as a relative by marriage (his sister is married to one of Khamenei's sons) he had the ear of the Supreme Leader, and his championing of yet another outreach to an American administration was crucial in thwarting any hard-line opposition to it. Any doubts as to the veracity of his communication could have been removed with a simple phone call, but back then the United States didn't "talk to evil." The letter, naturally, went unacknowledged and unanswered, and once again, as the United States began to deal with a post-Saddam Iraq, it wasn't just the United States (that might have benefited greatly from Iran's influence, and indeed help, in Iraq) that lost an opportunity, but also Khatami and the reformists, who were the ultimate losers for proving to the conservative opposition yet again the impossibility of dealing with America on an equal footing.

By now the Republicans had shed their reputation in Iran as the party of pragmatic deal-makers, and Bush's re-election in 2004 and a continuation of hostile U.S. rhetoric toward the Islamic Republic—still unanswered by Khatami—was a sign to conservatives that the only way to deal with the United States was to confront it. Still, the Supreme Leader followed Khatami's lead to a large extent, allowing him to suspend uranium enrichment in exchange for what promised to be a package of incentives from the West, including the United States, but the package wasn't delivered until the Iranian elections of 2005. And even then it was an ambiguous offer of future considerations if Iran agreed to forgo immediately its right to produce nuclear fuel on its own territory. Many argue that the Supreme Leader was willing to go along with his government's overtures to the United States, including sending the message to the Bush administration through the Swiss, only out of mere self-preservation—a fear that America might move against Iran militarily as it had against the Taliban and then Saddam. That is probably true to some extent in that in 2003 and 2004, Donald Rumsfeld's boastful "democracy is messy" years, Iran was seriously considering the possibility that whoever said "real men go to Tehran," a quote attributed to a senior U.S. official, wasn't kidding. But by the middle of 2005 when the West finally delivered its incentives package to Iran, whatever fears Iranians had of a U.S. invasion had largely disappeared, along with U.S. credibility, in the aftermath of the "messy" democratic experiment in Mesopotamia.

Khatami was in his last days as president, and the reform candidate

Mostafa Moin had lost spectacularly in the first round of the elections, but Ali Larijani, Iran's newly appointed chief nuclear negotiator, wasted no time in denouncing the Khatami administration as having been prepared, in its eagerness to deal with the United States, to "trade away a pearl for a lollipop." Of course Khatami would have rejected the incentives package just as Ahmadinejad did, and would have restarted the enrichment program as he did, but Iranian conservatives smelled blood and rushed to denounce Khatami's legacy as one of bending to the will of the West. This group of nations appeared to want to deal with Iran, but in fact put obstacles in Khatami's way every time he came close to achieving a breakthrough. It was a West that wouldn't even grant permission to Airbus to deliver a presidential aircraft to Khatami, one his administration had ordered and paid for but sat in a hanger in France because of U.S. objections to the deal, objections that were curiously removed once he was no longer president. (It is now the plane Ahmadinejad travels on for his yearly visits to New York.) The era of an open Iran—one where Jack Straw, the hapless British foreign secretary, made frequent trips to; one where even Prince Charles visited in the aftermath of the Bam earthquake of 2004 and met privately with President Khatami—seemed to be over.

And yet, it still wasn't quite over—not yet. President Ahmadinejad took a more confrontational approach to the nuclear issue and later toward Israel, but the Supreme Leader, while preferring Ahmadinejad's style to the mild-mannered Khatami's, kept his options open. Not only did he continue to meet with Khatami, Kharrazi, and other reformists, but also he sanctioned a 2006 trip by Khatami to the United States, ostensibly a private visit but one that he knew could be a test of what the Bush administration might agree to with respect to Iran's nuclear program, and even with respect to the possibility of a "grand bargain." At one gathering at Ambassador Zarif's residence in New York, in an elaborate dining room with an unnoticed Monet hanging on the wall,

Khatami gave a talk over dinner to the Council on Foreign Relations, one that focused on the nuclear issue.

In his talk, Khatami fiercely defended Iran's position on enrichment, and even Ahmadinejad's foreign policy (which was realistically not that different from his), but suggested to the audience, which included Richard Haass, the president of the council, that if the Bush administration agreed to allow Iran a pilot program for uranium enrichment, Iran might be willing to limit it to 164 centrifuges spinning and keep it as a research and development project as long as negotiations continued. In the audience also was George Soros, a member of the council, who came up to me after dinner and asked if he could make Khatami's suggestion public.

"No!" exclaimed Khatami, when I asked him.

"But that's the only way to embarrass the Bush administration, to show the American public that Iran isn't so unreasonable after all," said Soros, and I translated for Khatami.

"No," he repeated, shaking his head. "I'm a private citizen and I don't speak for the government, and these things should be kept private." His implication was that the Bush administration would know that whatever Khatami said had the blessing of the Supreme Leader, and the Council on Foreign Relations was a good enough conduit to the White House, but Iran wasn't about to put its cards on the table publicly, only to be embarrassed yet again. Needless to say, nothing ever came of the dinner conversation, and the concept of either lifting preconditions for negotiations with Iran or allowing a pilot enrichment program, a face-saving solution for a proud Iran, never went further, not until an Obama presidency became a real possibility.

In 2009, after the presidential election in Iran and the unrest that ensued, and while over four thousand Iranian centrifuges were spinning happily away in Natanz, in one of the court proceedings against arrested "agitators," Kian Tajbakhsh, an Iranian-American who had once worked for Soros's Open Society Institute, claimed that Khatami and Soros (along with Zarif at his New York residence in 2006) had plotted the overthrow of the Islamic regime. Tajbakhsh knew nothing of Khatami's brief chance encounter with Soros the night of the dinner party at Zarif's residence, but the Iranian intelligence services *did*, for they probably had tapes of the short conversation (which Zarif was not a part of) as well as witnesses, as did, no doubt, the U.S. National Security Agency and the CIA. (The account of Khatami's trip to the United States in my book *The Ayatollah Begs to Differ* was also used by the hard-liners in Tehran as evidence of Khatami's treachery, and I was compelled to issue a forceful denial of any plotting or secret meetings between Soros and Khatami, which was picked up by most of the Iranian media in Tehran, save for the hard-line media that suggested a plot in the first place.) In any event, Supreme Leader Khamenei was intimately aware of what transpired during Khatami's trip to the United States as a private citizen, which was nothing, at least in terms of relations or negotiations between the Bush administration and the Islamic Republic. In 2007 I asked Khatami, at one of my meetings with him in Tehran, if he still, two years into the Ahmadinejad administration, talked to Ayatollah Khamenei. "Yes, indeed," he replied. "The difference now, though," he continued, contrasting the time when he was president and was unable to accomplish much of what he wanted to, "is that he *listens*."

Supreme Leader Ayatollah Khamenei may have started to *really* listen to Khatami and moderate voices only after they were out of office and therefore unable to execute policy, perhaps one reason why he also tolerated or even encouraged Ahmadinejad's frequent outreaches, clumsy as they were, to the United States. Perhaps the Supreme Leader agreed all along with Khatami's notion that rapprochement with the United States was advisable for and beneficial to Iran; it was just that he didn't want the reformists to take the credit for what would have been a popular initiative if it had come to fruition under their watch. Obama's election meant the Democrats were back in power, the party Iranians tended not to trust to make deals, but it also meant Iran lost its easy target, an American administration much of the world disliked. Obama's promises to close the detention center at Guantánamo, to stop CIA extraordinary renditions, to forbid torture, and to treat the world with respect meant a renewed American moral standing, and demonizing the most popular American political figure since John F. Kennedy was not going to be an easy task, particularly if Obama also followed through on his promise to negotiate with Iran without preconditions.

After the Iranian New Year in 2009, I was once again in Iran, this time after Roxana Saberi, an Iranian-American freelance journalist, had been arrested and jailed for spying. (Saberi, a onetime beauty queen from North Dakota with an Iranian father and Japanese mother, had lived in Iran for about six years, learning Farsi, reporting for various U.S. and British media, and doing the occasional translation work. Her arrest as a spy had come as a surprise to everyone, even some in the government with whom she had good relations.) One day I was invited, or really summoned, to the Ministry of Culture and Islamic Guidance, for "tea" with the head of the Foreign Correspondents Bureau, I was told—"tea" usually being the euphemism for questioning or an interrogation. Well, at least it wasn't at the Ministry of Intelligence, so it couldn't be terribly serious, I thought, likely just the government trying to ascertain how friendly or unfriendly to the regime I really was. Mohsen Moghadaszadeh, the gentle bureau chief, spent a good twenty minutes complimenting me, in keeping with true Persian ta'arouf, telling me how invaluable my contribution could be to Iranian journalism but more important to the understanding of Iran in the English-speaking world—"*could* be," perhaps a hint that he was giving me a little of that Islamic guidance his ministry was charged with imparting.

"It doesn't help the understanding of Iran," I said, "when someone like Roxana Saberi is arrested and thrown in jail on what appear to be unfounded charges, at least as far as the Western media is concerned."

"Let me tell you a story about Ms. Saberi," said Moghadaszadeh. "Two years ago, I asked her to tea, right here in this office, and she sat exactly where you are sitting." I was on a long couch at one corner of his expansive office, and he was in an armchair by my side. "I told her that the authorities do not see it fit, *salah nemeedoonan*, for her to continue as a journalist in Iran, and that I wouldn't be renewing her press pass." I took a sip of tea from the small glass in front of me, intrigued by his candid reference to the "authorities," another euphemism, in this case for the intelligence services, which he either was a part of or had to maintain close ties to because of his work.

"But why would the authorities not see it fit for her to continue her journalism?' I asked.

"*What* journalism?" said Moghadaszadeh. "She had filed a few reports at one time, but didn't have any assignments as far as we knew. She said she was writing a book, but how long does it take to write a book?" He looked at me, perhaps hoping I would shed some light on the creative process.

"A book can take a long time," I said, "and freelance journalism means assignments can be few and far between."

"Well, she was going to parties and doing all sorts of things that weren't compatible with being a journalist, or even an author." Moghadaszadeh was admitting that she had been under surveillance. I wondered for a moment if he was implying that I, too, was not only under surveillance but engaging in activities "incompatible" with being a writer, such as going to parties, which I did often in Tehran, but which I, silly me, thought was essential to my work.

"Given that President Obama has reached out to Iran," I said, "I think it can only be harmful to Iran to imprison an American who few people believe could be a spy or the slightest threat to the country's national security. The Bush era is over, and there's a real opportunity for both Iran and America now."

"She hasn't been arrested for no reason, I assure you," said Moghadaszadeh. "There's plenty of evidence, and it will come to light. I could tell you stories, but we'll leave it at that." He paused for a moment, as if weighing whether to continue. "Do you know what her reaction was when I told her the authorities didn't want her to continue as a journalist?" he said, staring straight into my eyes.

"No," I replied. He continued to stare at me for a moment before continuing.

"Excuse me," lowering his gaze, "and I'm truly sorry to use this kind of language, but she essentially said, well, she said she *didn't give a fuck.*"

"Really?" I said, surprised.

"In so many words," said Moghadaszadeh, and I wondered if he took Saberi's reaction as a personal affront, a reaction that I'm confident was less rude than he believed.

"I'm sure she didn't mean anything," I said, "she probably felt that Iran's form of democracy allowed her certain latitudes." Moghadaszadeh was silent for a moment, probably not wanting to contradict my assertion that Iran was a democracy, and then he changed the subject. He was curious about the American media's apparent obsession with Obama, and he wanted to emphasize to me that Iran was being as open to change in its foreign policy as could be expected, given that as far as Iran was concerned, it hadn't actually witnessed a change in American policy yet. It was early, I told him, and as Obama himself had mentioned, the U.S. government was a like a big ship that couldn't necessarily turn on a dime. He smiled at that analogy, and I was surprised that he hadn't heard it before.

"I hope the American media," he said, and he was referring to me too, "will portray Iran more fairly from now on, and that they won't automatically believe everything their government says about Iran."

A FEW DAYS later, I was at the Ministry of Foreign Affairs, attending the Monday-morning weekly press briefing for foreign journalists and Iranian journalists working for the foreign media. The ministry was a sort of ground zero in Iran's attempts to formulate a response to President Obama's outreach to Iran, as well as the government's most visible and constant face to the world, especially since few Iranian officials give interviews or hold press conferences.

The ministry's spokesperson at the time, Hassan Qashqavi, was the Iranian official journalists turned to for information during the Roxana Saberi saga, much to his chagrin (he was replaced in November 2009 by Ramin Mehmanparast). "It's not my job!" he told me afterward in his spacious office over the obligatory tea and biscuits served at every Iranian meeting. "The judiciary has its own spokesman and they are independent," he continued, frustrated by the incessant questions he would rather not answer (but true to Iranian form he does so none-theless, even if unsatisfactorily, for the expression "no comment" is virtually unheard in Iran).

Roxana Saberi's case continued to be headline news in the West but was mentioned less in the Iranian media, and Qashqavi pointed to it as emblematic of how the Western media covers Iran. "My statement on Roxana Saberi, when it was first reported that she was arrested, mentioned two issues, but the media only quoted the first," he said. "I said that her press credentials had expired, *and* that she had been gathering information illegally. The media left out the second part so that it appeared she had been guilty of only a very minor infraction, and when she was later formally charged with espionage, they made it appear as though charges were being made up along the way." As a onetime journalist himself, Qashqavi proudly told me, he was hoping Saberi's case would be resolved quickly and that she would be freed soon, but he suggested that double standards are applied to Iran in almost every instance of disagreement or conflict with the West. "No one cares about the Iranian diplomats imprisoned by the Americans in Iraq for over two years *without charge*," he said, "while we [ministry officials] are the ones who have to answer to their families when they come here regularly to get, no, insist on, any information about their loved ones." (The Obama administration freed the Iranian diplomats two months later.) I suggested to him that if Iran did indeed have evidence of illegal activity by Saberi, it should make it public or specify what it is she is accused of doing.

"Why," he said indignantly, "should we discuss issues of national security openly? Do the Americans provide evidence to the press when they send someone to Guantánamo, or when they arrest an Iranian in Iraq? Why is it that the media assume Iranians are always guilty and Americans always innocent? And why does Mrs. Clinton assume that Saberi is innocent, without knowing any of the details?"

"I agree," I said, "that there might be some double standards sometimes, but you know, with a new administration in Washington there's a real belief that things are going to change, and Iran can benefit greatly if it takes advantage of the opportunity, which I don't think will be there forever."

"And I agree," said Qashqavi, uncharacteristically for a politically conservative Iranian official. "In Ms. Saberi's case, you will see that we are not just making things up, but that there is real cause for her detention and the judicial inquiries. It will come to light later, but in the meantime, we will do everything to secure her quick release." Clearly, Qashqavi understood that the Saberi case could be a serious obstacle to future negotiations with the United States, especially if

Iran hoped to engage on equal footing. When Saberi was released less than a month later, the "evidence" that Iran claimed it had was revealed to be her possession of a document that she had taken from a quasi-governmental think tank, the Institute for Strategic Studies. The institute is run by the powerful Expediency Council and employs scores of former top officials from previous administrations who, unlike in the United States or in Europe, would have had no place to work in the private sector when their administration stepped down. It was scarcely the stuff of espionage, but the Iranian government felt vindicated somewhat that it hadn't been manufacturing a case against an American just as the new Obama administration had begun its outreach to the Islamic Republic.

WHILE QASHQAVI and other senior Iranian officials were busy debating the pros and cons of relations with America after the inauguration of President Obama, they must have also thrown the occasional nervous glance at the former U.S. Embassy a few blocks north of the Foreign Ministry as they drove home every day. A vast complex set on acres of prime Tehran real estate, the embassy had been transformed into a barracks for the Revolutionary Guards after the hostage crisis and a small museum testifying to the crimes of the "Great Satan" that oddly seems to be open only very occasionally and never when I have visited. With the United States under President Bush and Vice President Dick Cheney, there had been no question of improving relations, but with the new Obama administration there actually was much debate in Iran, before the election crisis of 2009, about what the future of Iranian-American relations would look like. Openly discussed was the idea that there might even be an American presence in Iran, after thirty years, at that same embassy.

One Friday afternoon in late May, less than two weeks before the election, I was driving through downtown Tehran, looking for Ahmadinejad campaign posters with an NBC crew. We stopped at a busy intersection where a huge Mohsen Rezai banner was being affixed to a light pole by workers. Rezai, an eight-year commander of the Revolutionary Guards and a member of the Expediency Council, a governmental body that arbitrates between Parliament and the Guardian Council (and serves as advisory body to the Supreme Leader), was the lone conservative challenger to President Ahmadinejad, and was running far behind in the few polls that were conducted in the weeks leading up to election day. I greeted two campaign officials, former Revolutionary Guards themselves, who were guiding the workers, and I told them that we were from the United States, asking if they knew where we could find an Ahmadinejad poster. "His campaign has given up on Tehran," one man in a crumpled gray suit said. "But there's one poster on a side street two blocks up—turn left there," he gestured up the avenue. His co-worker, a man in his early fifties and with a reconstructed jaw, I presumed due to injuries suffered in the Iran-Iraq War, invited us, me and my American friends with their elaborate camera and lighting equipment, to a Rezai rally that evening. "There'll be plenty of free food!" he said emphatically. I thanked them, said we would try to swing by, and went back to our car. "*Inshallah*," the man in the gray suit shouted after me, "this time next year, the U.S. Embassy will be open." I turned to see him and his co-worker beaming, and they gave me a friendly wave. What had been unimaginable a year before was being talked about only a few months into Obama's presidency, and not just by liberals.

BEFORE THE Iranian presidential elections, every Iranian official I came across was curious about what I, a visiting writer from New York, thought of President Obama's intentions with regard to Iran,

and without exception, everyone, including Qashqavi and Ali Akbar
Rezaie, the director general of the North and Central American desk
at the Foreign Ministry, and even many mullahs in Qom, were conciliatory in their tone and guardedly optimistic about a future détente.
Also without exception, every Iranian government official decried the
lack of attention the U.S. media paid to the ongoing sanctions against
Iran and the still-belligerent attitude, to them, from the U.S. government. On the one hand, they couldn't help but applaud Obama's
softer tone and respectful messages, and on the other, they were
dismayed by talk of "all options on the table" and threats of further
sanctions or military action unless Iran "behaved." The deputy minister of science, research, and technology, Dr. Seyed Mohammad
Hosseini (who became the minister of culture and Islamic guidance
in Ahmadinejad's second term), however, reminded me one day of a
passage from the Koran: "If there's even a *small* chance of a peaceful
overture being genuine," he said, "one should welcome and accept
it." Although before the June election Iranian officials weren't yet
convinced that Obama's overtures were entirely peaceful, they were
willing, or felt obliged, to give the United States the benefit of doubt.
Islam, after all, told them to.

The Iranian presidential election of 2009 changed the U.S.-Iran
dynamic, of course, in a way that had been wholly unpredictable. Some
on the American left (and many Iranians living in the United States)
had already heavily criticized President Obama for suggesting that as
far as America was concerned, there would be no difference between
an Ahmadinejad and a Mousavi presidency. He was right, of course, for
Mousavi was a regime insider and had made it clear in his campaign
that when it came to the nuclear issue, the most pressing matter to
Obama and the United States, his policy would not be very different.
In fact, he barely acknowledged that the nuclear issue was an issue
he had any control over; the Supreme National Security Council, of

which he, as president, would be only one member, controls such decisions. On other matters of great concern to the United States, such as Hezbollah, Hamas, Iran's influence in the region and beyond, and Iranian involvement in Iraq and Afghanistan, Mousavi also differed only slightly from Ahmadinejad, and again, they were areas where an Iranian president might have some influence but not areas where he would be the *decider*, to use George Bush's term again.

The decider on matters of national security, foreign policy, and military strategy is the commander in chief of the Islamic Republic, the Supreme Leader, and he isn't called *Supreme* for nothing. (According to some reports, Obama, in recognition of that supremeness, had sent one or two letters directly to Ayatollah Khamenei, but neither the White House nor the Iranian office of the velayat-e-faqih would confirm or deny it.) President Obama was correct in believing he would face a difficult foe and tough negotiator in Iran no matter who won the presidential election, but Mousavi supporters, indeed supporters of all three challengers to Ahmadinejad, recognized that it would be much easier for President Obama to break bread with Mousavi or one of their candidates, *any* candidate, than with a Holocaust-denying, Shia millenarian like Mahmoud Ahmadinejad. And there was the expectation, not just in Iran but across the world, that the next president of Iran would be negotiating at some point on behalf of his nation and his Supreme Leader with the new, black, and son-of-a-Muslim president of the United States.

President Ahmadinejad, perhaps unreasonably, held out hope that a face-to-face meeting might happen sooner rather than later. Well after the election and during a lull in the street violence, he reiterated his offer to meet with and "debate" Obama at the annual meeting of the UN General Assembly, where both he and Obama were due to deliver statements. Immediately after the flawed vote, Ahmadinejad had complained—whined really—that Obama did not congratulate him on his astounding victory, especially as he had congratulated Obama on *his* victory, a felicitation, he reminded us, that had not yet received so much as a simple thank you. Ahmadinejad was not going to forget the perceived slight, it seemed, but he was determined to engage Obama nonetheless. The White House, meanwhile, seemed at a loss. It was impossible for Barack Obama to ignore the brutality on the streets of Tehran and the overwhelming evidence that the Iranian electoral count was tainted. But he was also aware, much more so than his predecessors, that interfering in the internal politics of Iran might endanger the very groups the United States was inclined to support.

PRESIDENT OBAMA continued to walk a fine line, a *very* fine line, between expressing support for the opposition to Ahmadinejad, for the Green Movement, and not interfering in the domestic affairs of a sovereign nation. That balancing act exposed him and his administration to charges from all sides of the political spectrum (both in the United States and in Iran) that either he wasn't doing enough to support a democratic movement or, when he *did* express concern about government brutality, he was injecting the United States into Iran's internal affairs. Curiously some on the American right, such as former vice president Dick Cheney and Senator John McCain, who began criticizing the Obama administration for its tepid support of Iranian protesters and the Green Movement, were the very same politicians who had once, quite recently, called the leaders of the Green Movement terrorist supporters and enemies of the United States, and had encouraged the notion of a military strike against Iran.

Iran-expert exiles, by far the majority siding with the Green Movement, weighed in with the White House and on television and radio programs. Some demanded that Obama refuse to negotiate with an illegitimate president, while others advised caution in his

Iran policy. In the end, there was little that President Obama could do, other than fulfill his campaign promise to use diplomacy to end the threat of a nuclear Iran. Refusing to negotiate would enable the Ahmadinejad government to claim that the United States, as was the case with Hamas's election, only respected democracy if its preferred candidates won. Those who argued that human rights should be at the top of any U.S. agenda with respect to Iran were ignoring the fact that unless the United States *first* had some form of relationship with Iran, even if it began with a nuclear deal, arguing about human rights was going to be ineffective and possibly counterproductive. Iranian government officials pointed out to me time and again that President Obama's famous "Cairo speech," his first message to the Muslim world five months into his presidency, was delivered in the capital of a country not only where hundreds of political prisoners languished in jails, but also where security forces perpetually broke up labor strikes, street protests, and demonstrations against President Hosni Mubarak's government, using as much violence and bloodshed as in Iran, if not more—and with nary a peep from either the White House or the Western media. For some Iranians, the American measure of human rights was merely whether pop-singer Beyoncé would be able to perform a concert (yes in Egypt, as she did; *no* in Iran, where female vocalists can only perform live if they are background singers—in hijab). Nonetheless, as the Green Movement continued to show strength into 2010, the calls for President Obama to support the opposition grew, particularly from Iranian expatriates, but Obama generally resisted the temptation. The experts never adequately answered the questions of why the Iranian government, which had never listened to unilateral U.S. demands in the past, would suddenly change course if Obama rattled his saber. Doing nothing was not the worst option for President Obama, unlike all the bad options he faced in Afghanistan and Iraq, but pressure, especially after nuclear talks seemed to go nowhere, was building and it was going to be hard for the administration to remain as aloof as it had been in its first two years.

PRESIDENT AHMADINEJAD didn't ultimately get his one-on-one meeting with Obama at the UN in 2009, even though he sat patiently through Obama's speech—delivered before the revelation that Iran had built a secret nuclear site near Qom—listening intently through his earphones, perhaps in the hope that Obama would reciprocate and sit through *his* speech. But Ahmadinejad had the misfortune to be scheduled to speak much later in the afternoon. Before the Iranian president took the microphone, however, Muammar Qaddafi, in his first-ever address to the world body, spoke for over an hour and a half, ignoring the fifteen-minute unofficial time limit (as most leaders do) and causing his personal interpreter, one he flew in from Tripoli, to collapse toward the end, shaking and screaming, for everyone to hear, "I can't take it anymore!" Ahmadinejad's speech was delayed by well over an hour, and by that time some delegates might have felt as Qaddafi's interpreter did: the thought of another rambling, repetitive diatribe against the West and the UN Security Council by a Muslim leader would be too much to take. When Ahmadinejad took to the podium, only a handful of countries' delegates were in the room, so he spoke to an almost empty chamber (which was not shown on Iranian state television). Needless to say, neither President Obama nor the U.S. delegation were in their seats, and it is unlikely that they would have been, even if Ahmadinejad had spoken earlier. For as President Obama remarked later in the fall when signing another one-year extension of sanctions on Iran, "Our relations with Iran have not yet returned to normal." The Iranian president immediately condemned the statement as "childish" and a "grave blunder." (Ahmadinejad is, I'm sure, unaware of the racist implications of calling a black man childish, and he probably thought it actually much sweeter than the usual Iranian denunciation of American presidents.)

Ahmadinejad and his obedient foreign minister, Manouchehr Mottaki, recognizing Barack Obama's popularity even in countries where Iran held greater sway than the United States, had in fact tried hard on their 2009 visit to New York to strike a conciliatory, polite, and even admiring tone with respect to the American president. Their buddy Hugo Chavez had joked, after all, in his address to the UN, that the podium "no longer smelled of sulfur," a reference to his previous pronouncement at the world body that likened George W. Bush to the devil himself. In every public appearance and interview, Ahmadinejad and Mottaki went out of their way to praise Obama the person, if not the U.S. government, and to present themselves as the kind of statesmen their own people no longer seemed to think *they* were.

Ahmadinejad was in the middle of an interview with *Time* magazine the morning that President Obama, with Prime Minister Gordon Brown of Great Britain and President Nicolas Sarkozy of France by his side, announced to the world that Iran had a secret uranium enrichment facility under construction in a mountainside on a heavily fortified Revolutionary Guard base near Qom, unannounced and hidden from UN inspectors. Early in the interview, *Time*'s managing editor, Richard Stengel, broke the news of the upcoming announcement to Ahmadinejad, who smiled uncomfortably as he listened. "Mr. *Obama* is about to say this?" he asked incredulously. When Stengel affirmed it, Ahmadinejad's response was, "So, is *all* the information that Mr. Obama receives of the same nature?" Although not entirely a clear response, it was Ahmadinejad's way of saying that he believed Obama was being ill advised and fed inaccurate information. Not that Obama *himself* was in the wrong, but that he was being manipulated by other forces. It was clear to any Iranian that Ahmadinejad's reaction was genuine, even if his ta'arouf about Obama, unwilling to condemn him directly, was calculated. The Iranian president wasn't caught in a "gotcha!" moment as some believed, for Iran had already informed the IAEA two weeks prior of the nuclear site and believed it was well within its rights under the Non-Proliferation Treaty; rather, he was surprised that Obama would resort, in his mind, to a crude anti-Iran propaganda moment. *Obama*, hero of the world, he of the "extended hand," follow the standard U.S. foreign policy playbook? *Nah!* He must have been under the influence of bad advisors. Ahmadinejad and others in the Iranian leadership were perhaps shrewd enough to recognize that it was foolhardy to demonize Obama less than a year into office, but they were also thinking, unlike "tea partiers" in the United States, that "the black man with an African and Muslim name who might even hail from Bushehr can't be all bad."

IRANIANS WEREN'T the only people to be thrown off balance by the election of President Obama; leftists everywhere, including in the United States, were busy adjusting to the idea that their vehement denunciations of the George Bush era and an American foreign policy that harked back to the darkest days of imperialism were finally being heard, and taken seriously, across the globe. It was always a curious phenomenon that Americans on the far left generally sympathized more with the right in Iran—the hard-liners who believed America could do no good—than with the reformists and liberals on the Iranian left who believed in a more democratic society at home and greater interaction with the West, even a Satanic America, abroad. Leftists who in the 1960s and 1970s were quick to throw their support behind democratic movements in Latin America and elsewhere were generally and remarkably silent when it came to Iran, perhaps because Iran's anti-imperialist and anti-American stands were more attractive to their own philosophies than the idea of an Iran in the American camp, with a Starbucks and a McDonald's on every Tehran street corner, F-18s and Stingers in its arsenal, and ExxonMobil getting even richer delivering Iranian oil to American automobiles.

The 2009 election in Iran, or particularly the brutal and bloody aftermath, caused many on the American left to re-examine their view of the government in Iran, and many leftist luminaries (such as Noam Chomsky) threw their support to the Green Movement even as they continued to decry American interference in Iran's internal affairs and U.S. imperialist goals in the region. Many American liberals turned Green, literally on their Facebook profiles and figuratively in their expressions of sympathy for Iranian protesters, but very few advocated an American policy that would inject the United States directly into the Iranian crisis. Just as the extreme left began to view Obama with an almost equal disdain as the extreme right, however, some American leftists began to blame the United States for Iran's post-election disturbances rather than an increasingly fascistic Iranian administration. It came as no surprise, then, that some dissenters, both Iranian and American, in an America shocked by the events in Iran in 2009, claimed not only that the presidential election was free and fair, or as free and fair as those in the United States, but that any street protests, and accompanying media coverage, were part of a larger plot to overthrow the regime in Tehran.

I WAS PRESENT when a handful of those dissenters gathered in New York's Greenwich Village two months after the election, away from the glare of the media (with the exception of the bureau chief and cameraman from the Islamic Republic of Iran Broadcasting, or IRIB, network), to present the case for Mahmoud Ahmadinejad. They managed to attract a standing-room-only crowd: Iranians who curiously, with the exception of a lone hijab-clad young woman (in a green headscarf no less), did not adhere to Islamic dress codes, and progressive Americans of all ages, some in T-shirts emblazoned with the words "Arrest Bush" or "End the blockade on Cuba," who remain reliably and charmingly steadfast in their conviction that the United States is up to no good in its adventures abroad.

One speaker described the incongruity of the signs printed in English carried by Tehran demonstrators ("Where is my vote?"), pointing to it as an example of a pre-planned foreign plot, perhaps unaware that Ahmadinejad's own government hands out signs, also in English, at pro-government rallies. Another speaker claimed that "this was one of the *freest* elections in the recorded memory of the Islamic Republic," presenting Interior Ministry charts and figures that showed the breakdown of the vote tally, oblivious to the comedic aspect of presenting as irrefutably factual the numbers provided by the winner in a disputed election.

Sara Flounders, a director of the International Action Center, a progressive activist nongovernmental organization, or NGO, founded by Ramsey Clark, said she believed the events of the previous two months proved there had been evidence of American interference and malfeasance. However, an Iranian-American peace and human rights activist reminded her that "we in the progressive movement have to be very careful not to fall into the dichotomy of either/or, and it's hard for us to forget that we have an Islamic Republic that in terms of political process is *not* progressive, has been very oppressive, and at the same time we should remember that the Iranian government has been executing a lot of political prisoners in the past thirty years," her statement betraying the unease even some Iranian supporters of the regime felt with the events of the summer of 2009. "Unfortunately," Flounders replied in a cool and deliberate tone, "in a crisis, you *do* have to choose sides, and there *is* an either/or." The crisis for her was that the election unrest was an attempt to overthrow the Islamic Republic—virtually

THE AYATOLLAHS' DEMOCRACY 201

the last stand on the planet for reflexive anti-Americanism—and the side these activists wanted to be on was *not* America's, not even in the age of Obama.

This group represents a tiny minority, to be sure, but despite their mistrust of American intentions and President Obama's commitment to progressivism, Obama was actually doing precisely what they wanted. Progressives in America generally worry less about Iran's nuclear program than mainstream Democrats or Republicans do, some choosing to believe that even if Iran develops a bomb it has every right to do so, given the hostility that emanates from the United States and Israel, both of which, they are quick to point out, already have many nuclear bombs. And an America that speaks to Iran respectfully is preferable to an America that threatens and sanctions it, regardless of the nature of the Tehran regime.

Progressives must have been relieved then, when in October 2009 President Obama made good on his offer to negotiate with Iran without preconditions and secured what appeared to be a deal on Iran's nuclear program that could satisfy all sides. Ahmadinejad's government, keen as ever to conclude an agreement quickly and make friends with Obama, indicated its approval for what was to be an exchange of Iran's low-enriched uranium stock for the higher-enriched uranium it needed to fuel its medical reactor in Tehran. For a moment it seemed that both Ahmadinejad and Obama would be able to take credit for lowering the temperature in a crisis that was threatening to boil over to war, particularly since the election of the hawkish Benjamin Netanyahu as prime minister of Israel. With most of Iran's uranium supply removed from the country only to be returned as fuel rods, the threat of its building a bomb would be radically diminished as far as the United States and its allies were concerned. Unlike in past discussions, which had always included a demand for Iran to suspend enrichment activities, because no mention of enrichment was made,

Ahmadinejad immediately claimed a victory over the West. However, he didn't anticipate the criticism that followed from across the entire Iranian political spectrum, from staunch reformists to the hard-liners to his right. In many ways it was a taste of his own medicine: suddenly it was him and not a reformist who was being accused of bending over backward for the United States, and making deals that were not in Iran's interest. It didn't help that the U.S. government and the Western media portrayed the 2009 deal as one restricting Iran's ability to manufacture a bomb, implying a weaker Iran and undercutting any support there might have been for the deal in Iran.

No, Ahmadinejad wasn't going to get away with it—not even with a partner like Obama. The conservatives he had alienated jumped to declare the deal a mistake, with Ali Larijani, the speaker of Parliament going as far as saying, "The recent actions of this country [United States], presenting unimportant and irrational proposals in the nuclear issue which they have called just and fair, all indicate that the alleged change [in American foreign policy] was nothing but a deceitful symbol aimed at deceiving naive politicians." Ahmadinejad, *naive*? The reformists and the Green Movement meanwhile, sensing an opportunity not to be lost, also declared Ahmadinejad's deal an insult to Iran (echoing his description of Khatami's dealings with the West), positioning themselves as defenders of Iran's rights who, unlike the president, wouldn't be so easily seduced by the *man from Bushehr.*

The deal that was offered was in reality not that different from an idea floated during the presidency of Khatami, to send Iran's enriched uranium to Russia for conversion into fuel rods for its yet-to-be-built reactors. That idea had been anathema to conservatives at the time, including Ahmadinejad, who felt that reliance on foreign suppliers of fuel could only lead to diminished independence for Iran. Ahmadinejad in 2009 had made the mistake of believing he was the decider, perhaps because of his easy win at the ballot box (or easy win on Interior

Ministry computers), when in reality powerful men opposed to him still held sway with the real decider, the Supreme Leader, who would not be seduced so easily. Nevertheless, Ahmadinejad scrambled, looking for a way to salvage a nuclear deal while backing off from his initial assertion that what had been offered was a win for Iran. In an offer Foreign Minister Mottaki made just before Christmas, Iran floated the idea of a simultaneous exchange of its uranium for fuel rods, a gradual swap of uranium on Kish Island, in the Persian Gulf. But the United States was steadfast in its assertion that Iran either accept the deal as offered in October or face additional sanctions and penalties in 2010.

THE WESTERN MEDIA paid scant attention to Iran's counteroffers while the Iranian media made them headlines, indicating to Iranians that it was the United States, even under a new president, that was not following up on its promise to negotiate with Iran. As late as a week before Christmas 2009, President Ahmadinejad made another appeal for talks, almost pleading with the United States to consider alternatives to its original proposal. Again, this appeal made headlines in Iran but hardly warranted a mention in the Western mainstream media. "Iran is ready to strike a uranium enrichment deal if the United States and the West respect the Islamic Republic and stop making threats," was one headline in the state-controlled media. Ahmadinejad was quoted as saying, "Everything is possible, 400 kilos, 800 kilos, it's nothing," a reference to the amount of enriched uranium Iran was expected to ship out of the country under a confidence-boosting agreement, and "We are ready to sit down at the table to reach an agreement." He added that no deal could happen while Iran was being threatened, a return to the Iranian insistence, for years, that Iranians would not buckle under threats or intimidation, a hallmark, they were convinced, of the Bush administration's approach to Iran. "From the outset, delivering 1200

kilos of uranium was not a problem for us." At the climate change conference in Copenhagen at the end of the year, Ahmadinejad remarked,
"But they believe they can wave a stick to threaten us—those days are
over—they are threatening us now, with sanctions, with resolutions,
pressure, it's going backwards." Ahmadinejad was reiterating what every
Iranian official has expressed to me vis-à-vis American threats and the
concept of "carrots and sticks": fear would not drive their decision. "If
we want to make a bomb we would not be afraid of the United States,"
he said, "but we do not want to make a bomb."

For Obama doubters in Tehran, the actions of the administration
in late 2009 were a vindication of their belief that the new U.S. president was at best only willing to pay lip service to real change, especially after Iranian officials indicated a willingness to negotiate with
the United States further. Two days of face-to-face diplomacy, a deal
structured by the West and offered to the Iranians, and rejection of
any subsequent counteroffers qualified as change? Threats of "crippling sanctions" unless Iran did as it was told qualified as respectful
engagement? While the U.S. Congress set about debating petroleum
sanctions against Iran, and as the United States geared up to send
additional troops into Afghanistan, the Iranian government continued
to assail Obama's faux change in foreign policy.

Having voiced moral support for Iran's opposition, as recently as in
his Nobel Peace Prize acceptance speech, President Obama had, in
fact, made diplomacy more challenging. Not only had the opposition
voiced strong opposition to the nuclear deal as presented by the West,
they had warned Obama not to expect some advantage because of the
Iranian president's apparent domestic weakness. Mehdi Karroubi, the
most outspoken of the opposition leaders, said, in an interview with the
London Times only a week after Ahmadinejad's pleas in Copenhagen
for further diplomacy, that "we ask Western governments not to use
this internal situation as a bargaining chip with the present Iranian

Government to reach agreements which would undermine the rights of the Iranian people." Karroubi was indicating that any deal that looked good to the West would come under close scrutiny in Tehran, not just by Ahmadinejad but also by every other political figure with any influence with the leadership. In the same interview, he also warned the West, a code word for the United States and therefore Obama, not to interfere in the domestic squabbles in Iran, not to give in to the temptation to offer support, moral or otherwise, to the Green Movement. "The challenges in this country should be solved by its own people," he said, quite confident that the civil rights movement he led would be ultimately successful in its goals.

Meanwhile, Obama's critics in America, who had been quick to criticize his Iran strategy at the country's first vacillation, didn't understand that a nod and a wink from an Iranian president was meaningless, not deceitful. Iran's president was always going to need the approval of Parliament, powerful politicians, and the Ayatollahs before finally committing his signature to any memoranda of understanding. Obama, who *did* seem to understand initially, had kept his cool and vowed to continue his policy of dialog and patience in dealing with a country that had confounded the United States for over thirty years. However, as the end of the year approached, there had been no more meaningful dialog with Iran, not even on Afghanistan, a country where Iran had great influence and had hoped to be consulted, as it was in 2001, with respect to the war against the Taliban and al-Qaeda, which remained Obama's biggest headache.

In late 2009, though, Senator John Kerry floated the idea of visiting Iran, an initiative supported by the White House and another attempt by the Democratic administration, it seemed, to engage Iran, even if only on a "track two" basis. And again, supporters of the Green Movement outside Iran worried out loud that the United States might appease the mullahs, no doubt adding to confusion in an Obama administration still trying to formulate its Iran policy. In any event, after careful examination in Tehran, Parliament rejected the idea of a Kerry visit (which would have been ostensibly to meet Speaker Ali Larijani, as a fellow parliamentarian). Parliament spokesmen suggested, for the umpteenth time, that dialog was not something they were anxious to engage in; rather, they were looking for concrete signs that the U.S. administration was going to change its policy toward Iran. But perhaps the Iranians were really waiting for what some commentators and analysts began to hope for after the election of Obama, a "Nixon to China" moment to jump-start Iranian-American relations, not a visit by a mere senator. If President Obama were ever convinced of the value of such a visit, it would represent to the Iranians a leap in their international standing—placing them on par with China (although in 1973 China did not yet clothe or furnish the houses of the majority of Americans, it was nonetheless a power to be reckoned with). A "Nixon to China" initiative, though, is unrealistic for the foreseeable future, given the circumstances of a post-2009 Iran, but President Obama can, if he wants, find a balance between doing nothing and embracing the regime. This would require extensive use of ta'arouf, though, something notably lacking in Obama's first State of the Union address, in January 2010, in which he "promised" Iran (in a not-so-veiled threat) that it would "face consequences" if it ignored its "obligations."

NO DEAL between the United States and Iran, whether caught up in an internal political crisis or not, whether with a hard-line or liberal reformist president, was ever going to be easy, and Obama had already said as much. However, there was something perverse, at the beginning of 2010, and a year into the Obama era, about U.S.-Iran relations being worse than at the end of the Bush administration, about tensions over Iran's nuclear program reaching their height, and about pessimism on all sides for a peaceful solution to the crisis, let alone a détente in relations. Blame was being apportioned from and by both sides, but it was fair to say that Obama's election clearly hadn't been enough for some Iranians to recognize that he represented a departure from sixty years of American heavy handedness in its foreign policy, not enough anyway, to set Iran-U.S. relations on the right track.

Obama had recognized early on that it was the Supreme Leader who mattered in Iran, at least when it came to diffusing the nuclear crisis or working toward normalization of relations, not the administration in power, and much of Obama's outreach was directed, if not directly, to the Ayatollah. The Supreme Leader had cautiously maneuvered around Obama's outreaches and his extended hand, waiting for, as he himself said, "the day the relations with America prove beneficial for the Iranian nation." That day wasn't going to be chosen by Ahmadinejad or the opposition, but by the Supreme Leader alone. President Obama, his honeymoon deemed long over by the end of his first year in office, even by the progressive wing of his party, was going to have to be patient, and aware of Iranian politics *and* the Iranian psyche if he wanted progress both on the nuclear front and on relations with Iran in general.

In February 2010, only days in advance of the important holiday celebrating the anniversary of the Islamic Revolution, both former president Khatami and Mousavi once again warned the United States against interference in Iran's affairs. Khatami went as far as to say that the Green Movement was under no illusions that America had benevolent intentions toward Iran, *any* Iran, a clear reference to America's dealing with the nuclear issue. President Obama ignored the warnings, and issued, along with the Europeans, a pre-emptive warning of his own to Iran, demanding that it respect the rights of demonstrators marching and protesting on the important holiday. By now,

Iranians, both in the leadership and among the public, were as aware of Obama's domestic struggles as Americans were, and "tea party" was as well known a phrase in Tehran as in Washington. Obama, increasingly under attack in the United States and his message of "hope" less resonant with an impatient public, was also becoming an easier target for Iran, his message of "change" more readily derided. When President Ahmadinejad ruffled Western feathers by announcing, the same week as Iran's holiday celebration, that it would begin further enrichment of uranium for its Tehran reactor unless the West returned to the negotiating table, President Obama's harsh response that Iran would face strong sanctions for its "misbehavior" (for doing something fully allowed under the Non-Proliferation Treaty) elicited no reaction by the opposition and hardly a shrug by the government, confident that in a week when it most needed its people's support, they would rally to Iran's, and not Obama's, side on the issue of its nuclear program.

Ahmadinejad, during his speech to a huge crowd at Azadi Square on February 11, the anniversary itself, barely mentioned Obama. After he defiantly announced that Iran had formally become a nuclear state, he said, "We expected Mr. Obama to make changes. We are told that he is under pressure. Okay!" Ahmadinejad's informal ta'arouf recognizing Obama's domestic problems was followed, predictably, with advice for the American president. "He should act rightly and based on respect to nations," Ahmadinejad said, adding, in case the sympathies of some in his audience were still with the man from Bushehr, "Unfortunately, hope for changes by him is rapidly fading and turning to mishap. His conduct disappoints all." On that point, Sarah Palin and her fans in the tea party movement were firmly in agreement with the Iranian president.

AT THE HEIGHT, or more realistically the *depths*, of the Bush presidency, an American friend of mine wistfully said to me, after a long
evening of discussing America's woes, "Gee, I wish *we* had a Supreme
Leader"—in other words, someone to control the president and his
party. During President Ahmadinejad's first term, many Iranians felt
the same way, about the United States *and* Iran, where it was perhaps
a benison that there was still someone their erratic president had to
answer to. But America had moved on by 2009, and Iran had tried to
do the same, in the June 2009 election, its voters inspired with the
same hope for change that drove Americans to vote a young, relatively
unknown black man to the highest office in the land. The disappointment that ensued for many Iranian voters was almost too much to
bear, and for some of them, a Supreme Leader, or at least the power
consigned to him, had outlived its usefulness, but trust in the country,
and even its Ayatollahs, remained high. No matter how the Ayatollahs'
democracy evolved—with or without the Supreme Leader—Obama
would still have to appeal to not just a government and a people, but
to the Ayatollahs as well.

THE GOOD, THE BAD,
THE UNCLEAN

Those who think they can revive the stinking corpse of the usurping and fake Israeli regime by throwing a birthday party are seriously mistaken.

—President Mahmoud Ahmadinejad, May 8, 2008

We are opposed to the idea that the people who live there [Israel] should be thrown into the sea or be burnt.

—President Mahmoud Ahmadinejad, September 18, 2008

"Mahmoud Ahmadinejad Revealed to Have Jewish Past"

—Headline, *The Daily Telegraph*, October 3, 2009

On a scorching hot Friday evening toward the end of Tehran's summer of 2008, Fifteenth Street off Yousefabad Avenue, a mostly residential street almost parallel to Valiasr Avenue, Tehran's longest tree-lined boulevard (and once named Pahlavi Avenue for the former Shah's family), was quiet, as most streets are on Fridays, the Muslim Sabbath. A nondescript mid-century brick building near a street corner, adorned with familiar Persian blue and turquoise tiles, drew no particular attention or even a glance from the occasional passerby (or a passenger jumping out of a stopped car to buy groceries at the deli a few yards away), but for anyone who cared to notice, the lettering above the intricate tile work was, incongruously in a nation where almost everything is written in the Arabic script, Hebrew. The Yousefabad Synagogue (*Kenisa-ye Yousefabad*, in Farsi) is one of the largest, and perhaps Tehran's most famous, among the approximately thirteen active synagogues in the metropolis of twelve to fifteen million people (paradoxically, there is not one Sunni mosque). In what is a wealthy and upscale neighborhood, on Friday evenings at sundown the temple attracts enough Iranian Jews, young and old, to completely fill its three or four hundred seats; women are segregated off to one side, and men and boys overflow onto the balcony upstairs, or simply stand at the back, reciting their prayers.

That a Jewish community exists in Iran, let alone that synagogues and churches do, often comes as a surprise to most Westerners unfamiliar with the Islamic Republic. But Iran's experiment in Islamic democracy, one that has evolved in fits and starts ever since Ayatollah Khomeini proclaimed a new political system in 1979, would not have any legitimacy as a democracy or even quasi-democracy were it not for how it accounts for religious freedom, and for its religious minorities,

minorities that have existed and lived in Iran since its founding as the Persian Empire over twenty-five hundred years ago. If one of the fundamental principles of democracy is that all citizens of that democracy are equal before the law, then Islamic democracy has not quite taken hold in Iran, for, to borrow George Orwell's depiction in *Animal Farm*, some citizens, the Shia, are still more equal than others. Islam is generally thought to be intolerant of other religions, and it can be, much like all religions, depending on how it is practiced. But in Iran, Shia Islamic, despite its Shias being more equal, religious freedom has a funny way of existing side by side with extreme intolerance of un-Islamic behavior of any kind, which would, one might think, preclude religious freedom altogether, much like in Saudi Arabia, where it is illegal to be anything *but* a Muslim.

THE GATE to the Yousefabad Synagogue was half open at 6:30 p.m. the evening I ventured there, well before sundown, and other than a woman standing waiting for someone or something, in a full-length Islamic-correct *manteau* (lightweight overcoat that conceals the shape of the body) and a properly tied scarf covering all of her hair, there was no one in the courtyard. I wandered in and peeked through the open doors of the temple; a handful of men were scattered about, sitting and reading miniature prayer books.

"Excuse me," I said to the woman, who was eyeing me with some curiosity, "is Mr. Motamed here?"

"No," she replied sweetly, "he's not here yet."

"Dr. Moreh-Sedegh, or Dr. Naim or Dr. Raffi? Mrs. Hasidim perhaps?"

"No, none of them are here. They're probably coming soon though."

"Thanks." I stood in the courtyard waiting, occasionally looking into the synagogue but otherwise pacing directly outside and even stepping onto the sidewalk, hoping not to draw too much attention to myself, the lone Shia at the temple. One by one, and sometimes in twos and threes, men and women walked past me, entered through the gate, and stepped into the temple, the women using a separate entrance farther down the narrow courtyard. A small man in an elegant gray suit matching his hair color, his yarmulke fished out of a pocket and expertly positioned on his head, busied himself with straightening the notices on the bulletin board immediately by the front doors while throwing me an occasional glance. I stepped up to the board and helped him, pinning an errant flier back in place. He looked at me carefully.

"Can I help you?" he asked.

"I was invited by Mr. Motamed," I said. "I'm a writer."

"Mr. Motamed isn't here yet," he said in a friendly tone, "but please, go in and have a seat. No need to stand here outside."

"Thank you," I said, and I stepped into the air-conditioned temple. I searched through the box of kippahs by the door and chose a large size that I felt confident wouldn't slip off my head without the hairpins I now cursed myself for not bringing, and I then took a seat at the front of the congregation, on a bank of theater-like chairs that were set up behind long tables stacked with plates of fruit, dates, and prayer books. The men sitting across from me stared but said nothing. The man who had invited me in walked along the tables, straightening the stacks of prayer books and moving things around, and occasionally whispering something to one or another of the congregation. One by one, more men entered through the doors, took yarmulkes from the box or from their pockets, a prayer book from the table, and sat down on one of the chairs. "*Shabbat Shalom!*" they each said loudly as they entered, to a muted chorus of "Shabbat Shalom." One man stopped in front of me and said an emphatic "Shabbat Shalom!" clearly directed at his friend sitting behind me, to which the friend replied, "*Chakeram!*" in a strong Tehran accent and intonation, employing a street-wise Farsi expression literally meaning "I am your obedient servant," but not an expression one might expect to hear in a house of worship, Muslim, Jewish, or otherwise.

As the crowd grew, I heard the occasional "writer" slip off a tongue here and there; clearly people were talking about my unusual presence, perhaps some less comfortably so than others, but mostly they ignored me. My eyes focused on the women's section, where, to my surprise, only one woman, younger, very attractive, and with an extensive and expensive hairdo, had let her scarf slip down to her shoulders. She chatted with other women, all of them heavily made-up and dressed to the nines, but all of the other women obeyed the Islamic laws of the land demanding proper hijab, which in these circumstances happily coincided with orthodox Jewish notions of female propriety. As I was staring at her and the room was filling to capacity around me, a middle-aged man with a limp approached me. I looked up at him as he stood over me.

"Can I see you outside?" he asked.

"Me?" I replied.

"Yes, please." I followed him out the doors and we stopped on the steps to the temple. "Are you a member of the *Kalimi* [Jewish] minority of Iran?" he asked. He used the preferred Farsi word for "Jewish"—that is, the one Jews prefer, although Iranian Jews are not uncomfortable with the word most of their Muslim brethren and the state officially use: *Yahoudi*.

"No," I replied, "I'm a writer, and I was invited by Mr. Motamed." I took out my press card, issued by the Ministry of Culture and Islamic Guidance, and handed it to him. He stared at it for a while and handed it back to me.

"It's all well and good that you have this from *Ershad* [Culture]," he said, using the commonly abbreviated word for the ministry that issues credentials, "but I'm in charge here and nobody told me anything about this. Motamed would have had to send a letter, and I never received anything."

"No problem," I said, "I don't want to cause you any problems. I'll wait here outside for him."

"No, no," said the synagogue administrator, "please go back inside and wait there. But when the services commence, if you don't have your host here, I'll have to ask you to leave."

"No problem at all," I said. "But are you sure? I really *can* wait outside."

"No, no, you're my guest," he said, employing ta'arouf. I walked back inside and he gestured to an empty seat by the door. "Please," he said, "*befarma'eed*." My old seat had been taken so I sat down at the new one, next to an old man, probably in his late seventies, with cropped white hair and big, 1950s-style glasses.

"*Salaam*," he said to me, interrupting his prayers. He pointed to the page in his prayer book, a page with Hebrew on the top half and Farsi below it. "I'm reading from here," he said.

"You can read Hebrew, then?" I asked.

"Yes," he replied, "I can, like everyone else. But I don't understand any of it of course, and neither do the others."

"Sort of like Muslims who say their prayers in Arabic?" I said.

"Yes," he chuckled, nodding his head. "I can read it, but I don't know what it means unless I read the Farsi. See?" He pointed at the Farsi text. "It's in Farsi," he repeated, as if he were speaking to an illiterate person. "You can just read the Farsi."

I learned that the chief rabbi of Tehran was not going to appear that night, for he was attending to services at another Tehran synagogue. Instead, a young man, almost shouting desperately over the din of loud prayer-chanting, children screaming and playing outside, and others just talking loudly, delivered a short and seemingly half-hearted sermon about the importance of family and community. He was followed by a boy, no more than fourteen years old, who did his best to chant another prayer without the benefit of electronic amplification. I felt a slap on my shoulder and spun around.

"Be a *Yid* for five minutes," said a middle-aged man with a hearty laugh, "it won't do you any harm!" (He had used the Farsi pejorative "*Joo-oud*" for "Jew," which has no translation but is perhaps closest to something like "Yid.") I laughed, a little uncomfortably, and nodded vigorously, and then turned again to smile at him and his friends, who were standing a few feet behind me and laughing out loud. I noticed, looking around the room, that only about half the men swayed as they chanted and prayed, which, I thought, made my rigid torso just a little less conspicuous. I faithfully stood up whenever the congregation stood up, and sat down as they did, although I did not utter "amen" loudly along with them (or "*ameen*," as they pronounced it, and as the Arabs do).

As the services continued, I watched the administrator walk up and down, say a few words here and there, and then take to the lectern and recite another prayer, acting as the cantor. He seemed to pay no attention to me and was clearly unconcerned that I was still sitting in the congregation, an uninvited Gentile as far as he was concerned. Another old man, one who had been throwing glances my way ever since I first entered the temple, walked up to me from across the way and leaned over.

"If you're waiting for Motamed or Raffi or Naim, don't bother. They won't show up, and you needn't waste your time or anyone else's."

"They won't show up, huh?" I said, looking him directly in the eye.

"No, they won't. Don't waste your time."

"Thanks," I said, looking back down at my neighbor's prayer book. The old man walked away, a little hesitantly, perhaps disturbed that I didn't immediately stand up and leave. My neighbor leaned over to me, and pointed again at the page in his prayer book.

"See, this is where we are," he said. "This is the prayer."

"I see," I said, and then looked up to see the administrator rushing toward me, his limp even more pronounced.

"What did that old man say to you?" he demanded in a frustrated tone.

"He just told me not to bother to wait," I replied.

"Don't listen to him," said the administrator. "*I'm* in charge here, and you're my guest. Stay as long as you like, do whatever you want, and don't listen to anyone else. He's just a nosey old man."

"I don't want anyone to be uncomfortable," I said.

"No one's uncomfortable, and you are welcome here," said the temple administrator, ta'aroufing, but quite genuine. "Please," he added, as he shuffled off. I felt another playful slap on my shoulder.

"It's been longer than five minutes!" said the beaming man who had teased me before. "You've been *Joo-oud* for way more than five minutes!" He laughed heartily and stepped back to the wall. I turned and smiled at him and his friends for the second time, and put my right hand over my heart in the traditional Iranian sign of respect. They smiled back and bowed their heads.

A young man took a position immediately to my left, standing against the wall, and began to pray, shouting but carefully enunciating every Hebrew word, although with a Tehran Farsi accent pronounced enough that it sounded more like unintelligible Farsi slang to me. He had to shout even to hear himself, for by this time the noise the children were making in the courtyard outside the open doors had risen incrementally with the sound of the prayers being spoken inside, almost as if there were a competition to see who could drown whom out first. I felt my cell phone vibrate in my pocket and rushed outside to take the call. As I was speaking on the phone and trying to avoid children intent on crashing into me as they continued to scream at the top of their lungs, I spotted two very young, unarmed soldiers, army conscripts clearly, walk through the gates and take their positions against a brick wall. They stood there looking bored, waiting for the services to conclude, and as I finished my call, a stream of worshippers walked out of the temple, men through the main entrance and women from theirs. I fought the bodies and went back inside the synagogue, looking for the administrator. I found him chatting to a number of young men.

"Thank you very much," I said, and shook his hand. "I really appreciate it."

"Please," he replied. "You are most welcome." He did not mention the fact that no one had shown up to vouch for me, and that he had not bothered to expel me as a potential fraud. (In the spring of 2009 I sent my friend Richard Greenberg, an NBC producer, to the same synagogue, and a man, perhaps the same administrator, unceremoniously kicked him out, oblivious to his protestations that he was Jewish. Later, as he almost came to blows with the man, that man's behavior made him ashamed to say he was Jewish, he told me.) I followed the congregation as they collected their children, ignored the two young sentries, and ventured outside the gates and onto the sidewalk. I stood there for a few moments as they milled about, the men's heads suddenly magically bereft of yarmulkes and the women properly buttoned up, scarves covering their hair. There may be a synagogue behind those gates, I thought, but, after all, this is the *Islamic* Republic of Iran.

IRAN HAS BEEN officially called "Islamic" only since the revolution of 1979 toppled the monarchy, but it has always been an Islamic state, at least since the Arab invasion brought Islam to its largely Zoroastrian, but also Jewish and Christian (mostly Armenian), population. Shia Islam was made the state religion under the Safavid dynasty, whose kings ruled a resurgent Persian Empire from the sixteenth to the eighteenth century. Jews, who had by then lived in Iran for at least two thousand years, came under renewed pressure to convert, but as throughout most of Persian history, they were spared the harshest of treatment (or even banishment) if they didn't. (Iran's history, however, is not completely devoid of waves of large-scale anti-Semitism or sometimes brutal repression of Jews.)

Unlike other religious minorities, Jews have always had a special place in Iran's culture. Almost all Iranians, fiercely proud of their glorious past, can recite the history of Cyrus the Great, the founder of the Persian Empire and a king who freed the Jews of Babylon, providing them safe haven in his empire and even issuing an edict that they should return to the Promised Land and rebuild their temple. In fact, according to the Book of Ezra, Cyrus may have been the first Zionist, or at least *Gentile* Zionist, an ironic fact that President Ahmadinejad and his fellow Israel-obsessed hard-liners may either be unaware of or simply choose to ignore. But regardless of ancient history (or whether one should even read the Bible literally), Iran's Jews have lived on the land continuously for millennia, and are perhaps, along with the Zoroastrian minority, the most Iranian of all Iranians, who, for the most part, can barely trace their heritage farther back than a few generations. (Birth certificates, and even last names, only came into existence with Reza Shah's reign in the 1930s.)

It is perhaps partly this notion of belonging, a sense Iranian Jews have of nationhood right where they have lived for generations and generations, which makes those Jews who have chosen to stay in the Islamic Republic a resilient bunch. They are not easily frightened by a state that at times can seem inhospitable, if not downright anti-Semitic, such as when President Ahmadinejad's government not only denied the Holocaust but even organized and hosted a Holocaust-deniers' conference in Tehran in late 2006. Ahmadinejad may come across as an ignorant and bigoted anti-Semite, but even he and his cohorts go to great pains to profess respect for Jews and Judaism and to distinguish between anti-Zionism and anti-Semitism, anti-Zionism being the official state line since well before the firebrand president was elected in 2005 (and even to some extent during the era of the Shah, who although he maintained relations with the Jewish state, never extended full diplomatic recognition to Israel).

Iranian authorities, when on the defensive about their perceived occasional bursts of anti-Semitism, are quick to point out, rather proudly, that Iran has had a guaranteed seat in Parliament for its Jewish minority since the constitution of 1906 (as do the Armenian, Assyrian, and Zoroastrian minorities as well, but not the Baha'is), as well as the fact that Iran has the second-largest population of Jews in the Middle East—second only after Israel, that is. But the history of religious minorities and how they would fare under an Islamic government, even an Islamic *democracy*, has always been a curious one in the thirty years since it was established. Under the Shahs, particularly the Pahlavi dynasty, religious freedom was guaranteed and in some ways religious minorities benefited greatly—especially the Baha'is, whose faith forbids involvement in politics—partly because they didn't fall under suspicion of being supportive of Islamic anti-monarchy groups, who, along with the communists, posed the greatest danger to the state. The Jews of Iran, as another example, while living in a Muslim state never came under pressure or force to emigrate, like many Arab Jews did, from Syria and Yemen to Egypt and across North Africa, after the creation of Israel or after the subsequent Arab-Israeli wars.

The Islamic regime, first under Ayatollah Khomeini, continued the guarantee of religious freedom, as long as the religion was one of the state-recognized monotheistic ones, namely, Zoroastrianism (Iranians, even the clerics, recognize the Persian religion as the first monotheistic one and consider it a forerunner to the three major religions), Judaism, and Christianity, along with Islam. Despite that guarantee, and the relative protection religious minorities enjoy, there remains suspicion and even anti-minority sentiment (particularly against Jews but mostly against Baha'is), which the mullahs stir up when it suits them, but both are also deeply ingrained in many ordinary Iranians.

The accusation (and I call it an "accusation" because that is what it was) that President Ahmadinejad came from a family of Jews who converted to Islam, one that made the mainstream Western media in 2009, could have been leveled only by his enemies, some in the reform camp, or conservatives opposed to him. The rumor was nothing new and it took on a life of its own in the turbulent post-election period, but the very accusation was anti-Semitic in its suggestion that either a president with a Jewish past was unacceptable, or Iranian Jews could not be trusted to owe a greater allegiance to Iran than Israel, something that resonated in Tehran considering that some people had already accused Ahmadinejad of helping, rather than hurting, Israeli interests with every anti-Zionist outburst. It reflects the kind of anti-Semitism that has always existed in Iran, not as dark or hateful as European anti-Semitism, but a sort of below-the-surface unease with religious diversity in a nation that is 97 percent Muslim.

THE ISLAMIC CONSTITUTION, written after the revolution of 1979 and under the close supervision of Ayatollah Khomeini, did not eliminate the religious minority seats in Parliament, but it did rename the body the "Islamic Consultative Assembly," *Majles-e-Shora-e-Eslami* (from "National Consultative Assembly," *Majles-e-Shora-e-Melli*). Critics of the regime assert that the name change alone indicates a Parliament no longer responsible to the people, but only responsible to God; however, the *Islamic* assembly of Iran continues to have, as it has had for over a hundred years, a Jewish member, elected to the post by other Jews, and presumably one who feels no discomfort in assembling to consult

Islamic*ally* with his peers. Iran numbers its four-year Parliaments, and during the Sixth and Seventh Islamic Consultative Assemblies, the elected Jew in attendance was Maurice Motamed, an engineer by trade and the man who had invited me to the Yousefabad Synagogue for Shabbat services in the summer of 2008.

Maurice Motamed's eight-year stint in Parliament, begun in 2000, covered both the reformist Khatami years and the first term of arch-conservative Ahmadinejad. During his term most Westerners came to realize that Iran had a Jewish representative in Parliament, and that there were even any Jews left in Iran, a credit to his outstanding efforts to be more than just the "token Jew" in an Islamic assembly. He not only fiercely defended the rights of his constituents, but also, and perhaps to the surprise of some of his Muslim peers, strove to be a full and active member of the assembly by joining (non-Jewish affairs–related) committees and commissions, such as the Energy Commission and the Australian Parliamentary Friendship Committee. During his term in office he was able to get the support of fellow parliamentarians (and the president) in overturning such discriminatory laws as unequal blood-libel payments (today Jews can claim the same amount of monetary damages in the case of accidental death or murder as their Muslim counterparts, something they were unable to do even under the Shah, and which made them by definition not equal in the eyes of the law). He was also able to persuade the government to permit, albeit unofficially, Iranian Jews living in Israel to travel back to Iran unimpeded and without fear of arrest.

Maurice (sometimes transcribed from Farsi as "Morris") Motamed often came under fierce criticism from some in the Iranian Diaspora for his overt support of the Islamic system and particularly for his support of the anti-Israeli policies of his government, but he remained nonplussed and continued to do his job as he saw fit: a Jew serving his Jewish constituency and his nation. And while it may be easy to criticize from afar, it should be noted that Iran's Jews, who know better than anyone else what it is like to live as a minority in a Shia country, overwhelmingly re-elected him to Parliament and, according to some I spoke to, would have done so again in 2008 if he had chosen to stand for a third term. Motamed can still, after all, point to real gains in rights for minorities during his two terms in office, particularly for Jews (even as compared to the benign political atmosphere for Jews under the Shah), and to his fearless criticism of and objection to the insulting and often outrageous anti-Semitism exhibited by the state under the administration of President Ahmadinejad, whether it be a celebration of the anniversary of the publication of "The Protocols of the Elders of Zion" or the Holocaust conference of 2006, where an open invitation was made to cartoonists around the world to submit cartoons mocking the genocide.

After eight years as a parliamentarian, Motamed returned to civilian life and his engineering firm, Iran Topography, which he runs from a small suite of offices on busy Valiasr Avenue in midtown Tehran. He remains active in the Jewish community, though, and is still recognized as a senior statesman who has many close contacts with Iran's politicians (and a close relationship with former president Khatami, who attended services at the Yousefabad Synagogue in 2003 at his invitation, the first ever visit to a synagogue by an Iranian leader). I visited Motamed in his offices in 2008; a simple phone call from former president Khatami's office to his cell phone had assured my being received by him as a trusted friend. Motamed had, in his years in Parliament, granted many interviews to the foreign media, particularly during times when President Ahmadinejad made headlines with his vitriolic statements on Israel or his questioning of the Holocaust, but with headlines when I visited him being mostly about the U.S. presidential campaign, Motamed was busy only with his work as an engineer. His office was strewn with maps and various files relating to his consulting business, and other than a large Iranian flag and a framed photograph of him with Khatami, there was no evidence of Motamed's long tenure as a politician.

MOTAMED WAS BORN in 1945 in Hamadan, one of the world's oldest cities in midwestern Iran and a city with a once-sizable Jewish population. He was raised in Tehran and attended university there, but since the age of twenty-four or twenty-five, as he remembered it, he had been active in Jewish community affairs and politics as it affected the community. Since the 1979 revolution ushered in a strictly Islamic state, his activism grew more urgent and he decided to stand for Parliament to address, as he called them, the issues and problems that had arisen for Jews and that required a "professional approach" to solve. "Part of my job was to serve the community of Jews living abroad," he said to me, "and fortunately, well, you know five of my years in Parliament were under the presidency of Mr. Khatami, and we were witness to his, let's say, *kindness* to the religious minorities, and we were witness to a new direction in the relations with the religious minorities in the country. I developed a real affection for him during my tenure as a parliamentarian." He passed me a tray of cookies. "These have come directly from Hamadan!" he said enthusiastically, and I couldn't refuse the treat to go along with the obligatory glass of tea that had been brought in by an office servant. Iranian Jews, like all Iranians, remain obstinately proud of their hometowns.

"Iranians who live in Israel seem to be able to come and go as they please, don't they?" I asked him as I bit into the delicious confection. "Although obviously there are no direct flights between Tel Aviv and Tehran."

"This will be interesting for you," he replied. "About eight years ago, it was exceedingly difficult for Iranians to travel to Israel and to return. They would be subject to all kinds of problems including even prison terms and having their passports confiscated. As one of my early duties in Parliament, I wrote to the presidency, to President Khatami, and explained to him that for many reasons it was necessary for Iranian Jews to be able to freely travel to Israel and back. To visit family, or to receive medical treatment, but above all, as part of their religious duties." Motamed's iPhone rang loudly (though obviously not on the AT&T network, which cannot boast coverage in Iran due to U.S. sanctions), interrupting him. "Excuse me," he said, and took the call. "What were we talking about?" he asked distractedly after he hung up.

"The Jews who live in Israel," I said.

"Yes, yes. Fortunately, this letter of mine had a positive impact. His Excellency Khatami gave orders that a group of ministers should look into the matter, and the result was that for about seven and a half years now, Jews do not face the same problems they did. They travel back and forth, and they encounter no problems. What's even more interesting is that even Jews who have lived in Israel for thirty or forty years can go to the consulate in Istanbul or neighboring countries, and reclaim Iranian documentation and travel to Iran, without any problems."

"But why," I wondered, "do Iranian Jews who still live here even persist in staying in Iran, when they are living as a small minority in an officially Islamic state, with all the laws and regulations that that implies?"

"That's a question I've been personally asked many times," Motamed said wearily. "You see; this is *our* country. In my opinion, the reason Jews are often persuaded to leave a country is that old issue of anti-Semitism. It's unfortunately a worldwide problem—you can witness even in France or Belgium or Holland, the attacks on Jewish houses of worship or cemeteries. An Iranian Jew might look at that and say, 'Why should I leave my homeland to go somewhere alien to me, and where there might be anti-Semitism of the kind that isn't in my own country?' "

What about the state of affairs for Jews under Ahmadinejad, though? I wondered. Hadn't the issue of "wiping Israel off the map," the repeated Holocaust denials, made life more difficult for Jews and particularly the Jewish member of Parliament?

"Absolutely," said Motamed. "Being a Jewish member of Parliament is a very difficult job, one of the most difficult. When the Holocaust issue came up, I was interviewed by both the domestic and international media, and I expressed regret that the president is either uninterested in history or is unaware of it, and I considered Holocaust denial a great insult to all Jews everywhere. There was no reason for bringing up the Holocaust, and we can see that in the last few years how it has negatively impacted Iran's reputation, both the people and the government. I raised my objections not just as a Jew, but first and foremost as an Iranian."

I asked Motamed if he felt that Iranian Jews, in an anti-Israeli nation, are obliged to always declare an anti-Zionist stance.

He danced around the issue but finally said that his own stance has always been against extreme behavior by Israel, and for the rights of the Palestinian people. "Even abroad," he said, "if you look at any demonstration for the rights of Palestinians, you'll see Jews at the forefront." It is a tricky question for the Jews of Iran, the fact that their welcome in their homeland is conditional on their rejection of what Iran terms the "Zionist state." No Jew in Iran would want to go on the record defending Israel's right to exist, but I sensed that Iranian Jews would prefer not to be asked, as if the uncomfortable question lingers over them all the time. To answer the question means they either have to lie or have to be confronted with the age-old question of where a Jew's loyalty lies, an issue that should be more than obvious for Iranian Jews still living in the Islamic Republic of Iran, under an anti-Semitic president no less. Motamed's own loyalty to the state, to his country, was not questioned by even the most anti-Zionist, anti-Semitic officials, and he was clearly comfortable in his own skin, first as an Iranian, as he put it, and second as a Jew.

"What are you doing tomorrow morning?" he suddenly asked me as my time with him drew to a close.

"I have a few appointments in the morning," I answered.

"Come to the Sapir Hospital afterward. The board of directors holds its meeting tomorrow and I want to introduce you to them, and to the new member of Parliament, Dr. Moreh-Sedegh."

I wrote down the address and promised I would rush there after a meeting at the Foreign Ministry's college campus at the northern fringes of town, a good hour's drive away from the Dr. Sapir Hospital, the Jewish hospital of Tehran, in what was once the Jewish ghetto in South Tehran.

THE JEWISH GHETTO of Tehran of course no longer exists. Partly because of Jewish emigration and partly because of the upward mobility of Iranian Jews, it had become a mostly Muslim neighborhood, albeit still resembling a ghetto, since before the revolution. About eighty thousand Iranian Jews have left Iran since the Islamic Revolution of 1979, leaving a population of between twenty and twenty-five thousand Jews in Iran, the majority in Tehran (about fourteen thousand) but with sizable communities in Shiraz, Esfahan, Kermanshah, Hamadan, and Yazd, and much smaller numbers scattered throughout the country. It is estimated that three million Iranian *Muslims* have also emigrated since the revolution, but, according to Motamed, the reason for the higher percentage of Jews is that "circumstances are somewhat easier for the Jews to leave and settle elsewhere," both in terms of family connections in the West and in terms of obtaining coveted Western visas. But most big cities still have neighborhoods that were once, in the distant or recent past, Jewish neighborhoods and where a handful of less wealthy Jews, mostly very old, still live among Muslims.

The Dr. Sapir Hospital, founded as a charity clinic by a famous Jewish doctor over fifty years ago, is on busy Mostafa Khomeini Street in the Cyrus section of South-Central Tehran, a street lined with shops selling inexpensive goods ranging from pots and pans to hookahs to automotive parts. A large sign faces the street—the Hebrew letters visible—and in the alleys behind and around the hospital, tall, pock-marked mud walls hide the decrepit homes that once housed some of Tehran's Jews but are now almost exclusively Muslim, multifamily residences.

On Tuesdays, the board of directors of the hospital, all prominent Tehran Jews, meet in the conference room/office of the hospital director, Siamak Moreh-Sedegh, a surgeon who had been elected to replace Maurice Motamed as the Jewish member of Parliament just a few months prior. After a long, traffic-choked drive, I was directed to the small office directly outside the conference room, where a secretary dressed in black and full hijab, but with rouge and bright-red lipstick, offered me a seat while she went into the conference room to announce my arrival. She returned to her desk facing me, and within a few minutes a servant appeared with a cup of Nescafé, a subtle nod that she knew I lived abroad and was therefore, in most Iranian minds, disposed more toward coffee than tea. She asked me to wait a few minutes while the board finished some business, important and contentious business judging by the raised voices I could hear from behind the door. I tried to make conversation as I sipped the coffee I didn't really want.

"Have you been here long?" I asked her.

"About seventeen years," she said.

"And you like it?"

"Very much," she said enthusiastically.

"Are you Jewish?"

"No," she replied with a smile. "Very few here are, except the board, of course. But they're all *such* good people," she added. Another man walked into the room and said a few words to her. She got up from her chair and walked into the conference room; when she returned, she gestured that I should go in, and said a few more words to the man, who was by now seated next to me.

"Thanks," I said, gathering my things and walking into the conference room. Maurice Motamed stood up from behind the large table and shook my hands, and then introduced me to the board, composed mostly of doctors but also the hospital administrator, a Mrs. Hasidim, who was wearing a proper Islamic manteau and tight scarf on her head.

"Mrs. Hasidim will give you a tour of the hospital," he said, "and then you'll join us for lunch in the cafeteria downstairs." I followed Mrs. Hasidim (who is not a Hasidic Jew, who do not exist in Iranian Jewry) out of the room and to her office down the hall.

"What would you like to know?" she asked pleasantly.

"How long have you worked here?" I asked, quite unprepared to ask any questions of a hospital administrator, Jewish or otherwise.

"Forty-three years," she replied. "I started as a midwife—this started as an outpatient maternity clinic, you know. It was started really because a pregnant Jewish woman, all those years ago, once bled to death because a Muslim doctor wouldn't touch her, because of her being *najess* [unclean, in Islam]."

"Really?" I said, surprised.

"Yes, so it was decided that there had to be a place for Jews to go without worrying about the najess issue. Of course, those days are long past, and we've grown substantially."

"And how many Jews work here?" I asked.

"We have 230 personnel of whom ten are Jews, including two

doctors," she replied. "The vast majority of the patients are Muslim, of course. We used to have only a Kosher kitchen, but after the revolution the employees demanded a *halal* kitchen too, so now we have two kitchens." She looked at me, trying, I thought, to convey a little sarcasm with her expression.

"And how is it with the government of Ahmadinejad?"

"Well, we've been asked to cut back our connections to Iranian Jews in the United States, but the government continues to support us, donating funds every now and then. Otherwise, we're entirely supported by the Jewish community."

"Any Muslim donors?" I wondered.

"No," she said wearily.

"And have you ever thought of leaving Iran?"

"No, this is my home. I'm a member of the Tehran Jewish Committee, a member of the board of directors of this hospital; I have work to do. My children are here too." She paused and stared at me. "But I suppose now that I'm getting old, I might think about retiring abroad," she added. The lights suddenly went off.

"Another cutoff?" I asked. In the summer of 2008, Tehran had experienced major electricity shortages, courtesy of Ahmadinejad's economic planning, and hospitals were not immune, apparently, from government-imposed shutdowns almost every day.

"Yes," she said. "The generator should kick in any minute." She looked worried for a moment, and then the lights came back on, dimly. It was already warm in the building and over 100 degrees outside, but the air-conditioning would not come back on until power was switched on again, normally within an hour or two. "Come," she said, "let's take a tour and then go and have lunch." I followed her out the door and walked with her through the hospital, along its impeccably clean and orderly corridors and through its wards. She pointedly identified the one or two Jewish patients in their beds. She also whispered, as we said hello at a nurses' station, that "that tall one is the only Jewish nurse, or really midwife, left." We took the stairs down to the basement and to an empty cafeteria, where a long table had been set up for the board of directors, who wandered in one by one.

"The kosher kitchen, I presume?" I asked Mrs. Hasidim.

"Yes," she said with a smile.

"Perhaps you might tell your Muslim staff that today the grandson of an Ayatollah, a descendant of the prophet Mohammad no less, ate a kosher meal in your cafeteria," I said.

"No, I won't do that," she said rather sternly and devoid of humor. Some things, one quickly learns, are just not funny when it comes to religion. Not in Iran. Mrs. Farangiz Hasidim, a Jew who was living and working among devout Muslims, knew that better than me.

I RETURNED TO Dr. Sapir Hospital a few days later, to meet with Dr. Moreh-Sedegh for a longer chat. At the Safi car service office on the narrow street where I stay in Tehran, in a downtown neighborhood not too far from the hospital, I told the dispatcher that I was headed to the Jewish hospital. "Why, do the Jews have a *hospital*?" he asked, raising his eyebrows. I had heard the same question from a number of other Muslims in Tehran.

"Yes, you know, the Dr. Sapir Hospital, in Cyrus, on South Mostafa Khomeini Street," I replied. The dispatcher shook his head and leaned over the glass partition separating him from the drivers lounging about and waiting for a fare.

"The Jewish hospital?" he yelled, more a question than an order. "Sapir." An older man came round, nodding his head, and guided me outside to his car. Fifteen minutes later he pulled right up to the gates, almost running over two people who were trying to cross in front of us. "Sapir," he said triumphantly.

Siamak Moreh-Sedegh goes to work everyday at the hospital and also visits his office in Parliament, where he conducts political affairs on behalf of his community. When I entered his office at the hospital, he was sitting at the conference table, which was right in front of his desk and had a plastic seven-branched candelabra, or menorah, prominently placed in front of the telephone. He was drinking tea and chain-smoking cigarettes and shouting and cursing on the phone. Forty-one years old and overweight, Moreh-Sedegh is a jovial, back-slapping, one-of-the-guys type of man, and his demeanor on the phone was affable.

"We can smoke in here?" I asked, when he hung up, mildly surprised. (Iran, much like the rest of the Western world, has strict laws forbidding smoking in public places, including restaurants and cafes and, naturally, hospitals.)

"Here you can do anything!' he replied with a smile, lighting another cigarette.

"But . . . in a *hospital*?"

"We're not patients, are we!" he exclaimed. I lit a cigarette myself, and he picked up the ringing phone again.

"How's Mr. Khatami?" he asked me, when he hung up.

"Very good," I said, as the secretary walked in with a question for Moreh-Sedegh and a question for me. Did I prefer tea or coffee? "Tea," I said to her obvious satisfaction. The phone rang again, and he apologized and took the call. It lasted over ten minutes, with Moreh-Sedegh pleading with and even begging the party on the other end to not start a fight with an unnamed third person. As he hung up he picked up a file in front of him that had been left by the secretary while he was on the phone.

"Excuse me," he said, as he looked it over. "Ms. Salehi!" he called out. "What is this?" His secretary returned to the office.

"Doctor," she said, "you had said 50/50 on this bill, but accounting says the hospital would lose too much money if they only pay 50 percent, and this was the third Caesarian for the patient."

"It's no problem," said Moreh-Sedegh. "How much did the doctor charge?"

"Nothing," said Ms. Salehi, "because of your recommendation."

"So how much is the bill?"

"Just this amount. 320,000 tomans [about $350]."

Moreh-Sedegh started to write something on the file. "The-amount -of-160,000-tomans-to-be-paid," he said softly as he wrote the words, overruling accounting. He handed the file back to Ms. Salehi. Another doctor walked in, and Moreh-Sedegh introduced him to me.

"Today, my meetings are a privilege," he said with some measure of ta'arouf. "Some days it's just lowlifes!" Moreh-Sedegh and the doctor talked shop for a number of minutes, calling Ms. Salehi in to resolve an issue involving a patient, and once again the phone interrupted the conversation.

"Today is a day when our phone calls are all *bullshit* but our meetings are with gentlemen," Moreh-Sedegh exclaimed when he hung up. "Ms. Salehi!" he shouted. Another doctor walked into the room, adding to the chaos. Moreh-Sedegh was animated, lighting cigarette after cigarette, arguing and discussing hospital business and surgery with the doctors and Ms. Salehi, and alternately handling Jewish Committee of Tehran business on the phone. I wasn't sure if I should stay, but he was now smoking my cigarettes, having finished his own, and all I could think was that I was glad I had brought an extra pack. "Excuse me," he said to me every now and then.

"Don't write this stuff down!" pleaded one of the doctors, knowing that I was a writer. Between discussing gynecology and the interrupting phone calls, Moreh-Sedegh started to tell ribald jokes. Everyone laughed as he answered the phone again, for the umpteenth time, and when he hung up, the other doctors left, and he sat down, promising me his undivided and uninterrupted attention. We spoke for a while about the failings of the Ahmadinejad government, and then moved on to the question of the Jewish community in Iran.

"You seem an extremely busy man," I said to Moreh-Sedegh. "Did you want to run for Parliament or were you asked or pressured?"

"No. It's an interesting story, my entering the Parliament. Mr. Motamed said to me that his wife would probably not want him to stand for the seat again, because it was affecting his personal life. He said to me: why don't you register to run? If I can convince my wife, I'll run myself, otherwise you will and we'll have a good candidate either way."

"You were the hospital director, right?"

"The hospital director *and* the director of the Jewish Committee. But it wasn't for my own sake that I signed up, it was for the interests of the Jewish community."

"How do you manage to run the hospital and fulfill your duties as a parliamentarian?" I wondered, having witnessed the chaos of his workday.

"I'm lucky," he said, "that the hospital is close to Parliament. I get to the hospital at six in the morning, work until eight, and then get on a motorcycle and go to Parliament and work until noon, when the Majles breaks for lunch, at which time I come straight here."

"So how does the administration of Ahmadinejad, with his vitriolic statements against Israel, affect your work in government, now that you've had some experience?" I asked.

"Look, a specific thing happened at the dawn of the revolution, and we owe the Imam (Khomeini) for that, in that there was a real distinction made between Judaism and Zionism. Fortunately, this has been really well understood in the culture of society. In other words, fortunately even the most radical anti-Israeli sentiment in this country has never translated into anti-Semitic sentiment. You see, Jews in other countries may identify themselves as Jews before any nationality, but that's not true of Iranians. Our nationality is Iranian, and we own the politics of our country too. This is well understood by the population at large. I can say with authority that even under the administration of Ahmadinejad, there has been no anti-Semitism directed at the community."

"But Jews in other countries," I said, "even if they have no love for Zionism, don't feel any particular obligation to always state their stance vis-à-vis Israel."

"Neither do we!" exclaimed Moreh-Sedegh. "There's never been any pressure by the government or otherwise in that matter. Iran has never really had a Zionist movement, though. And that may be because in Iran there has never really existed *organized* anti-Semitism. Zionism can thrive in a Jewish community if there's a sense of anti-Semitism in the culture where they live."

"But there *is* anti-Semitism in Iran, even if it isn't organized."

"Look," said Moreh-Sedegh, hesitating for a moment. "There's anti-Semitism *everywhere*. But the issue is really whether it is organized and whether it can penetrate the culture. Throughout Iranian history *organized* anti-Semitism has not existed. During the worst anti-Semitic times, such as during World War II, Iran was actually a refuge for Jews, even European Jews. If you go back further, Spanish Jews escaping the Inquisition came to Iran! Jews from Kashan are descendants of those Spanish Jews. Some Jews from Yazd are descendants of European Jews escaping pogroms. Look, throughout Iranian history, the greatest protectors of the Jews have been the *Marja-e-taghlid* [Grand Ayatollahs] of Shia Islam."

"But don't things such as a Holocaust conference affect the culture, and perhaps negatively in terms of anti-Semitism, particularly among lesser-educated citizens?" I asked.

"Look, anti-Semitism can only thrive if there are roots. And there simply are no roots in Iran," he said emphatically, "and so we're not in the least bit afraid of anti-Semitism in Iran."

"So what are the issues facing the Jewish community?" I asked. "I mean, Jews still cannot become ministers or judges, for example."

"The biggest legal issue is one of the inheritance law [Iranian law states that if one beneficiary in a religious-minority household converts to Islam, he or she will inherit everything and other non-converting members receive nothing]. But that's a law that dates from the Reza Shah period and it's not paid much attention to," said Moreh-Sedegh. "Look, any minority living in a religious country faces certain restrictions. For example, gaining employment in a government office is harder for a Jew than a Muslim, but it isn't impossible. I'm the perfect example, where I attained the highest university degrees and was hired by the government [in his previous job]. . . . There are even Jews who are pilots, for example, which is a sensitive and strategic job. You know, after thirty centuries of living in Iran, we Jews are culturally purely Iranian. We speak Farsi in our homes, not any other language, we eat the same food, and the only difference between us and Muslims is the language we pray in."

"And Muslims pray in Arabic, also a foreign tongue," I said. "But I'm curious how you view the future of this community of some twenty or twenty-five thousand Jews in Iran, and the future of religious freedom under an Islamic state. I mean, Jews and other minorities are just not equal with Shias, even if there is tolerance for different religions."

"Look," said Moreh-Sedegh again, in his charming way of prefacing every sentence. "I can't predict the future. But I *can* say that the situation for Jews in Iran has actually improved day by day. For example, with the help of the Supreme Leader, the issue of equal blood money has been resolved, with the fatwa Ayatollah Khamenei issued. This was the main legal issue for Jews, a question of equality, and other issues we're hopeful will be resolved. Our opinion is that all religious minorities, including the Jews, are in an improving situation."

"But what if Israel were to be involved in a military attack on Iran? Wouldn't that jeopardize the Jewish community?"

"No, not even that would affect the Jewish community. We've seen analogous situations, such as during the Six-Day War when anti-Israeli sentiment was extremely high in Iran and yet no attacks on the Jewish community took place. Look, we're part of the Iranian culture, and whomever is the enemy of Iran is our enemy *too*, whether they be Arab or Israeli. During the Imposed War [the government terminology for the Iran-Iraq War of the 1980s], about thirteen Iranian Jews were martyred and many more wounded. Let me tell you something: if Iran were under attack, I'd be the first person to put my entire life and expertise at my nation's disposal."

"With the nuclear issue," I said, "do you feel as a minority that you are under pressure to tow the government line?"

"No, no! But we are completely with the nation in the exercising of its rights and in what's to the benefit of the country. You can see that we suffer from electricity shortages, from gasoline shortages—we need alternative sources of energy, such as nuclear. This is our right, and we Jews are no different from any other Iranian in defending and demanding those rights. Why would we be?"

"So you don't see any serious problems for the Jewish community in Iran?"

"No, in fact I see better and better times ahead."

"And the najess issue? Unclean, in an Islamic nation?"

"That's no longer an issue. After Imam Khomeini issued his fatwa about the 'people of the book,' the issue of Jews being 'unclean' has disappeared from the culture." Moreh-Sedegh's phone rang again, and he seemed a little distracted. I knew that he had made an appointment with someone on the phone earlier to have lunch at a hotel, and I didn't want to hold him up.

"I want to thank you for your time," I said, standing up. "I should let you get back to your work."

"No, not at all. I'm happy to answer any questions," replied Moreh-Sedegh. "But I do have a favor to ask you. Foreigners like to write about all the problems the Jews of Iran face, exaggerate those problems, and this works against us. Anything that is against the interests of the nation we see as against our interests."

I left Moreh-Sedegh, thinking he was a suitable replacement for the perhaps more sophisticated Motamed, that he was someone who, fiercely proud of being Iranian, was also willing to be a crusader for Jewish rights. Although no Jew living in Iran would, despite his contention that there are no restrictions, voice a political opinion contrary to Iran's stance on Israel, I believed him when he said that he would be among the first to defend his nation should Israel ever mount an attack. I think that most Muslims in Iran, even Moreh-Sedegh's fellow parliamentarians, believe it too. And although Jews and other minorities didn't face as much discrimination as in the past simply because they were considered "unclean," as his own job as a surgeon, tending to less sophisticated sick Muslims from the poorer neighborhoods, testified, Moreh-Sedegh was a bit too generous in dismissing the issue entirely, for too many Iranian clerics, and many ordinary Muslims, still believe that a Jew or a Christian is unclean, and therefore untouchable and unequal, until he or she converts. That is one reason why there are two kitchens at the Dr. Sapir Hospital.

I saw Moreh-Sedegh again in May 2009, only a couple of weeks before the presidential election. I had called him and asked if he would be willing to grant an interview to Ann Curry of NBC News, whom he didn't know. "If you insist," he said to me on the phone, "and how's Khatami, by the way? What a pity he isn't running!" He was gracious but cautious in his interview with NBC, his first with the American media, and not unexpectedly, he repeated what he said to me a few months earlier. "I don't like to interview with the American press because they tend to make it look like we Jews have a terrible time in Iran."

Moreh-Sedegh remained a parliamentarian after the disputed election of 2009, although as a minority representative, he is not considered in any political camp, neither reform nor conservative. Ahmadinejad, however, perhaps in an effort to rehabilitate his image with both Iranian and American Jews, included him in his delegation when he traveled to attend the UN General Assembly less than three months after his questionable re-election. Inexplicably, the United States delayed in issuing Moreh-Sedegh a visa, perhaps in an effort to dissuade him from appearing by Ahmadinejad's side, thus granting the president a minor propaganda victory, but the Jewish member of Parliament eventually joined the president's delegation in New York, which included other parliamentarians. The election crisis continued to dominate headlines in the West, however, and Moreh-Sedegh—much to his relief, I imagine—seemed to be of no interest to the media, if it even knew he was on American soil.

A FEW DAYS after my first meeting with Moreh-Sedegh in 2008, I decided to raise the question of anti-Semitism and religious freedom in Iran with a senior cleric who, after all, could be definitive about what an Islamic democracy would tolerate. I called on Ayatollah Mohammad Mousavi Bojnourdi, head of the Imam Khomeini Center for Islamic Studies and a cleric who had a close relationship with the founder of the Islamic Republic (originally Iraqi, he lived in Najaf for many years, as did Khomeini), I was aware that his extremely liberal views made him likely to be more favorably disposed to the Jewish community in Iran than some other, more fundamentalist Ayatollahs. He had, after all, happily sat with the chief rabbi of Tehran, Yousef Hamadani Cohen, and the Armenian bishop (as well as Maurice Motamed) at a farewell event for President Khatami held at the Ministry of Labor in 2005, which I attended. I was to meet Ayatollah Bojnourdi in his office on the campus of the theological institute, which was a short walk from where I stay in Tehran, and when he arrived a few minutes late for our appointment, he was sweating profusely from the hot Tehran sun. I waited until he settled in his office before I went in. His rotund figure was situated right in front of the air conditioner, which was blasting cold air on his face. I wondered if the Imam Khomeini Institute had its own generators, or if the government simply kept the institute on the grid, since a short while before, the electricity had gone out locally.

"Besm'illah-o-rahman-o-rahim," he began. He was well prepared, as the Ayatollahs always like to be, to talk, this time on the subject of minorities in Iran. "The three monotheistic religions," he said, "Judaism, Christianity, and Zoroastrianism, are, under the Constitution, protected in the Islamic Republic. They are completely free to practice their religion, their religious ceremonies, pursue their economic activities, but of course within the laws of the Islamic Republic of Iran. They are completely under the protection of the Islamic Republic; and in fact the republic is *obliged* to protect them, to support them. As long as they don't act against the laws of the state. If they do, they come *out* from under the protection. The laws we have now are applied to Muslim and non-Muslim alike. At any rate, the religion of Islam is a religion that respects all of the Abrahamic faiths, the Jewish, Christian, and Muslim, and they can all function within society, go to university, engage in commerce—there are no restrictions on them. As far as jobs go, there are certain posts where the *requirement* is Islam, where the laws of Islam state that the person must be a Muslim, but where there is no religious requirement, they can occupy those jobs."

"But given the current administration's very harsh rhetoric toward Israel," I said, "do you think that should Israel ever attack Iran, Iranian Jews might find themselves in a very uncomfortable position, particularly in danger of being attacked by some people?"

"The people have enough wisdom," said Bojnourdi. "What do the Jews have to do with Israel?" For a moment I thought that it might come as some relief to Jews worldwide that a senior Muslim cleric had just absolved them of any perceived sin with respect to Israel's existence. "Even rabbis," he continued, "denounce Israel. They say they are *mortad* [apostates]. Myself, when Israel was founded, I was a child, but I was in Najaf [Iraq]. All the rabbis there denounced the Israelis as apostates. Jews don't occupy land; Jews don't disturb the peace, or deny the rights of others! The *Marja-e-taghlid* [Grand Ayatollah] of Iraq at the time Israel was created, Ayatollah Esfahani, issued a fatwa forbidding anyone from attacking the life or property of any Jew. The Jews were different from Israelis. We have no issue with Jews. The Torah is a sacred book to us. We're simply opposed to *Israel*."

"And just how do you see the future relations of Iran with the United States and Israel?" I asked.

"There is no place for relations, friendly relations, with Israel," he said coldly. "We consider them to have stolen land, to be occupying Muslim land, and they are committing genocide against Muslim people, the people of Palestine, the people of Lebanon, the people of Syria. They are an issue apart. As for America, if one day they stop threatening us, stop committing crimes against us, free our assets they have frozen, then we'll have nothing against them."

"But one of the conditions that the United States has for improved relations with Iran, spoken or unspoken, is that Iran not act in any way against Israel," I said.

"We haven't committed any act," said Bojnourdi. "We're just airing our opinion! We say Israel has occupied land, that Palestinians should be able to return to their homes, and the Jews who are there can remain. Let there be a free referendum for all the people of Palestine, including the Jews, to decide what kind of government should rule there [the standard line of the Iranian government]. But when Russians are brought in, when Germans are brought in—they're not Palestinian. The Jews who are Palestinian can of course remain there." Ayatollah Bojnourdi's cell phone, which had rung repeatedly with an Islamic prayer ring tone, rang yet again. He looked at his *abbah* (robe) hanging on a coat hanger, and where the cell phone was stashed. I sensed that he was eager to finish the conversation.

"Thanks for your time," I said, getting up from my chair. "I know you're very busy."

"Thank you," he said, not offering any more of his time, as he usually does. "The Jews of Iran are absolutely free," he repeated. "As long as they don't support Israel," he then added.

AYATOLLAH BOJNOURDI'S pronouncement that Jews are free to pursue any activity as long as it is legal rang in my head when I sat in a cab a few days later on the way to the Tehran Jewish Committee, *Anjoman-e-Kalimian-e-Tehran*, a legal and nonprofit organization set up and registered under the laws of the Islamic Republic of Iran. The Anjoman is the owner of the property and the manager of Dr. Sapir Hospital, and is the largest Jewish organization in Iran, its name being slightly misleading, for in truth it acts as the *Iran* Jewish Committee. Although membership is not obligatory for Tehran Jews (nor indeed any Iranian Jews), most do belong, and its members elect the Jewish member of Parliament, many of which have historically been directors or chairmen, such as Moreh-Sedegh was, of the committee. The Anjoman's headquarters occupies the third floor of a modern building on Sheikh Hadi Street, in a nice neighborhood in the less grimy part of midtown Tehran, opposite the Firooz-Koohi high school. There were no guards outside the building, nor any on the landing at the third floor, and the doors to the offices were wide open, much like the welcoming gates of the Yousefabad Synagogue.

The day I visited, Farhad Aframian, a board member and head of the Cultural Committee, was sitting in the expansive conference room, on a brand new chair whose plastic covering, like that on the others around the table, had not yet been removed. Farhad, an affable young man I had previously met at Sapir Hospital, welcomed me (even though my appointment was with Dr. Rahmatollah Raffi, the then director of the Anjoman) and handed me three issues of the committee's magazine, *Ofegh Bina*, of which he was the chief editor. The back (or front cover, depending on whether one is looking at the English, or the Hebrew and Farsi sections) of the March 2008 issue of the self-described "Culturl [sic], Social and News magazine of Tehran Jewish Committee," published quarterly, contained the following statement (in all three languages and scripts):

The news is short, but has a long story. 40 Iranians (the real number is 27) immigrated to Israel. I'm speaking to all Jewish Iranians. During all your life, do you ever remember any second in which you have been Iranian, nor [sic] Jewish? Or do you ever remember a second in which you have been Jewish, nor Iranian? Being Iranian and being Jewish, at least for us are not two concepts, patched together. It's the story of head and body; if they are separated, neither head is head nor body is body. The Jewish Iranian will always be Jewish Iranian. Denying his Iranian identity is actually denying his Jewish identity. Do the conspirators and/or their audience not know that if a Jewish Iranian denies his being Iranian, he will no more be Jewish, too?

The editorial, which continued inside the magazine, referred to a number of Iranian Jews who immigrated to Israel in December 2007, whose arrival in Tel Aviv was broadcast by the Israeli and foreign news media, and whose statements about persecution back home in Iran were widely used in anti-Iran media reports. At the time, Iran's Jewish community quickly sprang into action, condemning the groups responsible for offering the immigrants $10,000 each to go to Israel (earlier in 2007, the amount was doubled from $5,000 because no Iranian Jews had accepted the original offer, and at that time both Maurice Motamed and Siamak Moreh-Sedegh openly condemned the relief groups and the Israeli government for their attempt at "buying" Iranian Jews' "identity"). The community also condemned what it maintained were lies the immigrants told on their arrival in Israel, lies, it said, written for the immigrants by their sponsors. (To be fair to both the Tehran Jewish Committee and the Iranian government, some of the statements were indeed demonstrably false, such as the claim that the Ahmadinejad government had shut down Jewish schools and forbidden the teaching of Hebrew.) The Anjoman and the Jewish member of Parliament view it as their responsibility to protect the interests of Jews living in Iran, and, as almost every one told me, any story less than sanguine about the life of Jews in the Islamic Republic only hurts the Jewish community, first, by drawing unwarranted and negative attention to it, and second, by casting aspersion on the loyalty of Iranian Jews to the nation. There is no doubt that most of the Jews who remain in Iran, working, living, and even prospering among their Muslim fellow citizens, are loyal, nationalistic Persians who *like* living in their homeland. However, it must be a tedious chore to have to constantly be on guard against any suggestion, even if it comes from well-meaning foreign sources, that they would be happier either under a different regime or living in a different country.

Only a few days earlier, Farhad Aframian had had an engagement party and celebration to which he had graciously invited me, but I had been unable to attend, though not because of what Mrs. Hasidim had told me when I visited the Jewish hospital. The government of President Ahmadinejad had requested, she explained, that Jewish groups not invite Muslims to their functions, which were allowed by law to serve alcohol and to feature pop music and mixed-gender, unmarried dancing, all of which is proscribed to the general population but in any event is flouted in many Muslim homes. Farhad was adamant that life for Jews in Iran was really quite good and that he had no intention of leaving, and, he said, he had visited European cities such as Paris and Vienna, where he thought anti-Semitism was more pronounced than in Tehran. Farhad was proud of his magazine and has ambitions in the media world. He handed me another set of magazines to give to former president Khatami, whom he knew I was related to and would be seeing while in Tehran.

Khatami is immensely popular in the Jewish community, and not just because of his landmark visit to the Yousefabad Synagogue. His outreach to all minority groups in Iran, his calm demeanor, and his nonconfrontational approach to foreign policy, as well as the general liberalization in post-revolution Iranian society that took place during his eight years as president, resulted in an optimism among Jews that they had not felt since the overthrow of the monarchy. Although Jews in Iran tend to stay away from politics, I sensed from everyone I spoke to, on or off the record, that they were looking forward to a potential Khatami candidacy in the presidential election of 2009, which, along with the U.S. presidential election, was the most talked-about issue of the day in the late summer of 2008. Farhad and I chatted for a few minutes until Dr. Raffi, an active surgeon and director of the Anjoman, entered the conference room, apologizing for his tardy appearance. Farhad got up to leave us to ourselves.

"Next time I'll take you to the Kosher Kebab restaurant 'Tapoo' on Felestin [Palestine] Street for lunch," he said before he walked out.

"Palestine Street?" I asked. "A government sense of irony?"

"No," he replied with a smile. "The Jewish high school, '*Moussa ben Amran*,' is also on Felestin Street, which used to be Kakh [Palace] Street, and where the Israeli Mission was located before the revolution. Now the Palestinian Embassy has taken its place—hence Felestin Street."

Dr. Raffi and I sat down at the end of the huge table, under a gold-leaf-framed, oversized page from the Torah, dual portraits of Ayatollahs Khomeini and Khamenei, also framed in gold, and near a large Iranian flag in the corner.

"We're an umbrella organization for all of Iran's Jews," he told me, "and we coordinate with Jewish associations in cities such as Shiraz, Esfahan, and Kermanshah, but also much smaller cities such as Rafsanjan, where there may only be a few Jews living. We pay for the expenses of these associations, and the government of the Islamic Republic is supposed to give us 300,000,000 tomans a year [about $320,000], but with the new government budgetary plan, it has unfortunately been reduced by 20 percent. We try to spend none of that money in Tehran, but rather on the Jewish associations in other cities and towns."

"Well," I said, "that can't be enough to cover expenses, can it?"

"Not in the least!" replied Raffi.

"So where does the rest come from?" I asked.

"From some land that we used to own and have sold—the interest on the cash in the bank, we also receive some small donations, and we have income from rent on some stores we own. We spend it all."

"And are you involved in any political activity?" I asked.

"None," he said emphatically. "The Tehran Jewish association is not involved in any political activity whatsoever! We live under the Islamic

Republic of Iran, comfortably," he added, "and our activities are cultural, societal, etc. Because we have a Jewish member of Parliament, all political issues are handled by him."

"What are your relationships like with Iranian Jewish groups outside Iran, such as in California or New York?" I asked him.

"We have friendly relations, but that's it—just relations," said Raffi. "We have very good relations with the Jewish Federation of California, for example, but there's no kind of monetary assistance, neither asked for nor volunteered by them, but we maintain contact so that we are aware of each other's activities."

"And do you have any contact with Iranian Jews who've settled in Israel, but travel regularly to Iran?"

"No," said Raffi, firmly. "There are Jews who take that risk, for it's illegal, and the government seems to turn a blind eye, but we're really trying to persuade the government that it should be easier for Jews to go to Israel, not to live, but to visit the holy sites such as the Wailing Wall. Iranians who make pilgrimages to Mecca aren't Arab, after all, but they do so because of their religion. The same would be true for us: it wouldn't make us Israeli, but we should be able to freely go and visit our holy sites. In fact, I maintain that if that were the case, no Iranian Jew would ever settle in Israel," he said. "But we have no contact or association with Jews who live in Israel," he repeated.

"Can you go to Israel yourself, for religious reasons. Can you get permission from the government?" I asked.

"If they give permission—it's not official, but if they give permission, we'll go, and if they don't, we won't. We don't put any pressure on the Islamic Republic to give that permission—even the fact that they turn a blind eye to those who do travel, that's good enough, a small thing is better than none."

✥

I WANTED to visit a couple of ordinary working-class Jewish families in their homes during my stay in Tehran in 2008. The opportunity presented itself when Ali, who works for my friend Khosro (whose house I stay in), asked me one day if I would like to meet some regular Jews, friends of his, he told me, who were not very high up on the social ladder but were exactly the kind of Jews who might one day require the services of Dr. Sapir Hospital or might decide to emigrate to the United States or to Israel. I had said yes, of course, and he was to arrange to take me to their homes one afternoon. On the day before our appointments, Ali called the house to say the Jewish families had begged off.

"To tell you the truth," he said, "they're a little afraid. How do they know how a foreign writer will portray them, or what will come across? They're not looking for trouble."

I was disappointed, but I understood. My experiences with the Jewish community in Iran were no different from other experiences: the paradoxical nature of the government, the people, the culture, and the society at large is as confusing as ever, and peculiarly Persian in character. Synagogues, hospitals, committees, kosher restaurants, and Hebrew schools operate freely in a Muslim theocratic state, but the government celebrates "The Protocols of the Elders of Zion." The president denies the Holocaust as "fake" and a "hoax," but the Jewish member of Parliament openly and fearlessly criticizes him, and a government-run national television station runs a smash-hit mini-series (*Zero Degree Turn*) about an Iranian diplomat who saved many Jews from precisely that Holocaust (based on a true story). Jews are completely free, but not free to support Israel. Jews are equal citizens, except when they're not. Iranian Jews must not travel to Israel, except when they do. Iranian-Israelis are not welcome back in Iran, except when they are. Iranian government censors block the *New York Post* on the Internet, but not the *Jerusalem Post* and *Haaretz*. It is almost a necessity to be Iranian to understand, and to be Iranian in order to be comfortable with Iranian life and all of its paradoxes. And Iranian Jews are nothing if not Iranian. But for Iranian Jews, particularly those who, like Dr. Raffi, also live in the United States (in his case, Los Angeles), if only part-time, there is yet another paradox to consider: the United States, their second home, is a frequent critic of Iran and an avowed opponent of the Islamic regime under which they live in relative freedom, but it is an ally and friend, no *best* friend, with Saudi Arabia, where Jews are not even technically allowed to visit, let alone live.

Dr. Rahmatollah Raffi and Farhad Aframian, two generations of Iranian Jews who choose, despite their ability to leave and settle elsewhere, to live and work in Iran, one day gave me a ride from Sapir Hospital to a street corner near my home. As Dr. Raffi drove through the narrow alleys of the onetime Jewish ghetto and then along traffic-clogged main roads, as aggressively and expertly as any Tehran cabbie, we talked about Iranian politics, the subject of the day, which it always seems to be in Iran among any group of Iranians, regardless of race, religion, or creed. And as he pulled up to the corner of Manouchehri and Ferdowsi, across from the heavily fortified British Embassy, Raffi turned to me and said, as an Iranian Jew discussing the politics of the Islamic Republic of Iran, *"Amm'a, ma razzee hasteem"*— "But, we are *content*."

IRANIAN JEWS may be content, or merely content—and perhaps they would be even more content, as many have told me, under a reformist president like Khatami or Mousavi, although not for religious freedom reasons. But that is not the case for Iranian Baha'is, whose population is ten times that of the Jewish population inside Iran. Unlike Christians and Zoroastrians, and much more than Jews, Baha'is have been persecuted in Iran, even under the monarchy, ever since their religion was founded in the nineteenth century, by a Muslim cleric

named Baha'ullah. (Christians and Zoroastrians, it might be said, actually have a somewhat easier time than Jews, for they do not have Israel
hanging over their heads, like the sword of Damocles. Most Iranian
Christians are Armenian, and there has never been the suggestion that,
even after the independence of Armenia—which happens to enjoy very
close relations with the Islamic Republic, closer in fact than neighboring Azerbaijan, a Shia land— they might be more loyal to that nation
than their own. And Zoroastrians, being the purest Persians, have no
such worries either.) The clergy consider Baha'is, who are as Iranian
as any Muslim, heretics, and although the last Shah, Mohammad
Reza Pahlavi, granted them almost complete religious freedom, many
Muslims for generations, regardless of religious conviction, have viewed
them with suspicion. Those who accept their Ayatollahs' pronounce-
ments simply believe they are a heretical branch of Islam that must
be eliminated, and some of those who are less religious, even secular,
have bought into the propaganda that Baha'ism is a political movement disguised as a religion, with the intent of destroying Islam. Ever
since the late nineteenth century, Iranians have been taught that the
British (always the bogeymen) created the Baha'i faith to weaken the
influence of Shia clerics in Iran, as part of a plot to keep Iran under
British control.

The fact that Baha'is are proscribed from political activity by their
faith, something conspiracy-minded Iranians view as suspicious to
begin with, has made them an easy target for authorities, and the fact
that their prophet is buried in Israel and their holy site is in Haifa
(which was a British mandate when he died) makes them almost more
of a target than Iranian Jews. During the era of the last Shah's father,
fundamentalist clerics and townspeople, but not the government, instigated pogroms of Baha'is, but under the Islamic Republic, the harass-
ment and persecution of Baha'is has been institutionalized. As an
unrecognized minority, they cannot attend university if they proclaim

their faith, they cannot hold government jobs, and they cannot organize or meet as a group, although the government denies that these restrictions exist (and they don't on paper or in the law).

Occasionally, Baha'i elders, leaders of the community, are arrested and charged with spying for Israel, as were seven of them in 2008 and 2009, and other Baha'is have been executed for spying or treason in the thirty-year history of the Republic. The Islamic government denies that it persecutes or arrests anyone for religious reasons, but the fact remains that Baha'is are afforded none of the protection that Ayatollah Bojnourdi claims is offered to Jews, Christians, and Zoroastrians in their own land. Unfortunately, few Iranians, even human rights activists, stand up for their Baha'i compatriots, perhaps because they know they would not have the support of the people, a people who are still heavily prejudiced against the faith. In the aftermath of the 2009 election, Baha'is arrested and accused of sedition or being agents of Israel received scant attention from either the opposition, normally quick to denounce all post-election arrests and trials, or Iranian human rights activists in general, with few exceptions. While there was sympathy among the masses, even conservatives, for protesters accused by the state in show trials, there was little evidence of sympathy for the Baha'is.

In the Ayatollahs' democracy, where religious freedom for four faiths is supported and guaranteed by the constitution (and there is freedom for other faiths, such as Buddhism and Hinduism, as long as they are not practiced by Iranian converts), a mere vote, ballot initiative, or referendum will not be enough to guarantee Baha'is complete freedom to practice their religion in a country with a deeply religious Shia population. Democracy might demand equal protection under the law, but sometimes democracy can also lead to mob rule. Some clerics (such as Grand Ayatollah Montazeri, while he was alive) do not support the oppression of Baha'is, and millions of ordinary Iranians don't either, but as promising as an ideal Islamic democracy might be to many Iranians, unless it affords Baha'is (and any other religious group, including avowed atheists) at least the same protection and marginal equality as other minorities, something the Green Movement has taken no stand on, it risks never quite measuring up to democracy at all.

NOTHING IS TRUE;
EVERYTHING IS FORBIDDEN

Time with whose passage certain pains abate
But sharpens those of Persia's unjust fate.
—WILLIAM MORGAN SHUSTER,
The Strangling of Persia, 1912

"A mullah is waiting by the side of the road, his arm raised," the storyteller says, "and taxis fly by without stopping for him. At long last a taxi stops, and the mullah gets in. 'Thank God!' he exclaims, 'finally, a driver who'll stop for me!' The taxi driver says nothing and drives for about two minutes along the straight road before stopping again. He turns around and snarls, 'Get out!' The mullah is shocked. 'But why?' he asks. 'You stopped for me, and now you're kicking me out? Why, pray tell?' The driver shrugs his shoulders. 'Because,' he says, 'you were in the shade there, and *here* you'll be in the hot sun.'" The storyteller was a mullah himself, and he laughed heartily along with his audience, all pious men.

That was in 2007, twenty-eight years after the mullahs, both liberals and hard-liners, took over the affairs of state. Iranians have long had to confront "nothing—or everything—is true [the state], and everything

is forbidden [to the people]," a rewording of Hassan'e Sabah's alleged
deathbed pronouncement. However, since the creation of an Islamic
state, the force of the edict has taken on added religious authority,
one that is not so easily dismissed or mocked—even at times of great
unrest. It is not that the clerics, the mullahs and Ayatollahs, don't know
how unpopular they can be among ordinary people, and taxi drivers in Iran are often the stand-in for ordinary people—working class,
struggling to make ends meet—it is that the clerics know it doesn't
matter much. It hasn't mattered because the relationship between a
Shia people and their clergy is a complicated one, and difficult for
outsiders to understand. This is one reason why the Shah, who was
educated mostly abroad and then lived inside a bubble when he was
back in Iran, underestimated the power and draw of the mosque, as
did his father, who viewed the clergy with such disdain that he publicly
upbraided mullahs at every opportunity, even forcing them to remove
their turbans and excluding them from political life. No tears were shed
on his downfall, even though the always-despised British engineered
his abdication and exile.

Iranians may make fun of their mullahs, men who are quick to tell
them what is true and what is forbidden, but they have also always
revered them, or at least some of them, and anyone who underesti-
mates the reverence many Iranians have for their Ayatollahs—"signs of
God," as some literally believe—will soon come to regret it. It is true
that Ahmadinejad's early appeal was partly due to his being a layman
in a clerical political culture; some clerics, he constantly reminded
audiences, were corrupt and interested only in personal gain, not in
leading their flock. These same corrupt clerics, he claimed in his campaign for re-election, orchestrated the challenge to his presidency, and
their leader was Ayatollah Rafsanjani, who is reviled by many ordinary
Iranians more for his reputed Forbes-list wealth than for anything he
might tell them isn't permitted under Islam. And yet, in the wake of

the 2009 election, and more particularly in the wake of the extremely violent suppression of public demonstrations and protests, the heroes of the opposition and the hope of many Iranians for a better future were again as they were in 1979, the clerics.

Ahmadinejad and Mousavi were two lay presidential candidates, but importantly, each had mentors in the clergy without whom they would not have reached their positions of power. When the country's leadership effectively split into two political camps for the first time in thirty years, supporters of both sides looked to the clergy, *their* clergy, in the hopes that they might prevail. The disturbances of 2009 were more significant than previous bouts of unrest and government crackdowns not just because of the sheer numbers of citizens who took to the streets, but because of the support those people had from some of the top clergy in the country. It is a peculiarity of Shia Islam, similar though it can be to the Catholic Church, that there is no Pope-like figure, no ultimate religious authority above all others— although the Supreme Leader and his strongest supporters would like him to be just that— who can become the object of either adulation or scorn for the population at large. Shias can choose to follow any one of the two dozen or so Ayatollahs, or the handful of Grand Ayatollahs, whose opinions and decrees, fatwas, hold great sway over a large segment of the population, even as that same population might mock other clerics, or the institutionalized clergy in general. And as for what is forbidden, Shias, like Catholics and unlike Sunnis, conveniently have their Ayatollahs to absolve them of their sins. Iranian secularists have often looked to Ayatollahs for support too—those Ayatollahs who might give religious sanction to their political beliefs—without which they realize they have little hope of winning over the majority of the population.

ONE OF THE most vocal opponents of the Supreme Leader and of the Ahmadinejad government, the renowned filmmaker Mohsen Makhmalbaf, dedicated his 2009 Freedom to Create Prize, awarded in London in November of that year, to an Ayatollah: Grand Ayatollah Ali Montazeri, once Khomeini's designated successor but since 1989 the loudest clerical voice of dissent in Iran and in the aftermath of the 2009 election the highest-ranking mullah challenging Khamenei's endorsement of the fraudulent election. Montazeri, who died of natural causes a month after Makhmalbaf's gesture, had long been a hero to those opposed to the velayat-e-faqih as it is structured, but he had been sidelined, even kept under house arrest for a number of years at the end of the last century and into this one. He was, however, in 2009 still perhaps the most senior cleric among the Ayatollahs in Iran, and his fatwa after the election declaring the Ahmadinejad government illegitimate was a boon to the opposition, as it carried weight among his pious, even conservative, supporters far and wide. Largely forgotten in the last few years, he suddenly became relevant again after the election, his funeral an opportunity for all Iranians to protest what they believed was a government no longer of the people but of a few clerics and their supporters in the military.

Ayatollah Rafsanjani, the most prominent cleric who had supported the opposition to Ahmadinejad and had tried to see if he could reverse the election results in June 2009, knew, when he explored the possibility, that he needed much more than the still-sidelined Montazeri to mount a challenge to Khamenei. Montazeri held no official office and had long been banished from membership in the important organs of state. (Montazeri did provide at least some religious sanction for a challenge, and his position no doubt had some influence on some of the more liberal Ayatollahs that Rafsanjani intended to persuade to his side.) Rafsanjani might have initially prevailed on the Supreme Leader, before he took off on his journey to Qom to meet with his fellow

Ayatollahs, to back down from his support for Ahmadinejad's question-able re-election. And the Supreme Leader might have listened to some of his arguments, for he did order an investigation into the allegations of fraud three days after the election, charging the Guardian Council with recounting a certain number of votes before it certified the final result. However, it soon became clear to Rafsanjani that whatever steps were to be taken, there would be no voiding of the result and no new presidential election as the opposition had demanded, especially given that Khamenei had already called Ahmadinejad's victory a "divine assessment." God does not change His mind in the Islamic Republic, we were told.

As chairman of the Assembly of Experts (the body that can impeach the Supreme Leader), though, Rafsanjani could at least see if he might have the support of the majority of the clerics in the assembly to per-suade the Leader to change *his* mind, maybe only about whether God's message was jumbled in its delivery to him. Perhaps the threat of a special assembly meeting might have been enough to force him to back down, too. We will never know the details of any meetings Rafsanjani had, for he is the most secretive and taciturn politician in Iran, but what we do know is that he was unsuccessful in persuading the assem-bly to take a stand (although Rafsanjani maintained his opposition to the status quo for a considerable amount of time). Perhaps the clerics who were dismayed by the Leader's actions didn't want to rock the boat any further; perhaps the Leader had his own proxies working against Rafsanjani in the assembly at the same time. In any event, the assem-bly had never, in its brief history, taken any steps against the Supreme Leader. In fact, it hardly ever met. In June 2009, when its function was most needed (a time, one might say, akin to the U.S. Supreme Court's role during the disputed U.S. election of 2000), the "stabil-ity" and "good of the nation" trumped all other considerations, but the assembly remained quiet until months later, when it met and validated

the Supreme Leader's qualifications as valih-e-faqih. It was a majority vote, taken with the notable absence of the chairman, Ayatollah
Rafsanjani. And it put to end any notions that Rafsanjani might have
the ability to alter the course set by the Supreme Leader, regardless
of religious sanction provided by Shia luminaries such as Montazeri
or Grand Ayatollah Sanei. Despite that, Iran had not yet become a
Stalinist dictatorship. There still existed some room for dissent at the
very top of the leadership, and the leadership, even Ahmadinejad with
his questionable election, enjoyed a considerable amount of support
from the people.

WHILE RAFSANJANI was busy rallying, or trying to rally, fellow clerics
to his side, Mousavi, Karroubi, and Rezai, the three losing candidates
challenging Ahmadinejad and all a part of the leadership, along with
Khatami, the elder statesman of the reformists, were vocally denouncing the election and calling for their supporters to protest and demonstrate. The two clerics and two lay politicians, all of them staunch
revolutionaries and politicians, simply didn't believe that "nothing was
permitted" in their republic. Their supporters didn't believe it either,
for on Monday, June 15, some three million or more came out onto the
streets of Tehran (according to Mohammad Qalibaf, the conservative
mayor of Tehran and onetime Revolutionary Guard commander) in
relatively peaceful protest, bringing the capital to a complete halt. Two
days of protests and demonstrations, not just in Tehran but throughout
the nation, had already focused the Western media's attention on Iran.
The country's immediate suspicion of the media also drew attention,
especially as the government began to harass and intimidate journalists as soon as it realized that little of the coverage would be favorable
to Mahmoud Ahmadinejad or the governing administration. *Nothing
is true.*

The Supreme Leader, apparently unmoved by either the protests or Rafsanjani's machinations—of which he was undoubtedly aware—scheduled himself to address the nation on Friday, June 19, as permanent Friday Prayer Leader of Tehran, a title that the valih-e-faqih holds by definition. Ayatollah Khamenei rarely leads the Friday prayers, preferring to appoint a substitute leader from a rotating group of mullahs, almost all fiercely loyal to him and almost all, with the exception of Rafsanjani, hard-line conservatives. Friday prayers and the political sermon, its talking points faxed to the speaker by the *Rahbari*, the Supreme Leader's office, are when the nation and the world at large hear Iran's policies, opinions, and intentions. When the Supreme Leader himself speaks, they are hearing it straight from the horse's mouth. And he wanted the nation to hear it directly from him, now more than ever. To hear what was true, and what was permitted.

It is impossible to know what was going on in the mind of the highest-ranking official in the Islamic Republic in the days leading up to his sermon, for few people have access to him, and fewer still would venture any opinion on him or his motivations. Some in Iran and outside the country believe he lives his life so isolated that he is unaware of what is going on in, or even outside, the country. If that is true (and if he relies only on the Iranian state media for information), then he is as ignorant of popular opinion as the Shah once was. Importantly, however, while the Shah had only yes-men surrounding him, the Ayatollah still hears from dissenters and those in opposition to either his or his allies' policies.

In late 2008 while I was in Tehran, I heard a disturbing anecdote that could be true, but it could also be an exaggeration, as many things in Iran are. A doctor who attends to Khamenei told a friend of a recent visit to his compound for a regular checkup, and as he was waiting for the Supreme Leader to enter the room, the Leader's aides said to him, "Now don't say anything to the Rahbar. Even if he asks you a question, don't answer." The doctor was incredulous; as a friend of the Leader for many years, from before the revolution, he couldn't very well ignore his questions. "Well, don't answer anything non-medical-related," one aide said. Presumably, the aides didn't want any opinions on the state of the economy or the popularity of the Ahmadinejad administration reaching the Supreme Leader's ears, especially not from an outsider. If true, the Leader is more isolated than anyone thinks, and he could have even been unaware, when he declared the election a "divine assessment," that it might have been marred by less-than-divine inter-vention. Nonetheless, the Supreme Leader was smart enough not to make the same mistakes the Shah made when he faced angry crowds of unhappy Iranians. "I've heard the voice of your revolution," the Shah had said on state television in late 1978, which as far as many Iranians are concerned was an invitation to a *real* revolution. The Supreme Leader, one of the revolutionaries who smelled blood thirty years ago when the Shah showed a weak hand, was not going to admit that anything resembling a revolution was going on. Quite the opposite, for on Friday, June 19, he declared that the state would crush any revolt, any protest, and any activity that was deemed to be illegal. *Everything is forbidden.* In other words, people would be hurt if they continued to protest, and it would be nobody's fault but their own. *"Bring it on!"* the Supreme Leader of the Islamic Revolution had said, *"if you dare."*

But bring it on they did. Neither Khatami nor Mousavi nor Karroubi backed down (and Rafsanjani quietly went on with his business), for this was not about a revolution as far as they were concerned; it was about the very least a democratic republic could guarantee—the vote of its people. True to his word, the Leader unleashed his forces on dem-onstrators, and scores of ordinary people, men and women, were killed, beaten, or arrested and imprisoned. *Nothing is true.* The most famous of them, Neda Agha-Soltan, a young woman whose death the very next day was captured on video and shown on televisions throughout the world, became a rallying cry for Iranians everywhere, but still the government did not back down. Every protest, every demonstration, was met with a brutal response by the Basij, specifically charged by the Supreme Leader to restore order to the republic. For many in the West, and some in Iran, the clampdown by the Revolutionary Guards and the Basij became symptomatic of the Guards' overall takeover of the country, which started years ago and accelerated during President Ahmadinejad's first term. Although it is unclear if Ahmadinejad was ever a Revolutionary Guard himself (he was certainly a Basij), it is taken as fact that he was, and he *has* placed many former Guardsmen in key positions in Tehran, including in his cabinet. But to look at the post-election landscape in Iran and to call it a Revolutionary Guard takeover of the state, as some did, was to oversimplify matters.

The Revolutionary Guards, which are tasked with guarding the "revolution," have always answered to and been loyal to the Supreme Leader, and in the post-election crisis, it was no different. There is no question that in the rank and file of the Guards many officers and enlisted men might have voted for a candidate other than Ahmadinejad; in fact, according to election statistics in the past, the Guards voted along remarkably similar lines as the general population, with over 70 percent voting for the liberal Khatami in his landslide election of 1997. But at the very top of the command, the officers take their direction from the Supreme Leader, and whether they preferred one candidate to another, it didn't matter once the Supreme Leader declared Ahmadinejad the winner.

By the time the Guards entered the fray, the Iranian government had already set out a propaganda plan to counter accusations that the presidential vote results were fraudulent: Western countries, with the support of the foreign media, had instigated riots and demonstrations to begin a "velvet" or "color" revolution along the lines of those in Eastern Europe, and any disturbances or unrest were simply manifestations of their plans. The British were especially targeted as the masterminds, and since the British have a perhaps undeserved reputation for controlling everything that happens in Iran, even among Iranians who should know better, it was thought that labeling the "Little Satan"—servant to the "Great Satan"—as the nefarious hand behind the unrest might actually work. It didn't, of course, except with the Guards and the Basij, but the Iranian propaganda machine plowed on.

As a few in the Western media began to unhelpfully label the demonstrations as the "Twitter Revolution" (because of the use of Twitter by Iranian citizen-journalists) and as the government periodically shut down cell phone and text messaging services, Secretary of State Hillary Clinton admitted publicly that the U.S. State Department had requested that Twitter delay a scheduled maintenance (that would have disrupted services) so that Iranian forces for democracy could continue to communicate on the ground in Tehran. It was a small gaffe, and an unintentional one (that she inexplicably repeated six months later, in a talk at Georgetown University, where she tried to demonstrate U.S. support for the opposition to Ahmadinejad), but the Iranian government leapt to describe her admission as "proof" that the United States planned and supported the unrest. It was hardly that, but Secretary Clinton did lend the Iranian government's line some credence, at least as far as its supporters were concerned, as well as those who might have supported the demonstrators but were wary of foreign interference in Iran, interference that even President Obama had acknowledged had a very long and unfortunate history.

If Ayatollah Rafsanjani had been successful in changing the Supreme Leader's mind about the election, or if he had gathered the votes in the Assembly of Experts to remove him, or to force him to retire, the Revolutionary Guards probably would have gone along with whatever changes ensued, as long as they wouldn't be directly affected. That Major General Mohammad Ali (Aziz) Jafari, the commander of the Revolutionary Guards, didn't congratulate Ahmadinejad on his "glorious" victory for two whole days after the Supreme Leader did, indicates that he may have been privy to some of the discussions among the clerical leadership and was waiting to see *whose* revolution he was meant to be guarding. Jafari, who was appointed to his post by the Supreme Leader in 2007, was not known to be in the Ahmadinejad hard-line political faction. In fact, he was close to both Mohammad Qalibaf, the conservative and popular mayor of Tehran and a rival of Ahmadinejad's (who he is reputed to despise), and to Mohsen Rezai, the conservative candidate who believed that the vote was fraudulent (although he withdrew his official protest twelve days after the vote, presumably because as a loyal military man, he recognized by then that his commander in chief was there to stay, and wasn't going to change his mind).

At the time of Jafari's appointment, many Iranians viewed it as the Supreme Leader's check *against* the influence of Ahmadinejad and his extremist allies. However, after the election of 2009, Jafari's name became synonymous with the crackdown and the enforcement of Ahmadinejad's rule. The general's comments in the months following the election indicate to many that he willingly took on the expanded role of enforcing security throughout the country, and his accusations that the reformers were looking to overthrow the Supreme Leader led some to believe that the Guards were complicit in vote fraud. But as a military man charged with protecting the revolution, and by definition the Supreme Leader, it would have been highly unusual for him to not follow his commander in chief's orders, and he likely *did* believe that the reformers were intent on changing the system to such a degree that the structure he knew, with Ayatollah Khamenei at the very top, would be threatened. For months, after Mousavi declared his candidacy and publicly embraced Khatami as his mentor, there had been talk in Tehran, quite openly, that a Mousavi win would in effect mean a sort of dual Supreme Leadership: on the conservative side Ali Khamenei, and on the liberal side Mohammad Khatami. Since President Ahmadinejad had already set the precedent of defying the Supreme Leader on occasion, the argument was that a Mousavi-Khatami allied administration would also exhibit a heretofore unseen independence, bolstered by support from Ayatollah Rafsanjani as well as a number of other influential senior Ayatollahs, and the office of the Rahbar would be weakened. Nothing is true? According to *which* Ayatollah?

When I was in Tehran in the months leading up to the election, I tended to dismiss this talk as harmless, typical of Iranian gholov. Aziz Jafari did not think so, however. In a speech to fellow senior Guardsmen in early September, he revealed that Khatami had declared back in February, some four months before the election, that if Ahmadinejad could be defeated, then the Rahbari, the Supreme Leadership, would be effectively eliminated. I hardly think Khatami would have used those words, for I have had many conversations with him about the politics of the velayat-e-faqih, and he has never, not even in absolute privacy and off the record, declared his opposition to the political structure of the Islamic Republic. Regardless, Jafari's speech proved that he and his intelligence division were listening to every one of those private conversations in Khatami's office and home. Khatami has never been silent about his view of the role of the Supreme Leader more as a guide than an executive, and ironically shares with Ahmadinejad a philosophy that the elected president should be allowed more leeway in executing policy. But Khatami, like Khamenei, is a mullah, and perhaps if Ahmadinejad were a cleric too, the Supreme Leader would tolerate his insolence less.

JAFARI AND his colleagues at the top of the Guard command would not necessarily oppose more leeway for the president (as evidenced by their comfort with Ahmadinejad), but they would oppose the president of Iran taking control of the military—in other words, becoming the commander in chief. They would also resist relinquishing the Revolutionary Guards' vast interests in the economy of the country, which have expanded under the presidency of Ahmadinejad. (It was under Khatami, after all, that the new international airport in Tehran, the Imam Khomeini airport, was inaugurated by the president one day and seized by the Guards the next, and then closed until they completed their takeover of operations at the airport, ostensibly due to issues of "national security." That the Guards ended up with all the concessions, including the duty-free shops, at the airport, worth millions a year, was not, in many Iranians' view, incidental.) While some in the West and in Iran continue to describe the post-election political situation as effectively a Guards' coup, that the Guards by their control of security as well as expanded control of the economy are the de facto leaders of the country and are more important than the Supreme Leader himself, that analysis ignores the fact that without a Supreme Leader and the religious sanction he gives, the Guards' very raison d'être is in question, an issue at the heart of Jafari's speech when he accused Khatami of plotting to overthrow his Rahbar.

One member of the Guards' senior command, though, General Qassem Soleimani, commander of the Qods Force (the foreign expeditionary arm of the Guards) since the beginning of the decade, was noticeably quiet during the post-election crisis. As a commander charged with the execution of foreign policy, he might not ordinarily have been expected to express any views on domestic events, but he is perhaps as powerful as Jafari—allegedly reporting directly to the Supreme Leader—and with the Guards seeing foreign plots behind the unrest and taking on the responsibility for national security, it would not have been surprising, either, to hear from one of the most powerful men in Iran. Soleimani, though, is from the same part of the country as Rafsanjani, he was taken under the Ayatollah's wing during his presidency in the 1990s, and he is known as a fierce soldier—a decorated war hero—who is loyal to the principles of the Islamic Republic and his commander in chief, factors that were not incompatible with loyalty to Rafsanjani as well, at least not until mid-2009.

Importantly, General Soleimani was the man responsible for nurturing Iraqi anti-Saddam groups based in Iran during the years leading up to the U.S. invasion of Iraq in 2003, and he developed close friendships with Jalal Talabani, the Kurdish president of Iraq, and a number of other important Iraqi political figures, making him indispensable in Iran's foreign policy formulations (in which Rafsanjani has also always played an important role). Soleimani has been, according to Iranian officials, a target of the U.S. military despite those friendships, and he no longer risks traveling to Iraq as he did after the fall of Saddam Hussein. When Talabani wants to meet with Soleimani, both men drive to their borders to speak face-to-face. (During one of those meetings, in March 2008, Talabani secured an Iranian commitment to help contain the Mahdi Army violence in Basra.) Soleimani's record, his devotion to the revolution and to Iran's national security, ensures that he is an important cog in the military apparatus, but he also commands the devotion of the men who have served with or under him—a friend of mine who served with him during the war with Iraq can barely bring himself to talk about Soleimani without shedding tears over his devotion to his men and his country.

The Qods Force commander is a powerful figure in Iran, to be sure, but it is his direct access to the commander in chief that makes him, along with Jafari, a critical player in deciding the future of the Islamic state. Could he have been unsure, in June 2009, about who that commander in chief might be, or whether his former patron Rafsanjani might prevail in his power struggle with Khamenei? Or did he simply choose not to enter the fray of factional politics because of his inclination to secretiveness and his sense of duty as one not charged with internal affairs? Answers to these questions would be speculative, but Soleimani is likely to be an overall commander of the Guards someday, and he cannot have had no opinion on what was transpiring in his nation, even as he was focused on promulgating the Islamic Revolution abroad rather than protecting it at home.

Guardians of the Revolution. Their revolution had a beginning, but it has no end. And they, Jafari and Soleimani and all their lieutenants and the tens of thousands of troops they command, along with an untold number of Basij, the volunteer army Ayatollah Khomeini created at the beginning of the Iran-Iraq War and now under the command of the Guards, are sworn to defend it to the death. The revolution might mean different things to different members of the Guards, all the way up the chain of command, but what they all share is an undying devotion not just to the revolution but to Shia Islam as well. The leaders of the Green Movement, Shias and devotees of the revolution themselves, recognize that, and know that in the years to come none of their goals can be accomplished at the expense of their faith. Nor would they want them to.

Shia concepts of martyrdom, but more important victimhood, concepts deeply imbedded in the Iranian psyche—even in the psyche of non-Shia Iranians—play a bigger role in the culture of politics than is imagined in the West. We are Shia, Iranians say; our sect has long been a victim of greater Sunni oppression in the Muslim world; our original saints, the blood of the prophet in their veins, were victims of cruel and despotic Caliphs a millennia and a half ago, and we still weep for them, on cue and on time, every year. For centuries we have been the victims of foreign imperialist ambitions, then victims of tyrant Shahs who suppressed any democratic movement that would limit their power. Our latest political model, an Islamic Republic we voted for, has been a victim of foreign plots to destroy it, our independence a thorn in the side of every greater power. We were victims of Saddam, much more so than you Westerners, and yet no one wept for us as he gassed our children and rained bombs down on our cities. We are victims of a Western attitude of superiority that deems nuclear technology to be safe in the West's hands, but unacceptable in the hands of Shia Iranians, even as European man has wreaked more havoc on the planet than any other species.

President Mahmoud Ahmadinejad, a man who embodied the democratic notion, never before tested in Iran's history, that all citizens have equal access to power, is the victim of scurrilous attacks by an established elite. Ayatollah Rafsanjani, representative of that elite, is a victim of Ahmadinejad's relentless attacks on him and, worse, on his defenseless family. Mir Hossein Mousavi, Mehdi Karroubi, and Mohammad Khatami are all victims of Ahmadinejad's and Khamenei's vengeful intimidation tactics and their attempt to remove the democracy from their Islamic democracy; their supporters are victims of a stolen election. Khamenei and Ahmadinejad are victims of plots, foreign and domestic, to illegally overthrow them, to remove the Islamic from their *mardomsalari'e dini*, their self-proclaimed Islamic democracy; the Revolutionary Guards and Basij are victims of violent, Molotov cocktail–throwing mobs of protesters. The peaceful protesters are victims of a brutal military apparatus determined to crush their rights to protest and peaceful assembly, guaranteed under the Islamic Constitution. Iranian exiles and those inside Iran opposed to an Islamic regime altogether are victims too, victims of fate, a fate they believe has led to the loss of the soul of their Persian nation. We are all victims, all of us Iranians, and no matter on which side of the political fence we fall, we understand our victimhood, as well as that of our leaders. And we mourn our victims like no other peoples, seeking unforgiving vengeance for every wrong, real and perceived, and wishing death to every enemy, even when the enemy is ourselves.

The millions of Iranians, and the leaders who have braved the stern and unforgiving dictates of a regime they helped to create, are looking to finally break free from what has defined their political lives, and when they are successful—and they will be, in an Ayatollahs' democracy or not—there will be, finally, no more victims.

Tamam Shud—The End

ACKNOWLEDGMENTS

A special thanks to Seyed Mohammad Khatami, Seyed Ali Khatami, Ali Ziaie, Fatemeh Ziaie, Amir Khosro Etemadi, Sadeq Kharrazi, Iman Mirabzadeh Ardakani, Alireza Tabesh, Mohammad Sadoughi, Saman Majd, Maurice Motamed, Kaveh Bazargan, Mehdi Faridzadeh, Karri Jinkins, Davitt Sigerson, Glenn O'Brien, Michael Hainey, Lindsay Edgecombe, Ken Browar, Ann Curry, Richard Greenberg, David Lom, Drew Levinson, Ali Arouzi, Mike Simon, Robert Windrem, James Toback, Michael Zilkha, Mehrdad Khajehnoori, and Andrew Gundlach.

I would also like to especially thank my editor, Tom Mayer; my agent, Andrew Wylie, and his associates Rebecca Nagel, Sarah Chalfant, and Luke Ingram at The Wylie Agency in New York and London; Helen Conford at Penguin UK; and Thomas Gagnon at The Lavin Agency.

INDEX